P9-EFI-707

BASEBALL'S GREATEST HIT

The Story of
Take Me Out
to the Ball Game

United States Postal Service commemorative stamp celebrating the one-hundredth anniversary of the song "Take Me Out to the Ball Game."

NORTH COUNTRY LIBRARY SYSTEM
Watertown, New York

BASEBALL'S GREATEST HIT

The Story of Take Me Out to the Ball Game

Andy Strasberg
Bob Thompson
Tim Wiles

CENTRAL LIBRARY
WATERTOWN

HAL•LEONARD®

Copyright © 2008 by Andy Strasberg, Bob Thompson, and Tim Wiles

All rights reserved. No part of this book may be reproduced in any form, without written permission, except by a newspaper or magazine reviewer who wishes to quote brief passages in connection with a review.

Published in 2008 by Hal Leonard Books
An Imprint of Hal Leonard Corporation
19 West 21st Street, New York, NY 10010

Printed in the United States of America

Book design by Damien Castaneda

Library of Congress Cataloging-in-Publication Data is available upon request.

ISBN: 978-1-4234-3188-6

www.halleonard.com

To our moms, who gave us music,
and our dads, who gave us baseball

One, two, three strikes you're out? This is a pitcher's song.
—Carl Erskine (Brooklyn Dodger pitching ace)

CONTENTS

FOREWORD

I REMEMBER WHEN Jackie Robinson came to New York and began stealing bases off the best pitchers in the league–I was ten years old and had the immense fortune of living with the Robinson family in the summer of '55. They came and stayed with us at our home in Stamford, Connecticut, while they were constructing their own, down the road and around some green corners.

That summer I would drive to Ebbets Field with Jackie and his family and mine, and sit and wait in the dugout for the game to begin. Nothing has been quite as thrilling since.

The Brooklyn Dodgers made me a special little uniform, and I would sit proudly in the dugout for many of their games, sometimes on Pee Wee Reese's lap, sometimes just trying to get out of the way, especially during the rhubarbs, which always made me tingle. I still don't know why arguments with the umpires were called "rhubarbs," but they made the blood pressure soar–and there was more gum and tobacco reached for and more of it chewed and at a faster pace than during the peaceful plays when the umpires' calls agreed with the perceptions of the pitchers and coaches. But when the rhubarbs broke out, it brought me into a new consciousness, like anticipating a punch. There was energy from blood being drawn to muscles, and it drew more punctuated lines between teams. It was the pure essence of battle.

During many of the games back then, the audience spontaneously broke out in the song "Take Me Out to the Ball Game" occasionally, to relieve the tension. And of course we sang it during the seventh-inning stretch, and sometimes if it rained, during the unexpected intermission.

Nobody knew the whole song, though. I never knew that there were *verses* until Ken Burns asked me to sing the song for his 1994 PBS series, *Baseball.* Ken wanted me to sing the whole song, the verses and the chorus, which is the part we all know. And then he asked me to sing a slow, plaintive version of just the chorus over the section about Jackie. It nearly broke my heart.

That year I did a few concerts, and always opened them with an a cappella version of the chorus. Jack Norworth, who wrote the lyrics to "Take Me Out to the Ball Game," didn't have singers in mind when he penned the words–there's nowhere to breathe, and the lyrics are all crammed together. When I got onstage and started singing, *Take me out to the ball game, Take me out with the crowd,* I sang it slowly, daring the song, and measured my heartbeat to give myself time to calm to the larger meaning.

People aren't used to hearing the song sung at that tempo, and they were hugely relieved at the end of it, having finished the phrases in their own minds so much earlier than I had singing it. That kind of tension builds a certain, attractive introduction to a concert. It gives the audience a chance to see what you're wearing, and if you've gained weight or had plastic surgery. In their minds they have already finished off the song before the first three words are sung. It's a good transition. Like singing "Happy Birthday" before the cake is eaten.

But "Take Me Out to the Ball Game" is more than just baseball; it is filled with metaphor. I think of the "game" as the whole ball of wax. Life is a game, and the stage I was singing on was just a smaller version of it. (And if I struck out, I would never go back. Well, at least not before I had a sandwich and a martini.) The "crowd" might be on your side, or the opposing side.

The song applies to so much. It is universal. It has the larger meaning, and the smaller meaning, resounding on each side of the brain. It has a melody that was born with us, and will live on forever–even though I'm a little worried that Cracker Jack might become obsolete. Perhaps it isn't what the twenty-first century considers a healthy snack.

Baseball is the great all-American sports institution and the song "Take Me Out to the Ball Game" is connected to it the way "Happy Birthday" is connected to the birthday cake.

Happy one-hundredth birthday, "Take Me Out to the Ball Game"!

Carly Simon

ACKNOWLEDGMENTS

ANDY: Once again my wife, Patti, earns the Non–Baseball Fan "She Must Be a Saint" Award. And my sincere appreciation to Bennett for keeping me company and not barking while I worked.

BOB: I'd like to thank my family—my sister Linda, my brother Mitchell, my dear aunt Barbara, and of course my two favorite ballplayers, Emily and Christopher.

TIM: I wish to thank my wife, Marie, for allowing me time to work and for reading drafts of the book and making critical comments. Thanks also to my mother-in-law, Carol Warchol, our friend Judy Steiner-Grin, and our neighbor Nancy Keller, who came to help with the baby during the crucial final weeks of writing.

We'd collectively like to thank the following individuals:

Dr. Martin Abramowitz, Greg Allen, Marty Appel, Alexis Arbisu, Dan Ardell, Jean Hastings Ardell, Judith Armitstead, Jeff Arnett, Robin and Steven Arnold, Mark Atnip, Kyle Austin, Bob Bailey, Gary Baker, David Ball, Susan Becker, Mary Bellew, Kim Bennett, Edward Benoit, Art Berke, Freddy Berowski, David Black, Ralph Bowman, George Boziwick, Peter, Joyce, and Lee Briante, Daryl Brock, Mike Brown, Rob Butcher, Ben Caffyn, Peter Capolino, Vic Cardell, Arnie Cardillo, John Cerullo, Susan Clermont, Bobbi Colins, Kim Cook, Bob Crotty, LaVonne "Pepper" Paire Davis, Allen Debus, Dennis Degenhardt, Barbara Diamond, Paul Dickson, Duane Dimock, Rob Edelman, Leslie Elges, Gregg Elkin, Eric Enders, Gene Felder, Lindsay Flanagan, Shannon Forde, Mike Foster, Bill Francis, John Franzone, Bobby Freeman, Dick Freeman, Fumihiro "Fu-chan" Fujisawa, Kathryn Fuller-Seeley, Jim and Vicki Gates, Mike Gazda, Paul Geisler, John Genzale, Jim Gordon, Joanne Graham, Gregg Greene, Bob Grim, Randy Grossman, Tim Gunkel, Deborah Gunn, Bill Habeger, Arnold Hano, Darci Harrington, Benji Harry, David Headlam, Gary Hellman, Roland Hemond, Chuck Hilty, Fr. John Hissrich, Marianna Hof, David Holtzman, Brad Horn, Mike Huang, Rob Hudson, Joanne Hulbert, Tom Hutyler, Jeff Idelson, Jane Janz, Jane Jarvis, David Jasen, Steve Johnson, Megan Kaiser, Ron Kaplan, Nancy Kauffman, Pat Kelly, David Kiehn, Walt Knauff, Jen Knight, Tara Krieger, Audrey Kupferberg, Lloyd Kuritsky, Patrick Lagreid, Tom Larwin, Maury Laws, Eric Leong, James Leroux, Gary Levy, Chris Long, Lee Lowenfish, Ted Lukacs, Doug Lyons, Jeffrey Lyons, Sue MacKay, Peter Mancuso, John Matthew IV, Skip McAfee, Jim McArdle, Jim McCarty, Andy McCue, Susan Mendolia, Aleta Mercer, Annie Merovich, Wayne Messmer, Erik Meyer, Scot Mondore, Steve Montgomery, Tony Morante, Peter Morris, Emmanuel Munoz, Michael Mushalla, Richard Musterer, Kurt Nauck, Elinor Nauen, Lindsay Nauen, Varda Nauen, Rod Nelson, Randy Newman, Bill Nowlin, Fred Obligado, Michael Oletta, Charlie O'Reilly, Cliff Otto, Dale Petroskey, Amanda Pinney, Elizabeth Price, John Ralph, Rich Reese, Rick Reiger, Greg Rhodes, Fred O. Rodgers, Stephen Roney, Micahel Rovatsos, Annie Russell, Charles Sachs, Stu Saffer, Robert Schaeffer, Gabriel Schechter, Elten Schiller, Ron Seaver, Mark Sheldon, Andy Shenk, Tom Simon, Brad Smith, Ted Spencer, Albert Steg, Dan Stein, Jim Steinblatt, Bill Stetka, Milo Stewart, Jr., Helen Stiles, Kimberly Stuart, Carey Stumm, Fred Sturm, C. K. Suero, Bart Swain, Marian Von Tilzer, Linda Thompson, Rick Thompson, John Thorn, Stew Thornley, Sara Velez, Linda Vessa, Bob Watkins, Jeff Weber, Mark Wernick, Rick White, Benjamin Walter Wiles, Howard and Sonya Wiles, Dave Winfield, Jim Young, and Rich Zumbach.

INTRODUCTION

THE HISTORY OF BASEBALL is unparalleled. There are few institutions–if any–that can claim such a rich history while still evoking so much passion. This compelling combination resonates stronger than ever today. A look across the landscape of our sport shows that our national pastime continues to thrive.

As we reach unprecedented new heights, we recognize that baseball is a game of great tradition, and there is no finer tradition within the game than "Take Me Out to the Ball Game." Like the game itself, the song is timeless. It is the staple of the seventh-inning stretch. I find it fitting that, with the notable exceptions of "Happy Birthday" and "The Star-Spangled Banner," "Take Me Out to the Ball Game" is the most frequently heard song in America. Such a fact illustrates the prominent place of baseball in our culture, a position that we embrace.

The genesis for "Take Me Out to the Ball Game" is a young woman's eschewing a show in favor of a day at the ballpark. In that sense, the song serves as a perfect display of passion for our game. Today, fans are attending Major League Baseball games in record numbers. Our overall record for single-season attendance has been broken for four consecutive years, culminating in a banner 2007 season. More likely than not, each of the 79,503,175 fans who attended a regular season game in 2007 had the opportunity to sing along or simply relish in the work of the song's co-writers, Jack Norworth and Albert Von Tilzer.

It is interesting that, according to lore, neither Norworth nor Von Tilzer had ever attended a major league ball game before they assembled this great piece of Americana. In doing so, I believe the song was a major factor in the transformation of a trip to the ballpark into a communal event for all to enjoy. As someone whose mother brought him to Yankee Stadium in 1949 to see the great Joe DiMaggio and who now takes his grandkids to the ballpark, I know that a baseball game remains a wonderful family experience. The ambience that emanates from "Take Me Out to the Ball Game" is inviting to one and all. Whether one is the kind of fan who is keeping score, or one who wants to enjoy the green grass and the sunshine, or one who is simply there to be with his or her family, "Take Me Out to the Ball Game" adds to the fabric of the experience for everyone, which is how baseball should be.

Before "Take Me Out to the Ball Game" was popularized during the seventh-inning stretch, the song first gained notice from audiences in movie theaters. Since then, it has been heard in more than 1,200 movies and television shows. More than 400 artists have recorded the song, from Bing Crosby and Frank Sinatra to Aretha Franklin and Carly Simon. It is quite special that such an influential song has its roots in the best game in the world, and it's yet another sign of how entwined baseball and our culture are.

All of us have heard the legendary Harry Caray lead "Take Me Out to the Ball Game" at Wrigley Field. While Harry is gone, the show in the *Friendly Confines* has gone on. Whether it is our civic leaders, stars of stage and screen, athletes, or other icons who have taken their turns at the microphone, "Take Me Out to the Ball Game" remains a profound tradition at the venerable ballpark in Wrigleyville. If there is another sight in our entire society quite like the scene at Wrigley during "Take Me Out to the Ball Game," I have yet to see it.

"Take Me Out to the Ball Game" is a distinguished part of the grand old game. I hope that you enjoy this exploration of baseball's anthem.

Allan H. "Bud" Selig
Commissioner of Major League Baseball

Take Me Out To The Ball Game
by Jack Norworth

Katie Casey was baseball "mad"
Had the fever and had it bad,
Just to root for the home ~~town~~ TOWN crew
Every sue — Katie blew
On a Saturday, her ~~young beau~~ YOUNG BEAU
Called to see if she'd like to go
To see a show But Miss ~~Kate~~ KATE said no,
I'll tell you what you can do —

—

Take me out to the ball game
Take me out WITH ~~the~~ the ~~park~~ CROWD
Buy me some peanuts and crackerjack
I don't care if I never get back
Let me root, root, root for the home team
If they don't win its a shame,
For its one, two, three strikes, your out
At the old ball game

THE RETURN OF
PEANUTS

BY IRA BERKOW

I BEG THE READER'S indulgence (and Andy's, Bob's, and Tim's, too) by quoting myself—I promise I won't be long. But this is how I began my "Sports of the Times" column in the *New York Times* for the October 11, 2001, edition, one month exactly after four American airplanes, hijacked by maniacal zealots bent on murder, changed our lives forever:

I want to miss "Take Me Out to the Ball Game." I want to miss the inanity of it, of the peanuts and the Cracker Jack and not caring if I never get back. And I indeed miss the time, a lifetime ago, a hundred thousand years ago it seems, in a world now so utterly unrecognizable, so relatively benign, that we

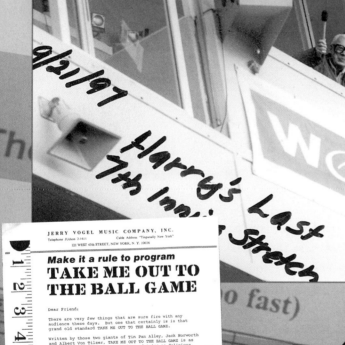

9/21/97

Harry's Last
7th Inning Stretch

JERRY VOGEL MUSIC COMPANY, INC.
Telephone JUdson 2-1611   Cable Address "Tinpanally New York"
121 WEST 45th STREET, NEW YORK, N. Y. 10036

Make it a rule to program

TAKE ME OUT TO
THE BALL GAME

Dear Friend:

There are very few things that are sure fire with any
audience these days. But one that certainly is is that
grand old standard TAKE ME OUT TO THE BALL GAME.

Written by those two giants of Tin Pan Alley, Jack Norworth
and Albert Von Tilzer, TAKE ME OUT TO THE BALL GAME is as
American as Ma's apple pan dowdy, and twice as delicious.
It's the only song that Americans can hear from Opening Day
in April until World Series time in October and never get
fed up.

The reason TAKE ME OUT TO THE BALL GAME is such a natural
born winner is that even if it were not about baseball it
would still be a great song. There is no known dance from
waltz cog to nerve tap that you can't do to TAKE ME OUT TO
THE BALL GAME. Even people who can't understand a word of
English love it. It's just a truly great song.

And when you add to all this intrinsic merit the happy
connotations of TAKE ME OUT TO THE BALL GAME and the good
times it stands for, you can see that you just can't program
it too often. So start programming it soon, and keep right
on going. And when you're looking for a tune for your next
commercial, keep it near the top of the list. Ask me about
our commercial usage rates. They're lighter than you think.

                              Always the same,
                                        Jerry
                                   Jerry Vogel

"THE OLD SONGS ARE THE BEST SON

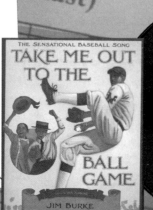

THE SENSATIONAL BASEBALL SONG

TAKE ME OUT
TO THE

BALL
GAME

JIM BURKE

SPORTING LIFE

The Ball Sticks
EVERY TIME

Ask to see Goldsmith Professional Fielder Glove. Professional and Amateur players say
they are just what they have
been looking for. Made large
and soft, of fine pliable leather,
full leather lined, with special
arrangement of padding making a deep Ball
Holding Pocket. Ready for use the minute you
take them from the box. Remember—

Base Balls . . . $.05 to $1.25   Fielder Gloves . $ .15 to $3.50
Base Ball Uniforms 1.75 to 15.00 Catcher Mitts . . .25 to 7.50
Basemen Mitts . . 1.00 to 4.00 Base Ball Bats . . .10 to 1.00

Write for free catalog of Baseball Uniforms shown in all colors
and styles. The Goldsmith Official League Ball is adopted by many
Leagues. Fully Guaranteed. Price $1.25.

Goldsmith Guarantees Perfect Goods or a new article in case of any defect,
dealer selling Base Ball goods. If he can't supply you
with Goldsmith's Guaranteed Goods, we will send goods
direct, prepaid, except here on receipt of catalog price.

THE GOLDSMITH GLOVE

P. Goldsmith's Sons
215 W. Pearl St. Cincinnati, Ohio

IRVING BERLIN

God Bless America
Land that I love
Stand beside her
And guide her
Through the night with a light
From above
From the mountains
To the prairies
To the oceans
White with foam
God Bless America
My home sweet home.

Irving Berlin

Handwritten lyrics to Irving Berlin's "God Bless America," a staple at many ballparks during the seventh-inning stretch, especially since September 11, 2001.

Legendary broadcaster Harry Caray.

could indeed forget our problems for three hours at a ballpark.

Now, at the seventh-inning stretch in baseball games, instead of the traditional "Take Me Out to the Ball Game," they are playing "God Bless America." I like "God Bless America," too. And I've been in ballparks in the last few weeks in which they've played it. . . . It is moving. The game stops dead in its tracks and we remember the atrocities committed at the World Trade Center and at the Pentagon, and the battle in the plane that crashed in Pennsylvania, as well as the bravery and goodness of so many in response.

But I miss the sweet song "Take Me Out to the Ball Game," that ode to triviality.

"God Bless America" halts the dream world to recall the nightmare. . . .

I hope the new seventh-inning song doesn't last past these playoffs and World Series. I hope we've had enough of what the song means to us at so raw a time that we won't need to be reminded of it again, or as often. It would mean returning, partially anyway, to a world we once knew. . . .

The following season, Bud Selig, the commissioner of baseball—wisely, as I viewed it—issued a directive to the ball clubs that "God Bless America" should be played only on holidays (Memorial Day, the Fourth of July, and Labor Day, particularly). It was more of a recommendation than an order, and most teams complied. Some clubs, however, like the New York Yankees, continue to this day to play "God Bless America" at the seventh-inning stretch—it's usually the famous recording by the robust Kate Smith—alongside "Take Me Out to the Ball

Kate Smith is to "God Bless America" as Harry Caray is to "Take Me Out to the Ball Game."

Game." It was Selig's obvious intent for baseball fans to, as the song implies, take time out for a few hours of unalloyed pleasure, and where the worst thing that can happen is that the home team doesn't triumph and that's "a shame." The world, or buildings, don't collapse.

I was born and raised in Chicago, grew up a Cubs

> *"I've often thought that 'Take Me Out to the Ball Game,' the theme song of our national pastime, would fit beautifully as our national anthem."*–IRA BERKOW

fan (one story among a multitude regarding the Cubs' futility went that one afternoon the public address announcer cried, "Will the lady who lost her nine boys please pick them up immediately. They're beating the Cubs 7–0"), and I learned that if the home team loses, the sun, barring showers, will shine the next day. When Harry Caray, with those outsized glasses and outsized personality, arrived at the ivied Wrigley Field in 1982, his croaky, invariably off-key, seventh-inning rendition of "Take Me Out to the Ball Game" quickly became a tradition. He leaned perilously out of the broadcast booth–Harry was widely known to enjoy a nip or two–his microphone acting as a conductor's baton, and the usual sellout crowd of some 35,000 turned to Caray as though he were some odd deity and, nearly piously, swayed as one as he warbled.

I've often thought that "Take Me Out to the Ball

Game," the theme song of our national pastime, would fit beautifully as our national anthem. No perilous fights, no bombs bursting in air, though there are indeed echoes of the land of the free and the home of the brave. And it has the added advantage of feasting on snacks.

No one, in our lifetime certainly, will ever forget the horror of September 11, 2001. I see no need, except perhaps for holidays, to be reminded of it on a regular basis at a ball game. For some of us, every time we see an airplane in flight is reminder enough. For some of us, every time we look at a tall building, it's a reminder. And beyond that there are the continuing media stories of the victims (from ordinary citizens to responders), of the victims' families, of the true-to-life heroes, of the construction of monuments, of the inevitable recollections on the anniversaries.

And "so," as I concluded in my column on October 11, 2001, "we go to the pleasure domes that are our playgrounds, and, unable yet to suspend disbelief, we sing with often moist eyes not 'Take Me Out to the Ball Game' but 'God Bless America.'

"It's what we need for now. After all, it's still letting us, with raised voices, 'root, root, root for the home team.'"

Now, some seven years later, what we need in the seventh-inning stretch is simply a full-throated call to "root, root, root" for our other home team, the one with the guys wearing ball caps, knickers, and cleats. Kate Smith, after all, is still there when we need her.

PROLOGUE

FROM THE *SMITHSONIAN* ARTICLE, "BASEBALL'S ANTHEM FOR ALL AGES," BY NANCY KRIPLEN

ON THE EVE of the 1956 World Series, a sickly, seventy-eight-year-old man lay in his Beverly Hills apartment watching television. The year had produced a "subway series"—the Brooklyn Dodgers versus the New York Yankees—and now, on his Sunday-night TV show, Ed Sullivan introduced some stars of the game: Yogi Berra, Sal Maglie, and Hank Aaron. As the studio audience applauded, the band played "Take Me Out to the Ball Game"—no words, just the disarmingly simple, soft-shoe waltz in the cheerful key of D major that the man in the bed, Albert Von Tilzer, had composed forty-eight years earlier. After Sullivan bid his audience good night, Von Tilzer's nurse turned off the TV and tucked him in for the evening. Sometime before morning, Von Tilzer died. It is nice to think that the final melody the old man heard was his own.

Albert Von Tilzer Is Dead at 78; Wrote 'Take Me Out to Ball Game'

LOS ANGELES, Oct. 1 (UP)— Albert Von Tilzer, composer of "Take Me Out to the Ball Game" and many other song hits, died today at his apartment after a long illness. His age was 78.

He teamed with Jack Norworth, lyricist, in composing baseball's theme song, and had been an outstanding name in the popular song field for nearly half a century.

Other popular tunes written by Mr. Von Tilzer included "Put Your Arms Around Me Honey" and "I'll Be with You in Apple Blossom Time."

Mr. Von Tilzer was born in Indianapolis. He was a charter member of the American Society of Composers, Authors and Publishers.

One of Five Brothers

Although Mr. Von Tilzer wrote the song that has become a baseball classic, he reputedly never saw a baseball game until twenty years after it was written.

He was one of five brothers who made popular-music history in New York at the turn of the century. He and his brother Harry were among Tin Pan Alley's most prolific composers.

Another brother, Wilbur, wrote the lyrics for Albert's first song hit, "That's What the Daisy Said." Wilbur and two other brothers, Jules and Jack, later became heads of New York music publishing concerns.

The brothers' family name was Gumm. Their father operated a shoe store, first in Goshen, Ind., and later in Indianapolis.

Harry, the oldest, left home at 14 to join the Cole Brothers Circus. He adopted his mother's maiden name of Tilzer and added the Von for a touch of class. His brothers followed his example.

Albert, who was born on March 29, 1878, studied in Indianapolis public schools. A self-taught pianist, he became musical director of a vaudeville show. After his brother Harry made his mark as a composer in New York, Albert followed him here.

Albert worked as a shoe salesman in a Brooklyn store and studied harmony, his first formal music training. His first published work was "The Absent-Minded Beggar Waltz," which came out in 1900.

Harry, meanwhile, had written many of the songs that made him famous—"A Bird in a Gilded Cage," "Wait Till the Sun Shines Nellie" and "I Want a Girl (Just Like the Girl That Married Dear Old Dad)"—and had organized his own music publishing house.

Albert went to work in the Chicago office of the business but stayed only a few years. In 1903, he organized a publishing house with his brother Jack.

He wrote a number of songs that sold more than 1,000,000 copies, among them "Take Me Out to the Ball Game." Mr. Norworth also wrote the words to many other of his songs.

Among Mr. Von Tilzer's other compositions were "O by Jingo," "Roll Along Prairie Moon," "Heart of My Heart" and "Oh How She Could Yacki Hacki Wicki Wacki Woo."

After having established himself as a composer, Mr. Von Tilzer toured the old Orpheum vaudeville circuit for several seasons. He then turned to musical comedy writing, producing such hits as "Gingham Girl," "Honey Girl," "Adrienne," "Bye Bye Bonnie" and "Somewhere." He moved to California in 1930 and lived there until his death. His brother Harry died in 1946.

The New York Times

Copyright © The New York Times
Originally published October 2, 1956

8

UNSUNG HEROES

I wrote a letter to God the other day and I said, "Dear God, why did you let somebody else write 'Take Me Out to the Ball Game'?"
—Harry Ruby (composer of such hits as "Who's Sorry Now" and "I Wanna Be Loved By You")

WHO HAS DONE the most to popularize baseball in our culture? Is it Babe Ruth, whose booming home-run bat thrilled fans–and made fans–in the Roaring Twenties while he redefined how the game was played? Was it Henry Chadwick, the first baseball writer, who did much to build popular interest in the game in the nineteenth century? Or perhaps it was Charles Schulz, who created the wildly popular *Peanuts* comic strip, which he drew for forty-nine years. A whopping 10

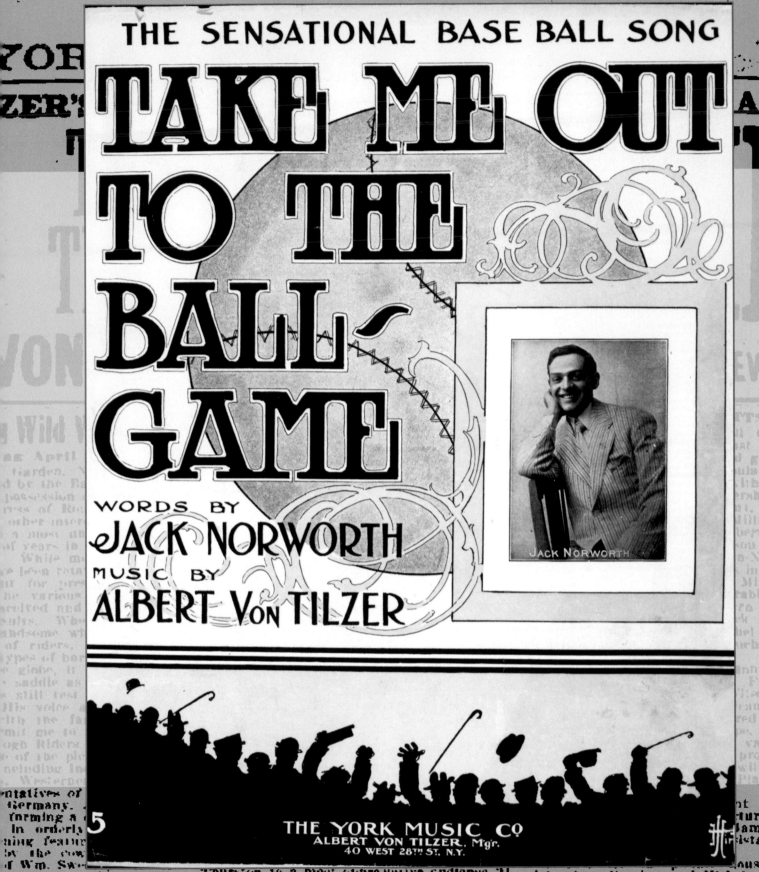

percent of *Peanuts* strips told stories of Charlie Brown's hapless baseball team—and the strip ran in approximately seventy-five countries.

What about Sy Berger, the Brooklynite whose leadership of the Topps chewing gum company popularized baseball-card collecting in the 1950s and beyond? If there were a Hall of Fame for promoting baseball—rather than playing it—all these would be worthy candidates, but they might all pale in comparison to an unlikely partnership of a sailor from Philadelphia and a shoe salesman from Indiana, who, according to one baseball executive, "did more to sentimentalize and popularize baseball in the heart of the American public than any other single factor in its history—with the possible exception of the fabulous bat of Babe Ruth."[2] It is worth noting that the executive in question was so quoted on the song's fiftieth anniversary, in 1958—and that the song has grown exponentially in popularity since then, largely due to another great baseball duo—Bill Veeck and Harry Caray—more on them later.

Jack Norworth, our Philadelphia sailor, and Albert Von Tilzer, our shoe salesman, wrote the immortal "Take Me Out to the Ball Game" in 1908, Jack handling the lyrics and Albert the music. Who were these unsung heroes, and how did they come to write baseball's anthem, often called the third most frequently sung tune in America, after the national anthem and "Happy Birthday"?

Jack Norworth was born John Godfrey Knauff in Philadelphia on January 5, 1879, the third child of Theodore Christian Knauff, a second-generation maker of pipe organs and an Episcopal choirmaster, and Louisa H. (Pearson) Knauff. As a boy, Jack sang in the choir at St. Mark's Episcopal Church, and presumably knew his way around a keyboard, given his father's occupation.[3]

While music was the family business, it was theater that called to young Jack, who recalled that "me and a couple of friends used to walk through a neigh-

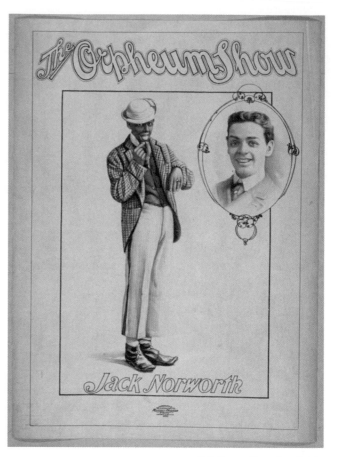

Jack Norworth performing in blackface early in his career.

borhood and wherever anybody was having a little party in their house we would go in and put on a little minstrel show for cake and ice cream."[4] To cure him of the theater bug, Jack was sent off to sea in early adolescence, spending two years aboard the school ship *Saratoga*, learning the sea trade. He then spent four years as a quartermaster on ships sailing back and forth from London to New York while he also "flitted from one port to another in Europe, Asia, Africa and Australia."[5] While at sea, Norworth wrote and directed shows for the sailors, and thus was prepared to embark on a theatrical career when he returned ashore before age twenty due to rheumatism. Still not interested in joining the family business, he later remarked, "I didn't want to work all my life for $5,000 a year and a white beard." [6]

Instead of a white beard, he chose the burnt cork

of black face, a ubiquitous theatrical motif of the time, for $25 a week in Camden, New Jersey, in 1898. To set himself apart, Norworth quickly developed his own persona, "The College Boy," which was an immediate hit.[7] He was soon in great demand, and moved to Brooklyn and its brighter footlights. The theater scene in New York was thriving and so was Jack. During one week in 1899, he was engaged, along with several other performers, to appear in two theaters on the same evening, which meant he had to take horse-drawn cabs from one theater "to the other at full speed and in the full glory of . . . stage make up."[8]

The following year, 1900, one Albert Von Tilzer (born March 29, 1878) moved from Indianapolis to New York. Von Tilzer came from a Jewish family of five brothers, all involved in the music business. His older brother Harry was the prolific kingpin of Tin Pan Alley (in fact, Harry later claimed that the phrase "Tin Pan Alley" was his creation, referring to the tinny sounds of pianos heard along 28th Street between Broadway and Sixth Avenue). Harry changed his family name from its original Gumm (shortened from Gumbinski) to Tilzer (his mother's maiden name) and added the Von for a touch of class. Albert and two other music industry brothers followed suit.[9]

There's no business like shoe business, which is what occupied their father, Jacob Gumm, who owned a shoe store in Indianapolis, with his large family living in the back. Auspiciously, the space overhead housed a small theatrical auditorium that played host to touring stock companies. This enchanted Harry, who ran away at age fourteen to join the Cole Brothers Circus.[10]

That same year, Harry wrote his first published song, "I Love You Both," and moved to New York, earning his passage there as a horse groomsman and arriving with $1.65 in his pocket. For six years, he worked as a pianist and singer at saloons, selling the songs he wrote to other performers for a couple of bucks each. His big break came when he sold a song, "My Old New Hampshire Home," to a publisher for ten dollars—the song went on to sell over a million copies, and the astute Von Tilzer accepted an offer to become a partner in a song publishing concern.[11] Harry is also noted for first publishing the compositions of two immortal American composers who began in Tin Pan Alley, Irving Berlin and George Gershwin.[12]

Growing up in Indianapolis, Albert Von Tilzer taught himself the piano and later became a pianist and arranger in Chicago for his brother Harry's publishing firm of Shapiro, Bernstein and Von Tilzer. In 1900 he moved to New York, first working in a Brooklyn shoe store and then directing a vaudeville company before joining his brother's newly established publishing house as an arranger. In 1903 he formed the York Music Company with another brother, Jack Von Tilzer. It was York Music that first published "Take Me Out to the Ball Game" in 1908. Norworth and Von Tilzer had first collaborated on the modest 1906 hit "Holding Hands" and went on to write several hit songs together, including "Honey Boy," "Good Evening Caroline," and "Smarty."[13]

In 1908, Jack Norworth met, and a week later married, popular stage singer Nora Bayes. The story goes that Jack was singing one of his songs in his dressing room and Nora popped in, saying, "I like that song, will you let me use it in my act?" Norworth replied that she could have the song if she would have him as well, and they soon began a personal and professional partnership that would last for the next six years, until they were divorced in 1913. It was the second of five marriages for each.

They debuted their mega hit, "Shine on Harvest Moon," in the Ziegfeld Follies of 1908, and the song now ranks as the only bit of

Left, Albert Von Tilzer *Bottom, right,* Nora Bayes.

Norworth's work that can challenge "Take Me Out to the Ball Game" in the musical memory of America. It was the title of the 1944 Hollywood motion picture based on Norworth's life, though if a biopic were to be made of him today, it would probably be called *Take Me Out to the Ball Game*. The two songs were very good to Norworth, who was quoted as saying, "My songs do very nicely by me. Because as soon as spring baseball training begins, the bands start playing 'Take Me Out to the Ball Game,' and that lasts right through the World Series. And then they start playing "Harvest Moon," and that carries me through until spring again."[14]

Jack and Nora were as big a celebrity pair in America as could be imagined. By today's standards, they might have the fame of a Brad Pitt and Angelina Jolie or a Garth Brooks and Trisha Yearwood. They were known as "the happiest married pair on the stage," and it was clear that the whole was more than the sum of the formidable parts: "That Bayes and Norworth together and Bayes and Norworth separate are different theatrical propositions from the box office standpoint is well known."[15] They were both talented and charismatic: "Their voices are exceedingly pleasing, but perhaps a better explanation of their hold on their audiences is that they have the valuable asset generally described as magnetism."[16] In his classic 1953 study, *Vaudeville*, Joe Laurie, Jr., called them the "top singing couple in America,"

adding that "nobody could touch them as to class, diction, looks, harmony, and showmanship."[17]

Offstage, the couple pursued life with vigor, renting out half floors of hotels, living in private railroad cars,[18] once being arrested eight times in a single week for speeding,[19] and even owning an airplane.[20] But the high life caught up with Jack and Nora, who were busy in vaudeville, stage plays, and recordings nonstop throughout their marriage. When they parted in 1913, Nora quipped, "We were known as the happiest couple on the stage. We were— on the stage." Within two weeks, Bayes was married to a man with whom she'd been in a recent play, and Norworth lasted three weeks before marrying an actress, Mary Johnson, with whom he'd appeared onstage.[21] Norworth's marriage to Johnson lasted until 1927, and produced his only children, Edward Fields and John Robert.[22]

Both Bayes and Norworth went "Over There" to future successes. Nora toured England in 1914 and continued headlining in vaudeville and appearing in legitimate theater in New York while also becoming the performer most associated with George M. Cohan's classic World War I tune "Over There."[23] Jack Norworth went to England in 1913 and stayed there for the better part of four years, touring, making records, and appearing in *Rosy Rapture*, a musical written by *Peter Pan* author J. M. Barrie, which featured Jack's star turn in the tongue-twisting song "Which Switch Is the Switch, Miss, for Ipswich?" He later became known for singing tongue twisters such as "Sister Susie's Sewing Shirts for Soldiers."[24]

Upon Norworth's return from England, he headlined on Broadway and starred in a musical review of his own making, *Odds and Ends of 1917*, which ran at the newly christened Norworth Theatre, 125 W. 48th St., owned by Norworth for four months. It was later renamed the

Interior of the Jack Norworth Theatre on 48th Street in Manhattan.

Belmont, and in the 1930s became a movie theater, which was demolished in 1951.[25]

Much is made of the idea that neither Albert Von Tilzer nor Jack Norworth ever attended a big league baseball game. There are sketchy references to Von Tilzer attending a ball game twenty years after "Take Me Out to the Ball Game" was written. Norworth constantly claimed that he didn't attend a ball game for decades after writing the song. He may have attended a game in 1938—again the references are inconclusive, but he is known to have attended a Brooklyn Dodgers game on June 27, 1940, at Ebbets Field, when the Dodgers hosted "Jack Norworth Day." In the evening, a testimonial dinner for Norworth was given at Brooklyn's St. George Hotel, with former New York City mayor Jimmy Walker serving as toastmaster.[26]

Norworth, however, may have been holding out on us all in order to promote himself and "Ball Game," as he called the song. In a 1951 column in *The Sporting News*, Oscar Ruhl reported on a reminiscing session at Al Schacht's restaurant, where vaudeville star Joe Laurie, Jr., reminded Norworth that he had taken him to his first big league game. "That's right," recalled Norworth, "we were both on the same bill at the Palace and you practically dragged me up to see John McGraw at the Polo Grounds. I don't think they even knew there was an American League club in New York in those days. But once I got the fever of going to big league games, I never got over it. In fact, after that, I wrote an umpire song, "Let's Get the Umpire's Goat."

There are several date clues in the statement: McGraw managed the Giants until 1932—so it had to be before that. The Yankees were not a big draw in New York, which meant it had to be before 1920, when Babe Ruth came over from Boston. Most telling, however, is the reference to "Let's Get the Umpire's Goat," written in 1909. Since that's only a year after "Take Me Out to the Ball Game," it seems entirely possible that Jack Norworth saw his first big league game in 1908, the same year he wrote the song—or perhaps even earlier.[27]

Norworth and Bayes tried for a second baseball hit a year after "Take Me Out to the Ball Game."

"If I die in Wentworth, Laguna won't get the publicity."–JACK NORWORTH

In a promotion for the Norworth biopic *Shine On Harvest Moon*, released on April 8, 1944, Jack Norworth was on hand, along with actors Dennis Morgan (who plays Norworth in the film) and Jack Carson, for opening day at the Hollywood Stars baseball team in the Pacific Coast League. Norworth threw out the first pitch to local sheriff Gene Biscalluz while baseball-loving comedian Joe E. Brown stood in wielding a bat.[28]

Albert Von Tilzer had moved to California in the 1930s, and Norworth followed him in the early 1940s, living first in Hollywood and later in Laguna Beach. In 1944, there was a gala performance at the Shrine Auditorium in Los Angeles, a two-night concert called "America's Music." Both Norworth and Von Tilzer were on the bill, but separately–an interesting twist. Not much is known of the relationship between the two in their later years. Von Tilzer performed "Take Me Out to the Ball Game," while Norworth did "Shine On Harvest Moon."[29]

While living in California, Von Tilzer appears to have kept a low profile. While this is probably due in part to the long illness referred to in his obituary, it is also an interesting contrast to Norworth, who moved to Hollywood and opened a retail store devoted to his lifelong hobby of collecting miniatures–the shop later moved with him to Laguna Beach. Norworth was also active in local service clubs, worked with a local community theater group, and founded and was honorary president of the Laguna Beach chapter of Little League, which gave the Jack Norworth Trophy out each year. The trophy read "Presented by The Cracker Jack Co. to the Most Valuable Player in the Little League of Laguna Beach."[30] Norworth could always be found marching in the annual Little League parade, tossing out boxes of Cracker Jack. During this period, Norworth also made frequent trips back to New York to appear on *Ed Sullivan* and other variety shows.[31]

While both men were show business giants, Norworth appears to have had the more outgoing personality and love of the limelight. When Albert Von Tilzer passed away first, in 1956, his obituaries often led with his role as composer of "Take Me Out to the Ball Game," going on to mention more than twenty other million-selling songs in the music business.[32]

Norworth was left alone to observe the fiftieth anniversary of "Take Me Out to the Ball Game" in 1958, and he appears to have benefited from, if not orchestrated, a raft of publicity surrounding the song's anniversary. He appeared at the Los Angeles Coliseum for another "Jack Norworth Day" from the Dodgers–perhaps he was the only man to be so honored in both Brooklyn and Los

L/122101-12/21/63-LAS VEGAS, NEV. -- "Take Me Out to the Ball Game" is the opening number sung by the Los Angeles Dodgers as they were joined by comedian Joey Bishop on stage at the Sands Hotel in Las Vegas, Nev., Saturday night. Jack Entratter, Sands president, brought Bishop and the baseballing world champion songsters together for the night club act which opened Saturday. The Dodgers are, from the left, Frank Howard, Tommy Davis, Ron Perranoski, Willie Davis, Don Drysdale and Bill Skowron. That's Joey Bishop at far left, out of uniform. UPI TELEPHOTO

KEITH & PROCTOR'S FIFTH AVE. THEATRE
BROADWAY and 28th STREET
Now Playing   A VERITABLE VAUDEVILLE SENSATION.   Now Playing

NORA BAYES and JACK NORWORTH

Norworth and Bayes were one of the most popular show business couples the nation had ever seen.

Angeles. That same day, July 11, 1958, was declared "Take Me Out to the Ball Game Day" by the Los Angeles city council.[33] And in contrast to the quiet, almost lovely death of Von Tilzer described in the Smithsonian story in "Prologue," Norworth went out with a bang. After coming out of a stroke-induced coma, his first words were reportedly "How're the Dodgers doing?"[34] He insisted on being taken home to Laguna Beach, as his condition was improving. Ever the showman, Norworth told fifth wife, Amy, to take him home. "If I die in Wentworth (at the UCLA Medical Center)," he quipped in perhaps his final joke, "Laguna won't get the publicity."[35]

RAPID TRANSIT CO.

Local Stations, shown
Sub=Power Stations,

16 10000   15000 FEET.

FEET.

04.

B O R O U

Q U

The Ball Game

"Take m
out to the
Ball Game"

BLACKWELL'S ISLAND

HIT OR MYTH?

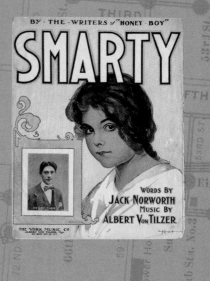

BY THE WRITERS OF "HONEY BOY"

SMARTY

WORDS BY
JACK NORWORTH
MUSIC BY
ALBERT VON TILZER

THE YORK MUSIC CO

I N THE NATIONAL BASEBALL Hall of Fame and
Museum's archives sits a piece of paper, crumpled and apparently
old, that is purported to be the original manuscript of the lyrics to "Take
Me Out to the Ball Game." Norworth claimed that in the spring of 1908
while riding a New York City subway, he spotted an ad for the Polo
Grounds advertising a ball game that day. Inspired, he took out a piece
of paper and wrote the lyrics to the song. Ironically, this wasn't the first
time Norworth claimed to have written a song while riding public trans-
portation. The song "Smarty" was supposedly written on Thanksgiving
Day. According to the story, "Norworth was standing in a swaying, dirty
day coach in Boston when he suddenly reached for an old envelope and
pencil and scribbled the lyrics to 'Smarty.'" Either Norworth frequently
wrote while on public conveyances or he knew a colorful story
when he had one and used it to suit his purposes.[1]

Whether that piece of paper is the same manuscript in the
collection of the Hall of Fame is not entirely clear. The Hall of
Fame came into possession of the manuscript in 1953 as a result
of a donation by Alexander G. Law, a miniature-ship model collector from Englewood, New Jersey, and a friend of Norworth's

THE BASE BALL CRANK
He's a bawling megaphone, a human idiot,
When will he cease to talk unmitigated rot,
When will he stop his senseless howl
Of strike and base and home and foul?
He talks of nothing else but ball.
That is he does not talk, he can only bawl.

S   O   N

Jack Norworth's manuscript for
"Take Me Out to the Ball Game,"
now in the collection of the
National Baseball Hall of Fame.

TAKE ME OUT TO THE BALL GAME
BY JACK NORWORTH

KATIE CASEY WAS BASE BALL "MAD
HAD THE FEVER AND HAD IT BAD,
JUST TO ROOT FOR THE HOME TOWN CREW
EVERY SUE — KATIE BLEW
ON A SATURDAY, HER YOUNG BEAU
CALLED TO SEE IF SHE'D LIKE TO GO
TO SEE A SHOW BUT MISS KATE SAID NO,
I'LL TELL YOU WHAT YOU CAN DO —

TAKE ME OUT TO THE BALL GAME
TAKE ME OUT WITH THE CROUD
BUY ME SOME PEANUTS AND CRACKER JACK
I DON'T CARE IF I NEVER GET BACK
LET ME ROOT, ROOT, ROOT FOR THE HOME TEAM
IF THEY DON'T WIN ITS A SHAME,
FOR ITS ONE, TWO, THREE STRIKES YOUR OUT
AT THE OLD BALL GAME

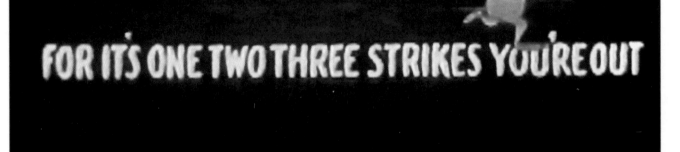

A cartoon mouse takes a swing in this video still.

FOR IT'S ONE TWO THREE STRIKES YOU'RE OUT

(both were miniature model collectors). In an October 29, 1953, letter to the Hall of Fame, Law wrote:

Dear Mr. Keener:

You may recall our conversation at the Museum on August 7th of this year. I promised you I would try to get for the Museum's Exhibition an autographed first edition of Jack Norworth's song, "Take Me Out to the Ball Game."

Jack not only has sent me the autographed and inscribed first printed edition, he has included his original, hand lettered manuscript as well.

I am enclosing both items herewith which, I hope will be given the prominent place both Jack and his song have earned among baseball immortals. Also enclosed you will find Jack's letter to me. You may consider this letter as a part of the entire donation since it authenticates both the song sheet, (autographed 1953)—and the original "Dressing Room" rough draft of 1908.

I would appreciate it if you will acknowledge receipt of these items both to Jack Norworth and myself.

Sincerely yours,
Alexander G. Law

Accompanying the letter from Law were the hand written lyrics, along with a letter from Norworth to Law, dated October 10, 1953:

Dear Al,

I am sending you the original draft of "Take Me Out to the Ball Game," but could not locate it at the time you asked for it. Sorry.

By now you have an original copy of the song, auto-graphed by me for the museum at Cooperstown. If they don't want it, you may have it with my compliments. But I think they should have it up there. It is a real museum piece. An original copy I mean.

I was rooting for the "Bums" to win the World Series. Doggone it. Maybe they will turn the trick next year.

All best wishes from Amy and myself to Balnch [sic] and of course that includes you.

Always sincerely,
Jack

Norworth would often send handwritten lyrics of his songs to friends and colleagues; however, in his letter to Law, he refers to the document as the "original draft." We didn't have the means to test-date the paper or pencil (mind you, we're writing about a song, not a crime scene), so we don't know if this "original draft" was indeed written in 1908. If it is the same piece of paper from Norworth's subway ride, Norworth must have either had a steady hand or the New York City subway offered a very smooth ride, for Jack's handwriting is exceptionally neat (one of us attempted to write the lyrics to "Take Me Out to the Ball Game" while riding the Broadway 1 train in Manhattan and the results were nearly illegible).

As to the much ballyhooed subway ride, Albert Von Tilzer's version of how "Take Me Out to the Ball Game" came to be mentions nothing about a subway. He claimed that the idea for the lyrics started with the phrase, "One, two, three strikes you're out."

"It had sock," Von Tilzer added. "I finally worked it into a song and Jack wrote the lyric."[2]

Albert's version of how "Take Me Out to the Ball Game" was conceived is quite plausible. The musical structure of the song is built around the *one–two–three strikes you're out* phrase. In fact, it's the high point of the song (see "What's in a Song?").

If it is indeed true that Jack wrote "Take Me Out to

Subway scenes like these were familiar to Jack Norworth.

the Ball Game" on a New York subway, it would seem logical that he and Von Tilzer would have touted the story. This was after all a mega hit in 1908. Surely there'd be an interview, a quote, a story, or a secondhand account of this famous subway ride. But there appears to be nothing—until 1958—exactly fifty years after the song was written, and five years after the Hall of Fame had acquired the "original draft" from A. G. Law.

It's curious that fifty years would pass before any word of a subway ride would surface. It's even more curious that the first mention of the subway ride occurred only after Albert Von Tilzer had passed away in 1956, leaving no chance for Von Tilzer to respond. But there it was—in 1958, within a year of his passing, Jack Norworth gave an interview in which he related, apparently for the first time, the story of how he came to write "Take Me Out to the Ball Game":

"I was on the New York subway one day," Norworth explained, "and saw a poster that read, 'Come to the Polo Grounds.' An idea occurred to me. There had been many baseball songs but none ever became popular. I took an old scrap of paper from my pocket and started writing. Fifteen minutes later, I had it."[3]

One common variation on the story is that Norworth, upon boarding a busy 9th Avenue El train, didn't even have room to read his newspaper, so he scanned the placard advertisements running across the top sides of the car, spotting the Polo Grounds ad.

POLO GROUNDS, 157th STREET AND EIGHTH AVENUE

Can be reached by Sixth and Ninth Avenue Elevated direct to the grounds, and Broadway Subway, stopping at 155th St., and a short walk to the grounds. Seating capacity estimated at 40,000.
Reserved Seats as well as Box Seats on sale by A. G. Spalding & Bros., No. 126 Nassau St. and No. 29 W. 42nd St.

POLO GROUNDS, NEW YORK CITY.   THE HOME OF THE NEW YORK GIANTS.

Vintage views of the Polo Grounds, home of the New York Giants and backdrop for the success of "Take Me Out to the Ball Game."

Another variation is that the ad he saw actually read, "Ball Game Today–Polo Grounds." These were indeed real ads. Except that the "Ball Game Today–Polo Grounds" sign had a counterpart, "Ball Game Today–Yankee Stadium" and Yankee Stadium wasn't built until 1923, fifteen years after the song was written.

We couldn't find any information that there indeed was an ad that read, "Come to the Polo Grounds" on any New York subway in 1908. We also couldn't find evidence of any ads about baseball placed inside the subway trains at that time. In fact, it's unlikely that these ads were inside the subway cars themselves. According to Charles Sachs, senior curator of the New York Transit Museum, "It's unlikely any ads advertising 'Ball Game Today' were inside the subway car themselves. Imagine the cost, the manpower, and the effort required to change or remove those ads on a near daily basis on each of the cars during the season. It would have wrought havoc." Mr. Sachs is correct: imagine the mob scene of outraged Giants fans outside an empty Polo Grounds, all because some poor transit worker forgot to remove an ad for a game from the day before.

Cary Stumm, archivist for the Transit Museum, proffers, "He could have seen such a sign: in the newspaper, on the outside of train itself perhaps, as a broadside stuck to a building the train was passing, or on a trolley down below the elevated. The possibilities are endless." There exists a tradition of placing ball game ads on the front of trolleys and elevated trains (Boston, Chicago, and Spokane did this, to name a few).

There is also a tradition of announcing the day's games in the local paper. A number of New York City newspapers announced games, including the *New York Times* and the *New York Tribune*.

The first ad appeared on April 13, 1908, it was for an exhibition game with the Jersey Giants, although newspaper advertising for "Ball Game Today–Polo Grounds" dates as far back as 1901.

In another interview from 1958, Norworth claims that after thirty minutes, he emerged from the subway

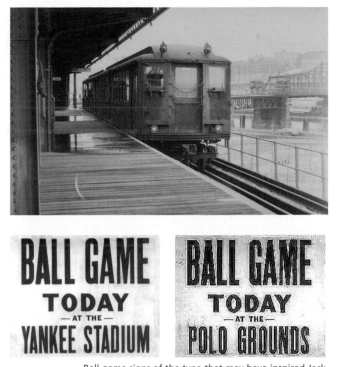

Ball game signs of the type that may have inspired Jack Norworth to write "Take Me Out to the Ball Game."

with *both* lyrics and music in hand. Whether laying claim to the words *and* music were intentional or not, or just an oversight, his songwriting partner, was, of course, Albert Von Tilzer, and Albert was duly credited with writing the music. Since Albert passed away two years prior to Norworth's interview, one could imagine that, had he been alive, he would have taken Norworth to task over the "words and music" claim.

But it is entirely plausible that Norworth wrote *both* the lyrics and music. Jack and Albert most likely had an oral or written agreement that any songs for which they collaborated would entitle each to an equal share of royalties and equal billing, regardless of whether one or both of them fully collaborated. Jack may have emerged from the subway with both lyrics and music in hand, to which Albert Von Tilzer put the finishing touches. But it's circumspect that Norworth would only mention this after Albert's passing.

As to what subway Jack Norworth was riding when he purportedly found inspiration, the best guess is that it was the 9th Avenue El (although technically the 9th Avenue El was an oxymoronic subway in that it was

"I was a professional songwriter. I thought it was time for a baseball song and an idea struck me which I thought was pretty good."–JACK NORWORTH

an elevated train, with but a small section traveling through a tunnel). Built in 1867, it was the first elevated railway erected in Manhattan, and traveled between South Ferry station and 155th Street (the last stop, and coincidentally the stop for the Polo Grounds, where the New York Giants played).

It is unlikely that Jack and Albert gave all that much time to composing "Take Me Out to the Ball Game." This was Tin Pan Alley and songs were not composed or written–they were cranked out, like a factory. If Norworth took thirty minutes to write the lyrics, it most likely took Von Tilzer the same, or less, to write the music. The goal of Tin Pan Alley was fame and fortune, not high art. Songs were written to be profitable, not pretty or pretentious. "Once you got a title, you had your song," Norworth once explained. "Lyrics were written so they'd fit with lantern slides and the simpler the better. When we dissected a song in the Alley before we turned it loose, it was judged by one standard: 'Could the hired help play and sing it.' Songs were written for the hired girls . . . catchy, tuneful, and easy to learn."[4]

The best estimate is that, in less than an hour, in the spring of 1908, Jack and Albert composed an immortal hit. In just a few months–by October–it became one of the top ten hits of 1908. By 2008, it will have been used in over 1,200 films, television shows, and commercials, from *Arsenic and Old Lace* to *The X-Files*; will have earned millions of dollars in royalties; will have been on the air on radio and television every single day of the year (including Christmas and New Year); and will have been performed over 2,500 times a year during major league seventh-inning stretches. There are hit songs and then there are songs that hit home runs.

Both Jack and Albert endured some criticism that they had never attended a ball game nor were they initially fans of the game prior to writing the song. Bob Addie, in a 1960 column in the *Washington Post*, put it best:

Jack Norworth wasn't a fan. Maybe that's the way it had to be. No father can talk objectively about

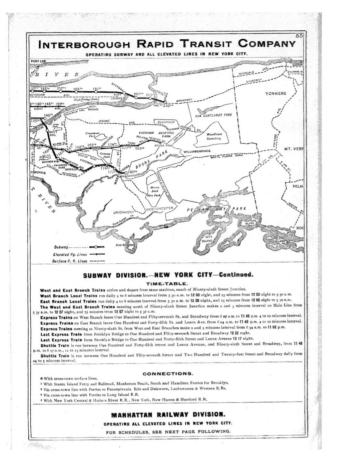

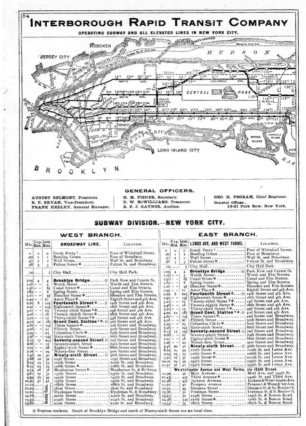

his own son. It had to be a fellow in show business, a professional at songwriting, who captured the essence of a baseball game, its ever-young appeal, the anticipation, the excitement, the wry humor and drama.[5]

Jack Norworth once said that he had written "more than 3,000 songs, seven of them good" (the seven he identified were "Shine On Harvest Moon," "Meet Me in Apple Blossom Time," "Smarty," "Come Along My Mandy," "Garden of Sweden," "Over on the Jersey Side," and of course "Take Me Out to the Ball Game"). So why a baseball song to add to his oeuvre? "Very simple," explained Norworth. "I was a professional songwriter. I thought it was time for a baseball song and an idea struck me which I thought was pretty good."[6]

Jack Norworth had no jackpot hits after 1908– "Shine On Harvest Moon" was perhaps his biggest.

Albert went on to write several more hits, but after 1908, Jack and Albert never collaborated on another song. It remains unknown why their collaboration ended. Oddly enough, some years later, both Von Tilzer and Norworth appeared in public at the same concert–but not together. Von Tilzer sang "Take Me Out to the Ball Game" while Norworth sang "Shine On Harvest Moon." They never appeared in public together thereafter, and although they both lived their latter years within miles of one another (Jack in Laguna Beach and Albert in Los Angeles), there appears no evidence that they remained in contact.

Their brief collaboration made them, however, like those Hall of Famers in Cooperstown, synonymous with the sport, forever linked to a particular time and place in America's past–for Jack and Albert it was the summer of 1908, Tin Pan Alley, a subway car, the old Polo Grounds.

Dedicated to J. A. Sternad

Take Me Out to the Ballgame

1. Ka - tie Ca - sey was base - ... fe - ver and had it bad,
2. Ka - tie Ca - sey saw all th... play - ers by their first names;

Just to ... ot for the home-town crew, ev'ry sou... Ka - tie blew.____
Told the um-pi-re he was wrong, all a - long____ good and strong.____

LONG-DISTANCE DEDICATION

MOST PEOPLE THINK the first line of the song is "Take me out to the ball game . . . ." The initiated know that the first verse begins "Katie Casey was baseball mad . . . ." But the first words of all, even above the title on the sheet music, are the mysterious "Dedicated to J. A. Sternad."

For years, this has been a source of idle wonder—and looking for a Sternad in the world of baseball has been fruitless. Nor did his name turn up in asking around, or in the more modern Internet searches. Perhaps he was nothing more than a red herring, a composer's joke, meant to drive people crazy a hundred years later.

But technology has now done what old-fashioned scholarship could not—one can now search the full text of old newspapers online, and in the *Chicago Tribune*, one J. A. Sternad reveals himself little by little. Even after finding several tantalizing mentions of him, one still wonders just who this fellow was.

A man after Jack Norworth's own heart, Sternad was a sportsman, a theater impresario, and a baseball lover. He first appears in 1907, directing a vaudeville-style theater benefit for the Elks club, to benefit a local sanitarium.[1]

In May of that year, Sternad is involved with the parade celebrating the world championship of the "Hitless Wonders," the Chicago White Sox team that defeated the heavily favored Cubs in the first crosstown World Series. An automobile enthusiast, (like Norworth), Sternad is listed as the man to contact if one wants to drive one's auto in the parade.[2]

A couple of days later, Sternad and two partners are listed as starting the South Chicago Amusement Company, incorporating a plan to run theaters.[3] But perhaps the most interesting and enigmatic trace left by Sternad is that of his pedestrianism—an athletic pursuit popular a hundred years ago that involved walking long distances at top speeds.

In early December, Sternad and five other men set out to walk the ninety miles from Milwaukee to Chicago, hoping to complete the trip in sixty hours or less, in response to a bet proffered by one Peter Schaeffer at the Illinois Athletic Club. The jolly party left Milwaukee at 7:10 a.m., one member not even wearing an overcoat. Schaeffer followed, in his motorcar, ready to pick up anyone who couldn't continue. They reached Racine at 2 p.m. Two men gave up here, going to bed, but Sternad and three others set out again. Within a mile, another man gave up. Eight miles north of Kenosha at 5 p.m., the group encountered a blinding snowstorm, and two of them got lost—they were later picked up by Schaeffer. Sternad continued bravely on alone, stumbling through the snow and reaching Kenosha at 9:19 p.m. In a state of exhaustion, he went to bed, and Schaeffer had won his bet.[4]

Sternad's last appearance in the *Tribune* is in 1911, when he incorporates the J. A. Sternad Vaudeville Agency, engaged in "general theatrical and booking business."[5] Doubtless the theater is the area in which he knew Jack Norworth, who was performing frequently in Chicago at this time, but it is intriguing to speculate on whether the two men shared a baseball interest. They were certainly both good-time guys.

THE
AMPHION

THE AMPHION Musical Society, in October 1880, erected its building at what is now #437–441 Bedford Avenue, Brooklyn, New York, as an opera house. It opened the same year under the management of C. M. Wicke. Not being a financial success, in January 1888 it was taken over by Knowles and Morris and operated as a theater. Edward Knowles remained the manager until 1897. The Amphion was the site of the first performance of "Take Me Out to the Ball Game," purportedly performed by Jack Norworth during a matinee.

A MAGIC
LANTERN RIDE

WITHIN WEEKS of its release in 1908, "Take Me Out to the Ball Game" was being sung by thousands of folks across America. But not in ballparks.

Oddly enough, "Take Me Out to the Ball Game" became famous in movie houses, thousands of them—from small nickelodeons to large, plush Ziegfeld-like cinemas—before the song was ever heard at a ball game. Why did people sing the song at movie theaters? Because of a short-lived phenomenon known as the "illustrated song play."

The song play consisted of a set of slides created to depict and illustrate a new song, sung by the house vocalist and accompanied by the house pianist. The slides, often referred to as "magic lantern slides," were 3¼ x 4–inch positive glass transparencies consisting of custom-made hand-colored scenes, one to each line of lyric.

The song play grew out of necessity. In the early days of cinema, there was an interminably long pause while the projectionist changed reels. For movie houses, the slides were cheap filler between reels to keep the audience entertained. But for members of the music publishing industry, whose patronage accounted for nearly 100 percent of song play slide production, magic lantern slides were a pivotal factor in a new song's success.

With the complete, undivided attention of an eager public waiting for the second half of their movie to begin, song pluggers had stumbled on a golden opportunity: the right time and place to introduce a new song to the public, and introduce it in a way that folks would not soon forget—with imagery. MTV and VH1—indeed the first music video—owe some gratitude to magic lantern slides.

Albert Von Tilzer's publishing house, the York Music Company, commissioned pioneer lantern slide

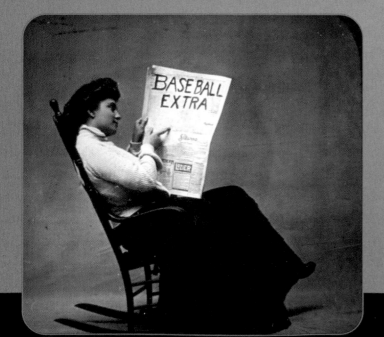

Lantern slides used to promote "Take Me Out to the Ball Game" were shot at the Polo Grounds in May 1909.

maker DeWitt C. Wheeler to illustrate "Take Me Out to the Ball Game" (Von Tilzer, a big fan of movie houses, later wrote "Let's Go into a Picture Show" with Junie McCree in 1909 to capitalize on the burgeoning popularity of movies).[1]

Wheeler selected the Polo Grounds as a backdrop for the song's heroine, Katie Casey. Production at the Polo Grounds was completed in one day, with two anonymous models each three dollars richer. Within a few weeks, sets of the song slides were in five-cent movie houses across the country, accompanied by house vocalists—usually semi-pros—introducing the new baseball song. According to one trade paper's review of the song slides, audiences frequently applauded the unique illustrations, a welcome change from the syrupy sentimental scenes typically used to illustrate love songs.

But something other than applause was expected by the York Music Company: an opportunity to insure that everyone left the movie house singing and humming "Take Me Out to the Ball Game." After the soloist finished the verse of the song about our heroine Katie Casey, accompanied by DeWitt Wheeler's colorful slides, the projectionist would put up the money slide: the lyrics to the chorus with the invitation by the soloist to, "sing along." If the soloist could convince an audible majority to sing the two choruses, it was pretty certain that after the show a good number of folks would be humming, singing, or whistling the tune all the way to their nearest music dealer to buy the sheet music. And that is exactly what happened.

Within a few years, millions of copies of the sheet music to "Take Me Out to the Ball Game" were sold. But by 1911, the song play became obsolete: most movie houses had acquired a second projector and there was no need to pause between reels. But "Take Me Out to the Ball Game" had already found its way into the hearts and minds of millions of Americans, long before the song ever found its way into a ballpark. As odd as it seems, Americans were singing "Take Me Out to the Ball Game" together in public over fifty years before they'd ever sing it together in a ballpark. Perhaps singing it at movie houses made sense—why sing "Take Me Out to the Ball Game" at a ball game when you're already there?

FACES OF "TAKE ME OUT TO THE BALL GAME"

IT WAS COMMON practice for Tin Pan Alley to print various versions of the same sheet music featuring different photos of vaudeville singers. Those singers were actively promoting the song–some were song pluggers, others were vaudeville touring stars, but all agreed to help promote the song for which they'd receive compensation, especially if the song was a hit. We estimate that there were over thirty different covers to the original 1908 publication, each featuring a different artist. Here is a list of the artists we were able to find:

Baby Florence Mascotte: famous child actress and singer.

Henry Fink: a singer and songwriter, who, with Al Piantadosi, wrote the musical *The Curse of an Aching Heart* in 1913.

Maude Gray: star of the New York stage, appearing in her sensational show *The Star of the Period* and later, in 1911, in the films *Sir George and the Heiress*, *Heroes Three*, and *It Served Her Right*.

Sadie Jansell: noted vaudeville singer and performer, who promoted many songs, often appearing on the covers of their sheet music.

Trixie Friganza: a "provocative" and "curvaceous" vaudeville star, most known for her role as the widow in the operetta *Prince of Pilsen*. She appeared on two covers of "Take Me Out to the Ball Game" in two different poses.

The remaining artists featured on extant covers of the song were:

Nora Bayes
Lulu Beeson
Frank Dooley
Wheeler Earl
Susie Fisher
Jack Kloville
Ida Burt Lawrence
John Marion and Grace Lillian
Nevins and Arnold
Jack Norworth
Harry Pen
Reynolds and Tucker
Richards and Grover
Meredith Sisters
Billy Sousa
Sam Williams
(two different poses)

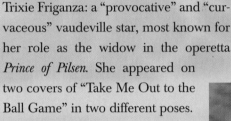

CHART
TOPPERS

"TAKE ME OUT to the Ball Game" was on the charts at number one for the longest of any song in 1908, a total of seven weeks, even though it didn't chart until October 31, after the crazy 1908 baseball season had ended with the Chicago Cubs winning the World Series. Oddly enough, folks were so enamored with the tune they continued buying hundreds of thousands of copies through the holiday season.[1] Here's a list of the other number one hits of 1908:

CHART DATE	WEEKS AT #1	TITLE	ARTIST
01/04/1908	5	"My Dear"	Harry MacDonough
02/08/1908	6	"Under Any Old Flag at All"	Billy Murray
03/21/1908	6	"As Long as the World Rolls On"	Alan Turner
05/02/1908	3	"Wouldn't You Like to Have Me for a Sweetheart?"	Ada Jones and Billy Murray
05/23/1908	5	"The Glow-Worm"	Victor Orchestra
06/27/1908	5	"The Glow-Worm"	Lucy Isabelle Marsh
08/01/1908	4	"Are You Sincere?"	Elise Stevenson
08/29/1908	4	"When We Are M-A-Double-R-I-E-D"	Ada Jones and Billy Murray
09/26/1908	5	"Cuddle Up a Little Closer, Lovey Mine"	Ada Jones and Billy Murray
10/31/1908	7	"Take Me Out to the Ball Game"	Billy Murray and Haydn Quartet[2]
12/12/1908	5	"Sunbonnet Sue"	Harry MacDonough and Haydn Quartet

BASEBALL IN 1908

HOW DIFFERENT WAS BASEBALL in 1908? Well, the Cubs were the best team in baseball. There are lots of differences between baseball in 1908, when "Take Me Out to the Ball Game" was written, and baseball a hundred years later. One of the great things about baseball, compared to other sports, is that a time-traveling team from 1908 could take the field today and hold their own against a modern team, despite many differences in how the game is played. Intriguingly, the strategies and tactics of 1908 might prove more of a challenge to the 2008 team than the strength and size of the latter would to the former.

A team from 1908 would be momentarily mystified–and certainly appalled–at the designated hitter rule (instituted in 1973, but suggested as early as the 1890s), which one suspects they would find unsportsmanlike, perhaps even unmanly. The pitcher should get in there and take his cuts just like any player, and perhaps if he does, he'll be less likely to brush back an opposing hitter since the same might happen to him in the next inning.

Our 1908ers would need to adjust to artificial turf–thankfully on the wane in the major leagues, and to night baseball, first played in the majors in 1935. The uniforms, though they went a little mod in the 1970s and early 1980s, aren't all that different from a century

Tinker to Evers to Chance: the infield of the 1908 Cubs.

ago. If anything, they are looser-fitting and more breathable, being made of lighter fabrics like cotton, instead of the more durable—and heavier, especially when wet with sweat—wool.

One major change the 1908 players would marvel at is the impeccable grounds-keeping in today's game. Back in their day, it wasn't unusual to have pebbles and rocks strewn about the infield, dull brown grass in high traffic areas, and even fans seated around the field for big games. One of the most privileged spaces in America today is a big-league ball field—it's almost impossible for the curious fan to walk on that pristine grass—but in 1908, it was common for fans to exit the ballpark by walking across the field toward big outfield gates. Just ask Fred Merkle, but more on him later. And the outfields themselves are smaller; as baseball fans have over the last few generations expressed a preference for offense over defense, the parks have continually gotten smaller.

The style of play is much different today, too. In 1908, the archetypal ballplayer was someone like Ty Cobb or Honus Wagner, a hustling contact hitter who could spray line drives to all fields, choked up on the bat—especially with two strikes—and never, never wanted to strike out. Batters struck out a lot less often

Fred Merkle of the Giants and Honus Wagner of the Pirates.

in those days, as the object of the game was to play "scientific" or "inside" baseball, advancing runners one base at a time, through singles, bunts, hit-and-run plays, and stolen bases, as opposed to hitting home runs.

The home run was a rare commodity in 1908, and it wouldn't become a big part of baseball until the rise of Babe Ruth in the late teens and early twenties. Johnny Evers, second baseman for the World Champion Cubs of 1907 and 1908, explained inside baseball: "It was as much a battle of wits as a trial of strength and speed. Everything was trying to outguess the other fellow and we used to spend hours doping out plays, but I guess most of the current players have stopped thinking. All they have to do now is walk up to the plate, grip the bat at the end, and take a swing."[1] Doping out plays, eh? Well, just ask Fred Merkle about that, but more on that later. . . .

One of the changes that Babe Ruth introduced to the game in the late teens was his philosophy that hitting more home runs meant opening up to the possibility of striking out more as well. The two are interrelated, as the kind of all-out swing that is required to hit home runs also means that players will miss the ball more often. His home run totals weren't the only thing off the charts—so were his unprecedented strikeout totals. As he said, "I swing big, with everything I've got. I hit big or I miss big. I like to live as big as I can." [2]

Pitchers in 1908 could legally resort to the spitball, the shine ball, and other trick deliveries, which weren't outlawed until 1920. While there are two schools of thought, we feel that today's larger, stronger pitchers, who stay in shape year-round instead of going to spring training to lose that extra twenty pounds they picked up over the winter, are generally capable of throwing the ball harder—faster than their counterparts of a hundred years ago.

Advances in equipment have changed the game as well. A glove or mitt in 1908 was basically meant to protect the hand, and would later evolve, by mid-century, into a device designed to help a fielder catch the ball. Today's large gloves would take some getting used to for the players of 1908, and vice versa. Little Leaguers today are still taught to catch with two hands, keeping the throwing hand near or behind the glove in case the ball pops out. This comes from the old days, when it was very difficult to catch a ball with just one hand. Catcher's mitts have changed a great deal, too, with the mid-century addition of a hinge, which eventually allowed for one-handed catching of pitches—another technological innovation that arguably allows pitchers to throw both harder fastballs and better breaking pitches. Of course, players from 1908 would not know what a batting helmet was, let alone shin guards and elbow guards designed to protect the batter from being hit by a pitch or a foul ball. Such aids also allow a player to step into the box with less fear, a decided advantage for hitters.

There are many knowledgeable baseball fans who feel that the 1908 season was the greatest season ever, so much so that there are three separate books devoted solely to the events of the season. The World Series was a relatively recent innovation, having been first played in 1903, and the American League itself was still a bit of an upstart, though teams from that league had captured two of the first four World Series. The 1908 pennant races are among the most dramatic ever, with both the NL and AL seasons going down to the last day and involving three very closely bunched teams.

In the NL, the three teams were the Chicago Cubs, New York Giants, and Pittsburgh Pirates. The season ended in a tie between the Cubs and the Giants, with the Pirates a scant half game out. In the AL, play came down to the final day of the season, with the Chicago White Sox and Detroit Tigers still in the hunt after the Cleveland Naps were eliminated the previous day. The Tigers beat the White Sox that day to clinch the pennant and their second straight World Series berth.

The Cubs and the Giants enjoyed perhaps the game's greatest rivalry up to that point, a rivalry that had been brewing since the mid-1880s. The two teams hated one another, and their contests were epic in nature. New York was led by the fiery John McGraw, and the Cubs by "The Peerless Leader" Frank Chance. The Giants featured the pitching of the incomparable Christy Mathewson and Hooks Wiltse, while the Cubs staff was led by Mordecai "Three-Finger" Brown, Ed Reulbach, and Jack Pfiester. The Cubs were also known for their scrappy double-play combination of "Tinker to Evers to Chance," a trio immortalized in the 1910 poem by F .P. Adams, "Baseball's Sad Lexicon":

> These are the saddest of possible words:
> "Tinker to Evers to Chance."
> Trio of bear cubs, and fleeter than birds,
> Tinker and Evers and Chance.

> Ruthlessly pricking our gonfalon bubble,
> Making a Giant hit into a double–
> Words that are weighty with nothing but trouble:
> "Tinker to Evers to Chance."

The season all came down to one fateful game in New York's Polo Grounds, the Giants hosting the Cubs, on September 23, 1908. The Cubs had swept a doubleheader against the Giants the previous day to move into a first place tie, and the pitching match up for September 23 was as good as it could be: Giants ace and future Hall of Famer Christy Mathewson against Jack "The Giant Killer" Pfiester, so nick-

The heart and soul of the Giants— pitcher Christy Mathewson and manager John McGraw.

BRIDWELL N.Y. NAT'L

Giants' shortstop Al Bridwell, whose hit sparked the most controversial play in baseball history.

named because of his 15–5 career record and seven shutouts against the archrivals. The day would go down as "the most controversial game ever played," [3] because it featured "the most famous play in baseball history."[4]

With two outs in the bottom of the ninth, the score tied 1–1 and Moose McCormick on first base, nineteen-year-old Fred Merkle stepped up to the plate for the Giants in a packed Polo Grounds. With a poise beyond his years, Merkle smashed a single, sending the winning run to third base. Even against "The Giant Killer," the Giants would seem to have the upper hand, as Al Bridwell, sporting a .285 batting average for the season, approached the plate.

Remember "inside baseball," and how Cubs second baseman Johnny Evers said he and his teammates would "spend hours doping out plays?" Well, Evers had a play in mind, should Bridwell get the game winning hit. It was, in fact, a play he'd tried three weeks earlier, in Pittsburgh, where umpire Hank O'Day, working the

game alone, disallowed it because he couldn't put his eyes in two places at once. He later admitted he was wrong and vowed to make the right call should the situation occur again.[5] O'Day was working this game also, along with partner Bob Emslie. You can bet that Johnny Evers knew this.

Bridwell lined the ball up the middle, knocking Emslie off his feet,[6] and sending McCormick trotting home with the winning run. The Giants had regained first place. The crowd poured onto the field, both in celebration and because the common practice was to depart through those outfield gates, and young Merkle veered off of his second base course to head for the clubhouse in centerfield ahead of the massive crowd. Far from being a blunder or "boner," as the press dubbed it, Merkle's base running was standard practice at the time.

But as the immortal Yogi Berra would say a generation or two later, "It ain't over till it's over," and as far as Evers was concerned, it wasn't over. He called for the ball from center fielder Solly Hofman, who overthrew the ball all the way to third, where it briefly was the object of a tug of war between two future Hall of Famers, Giants pitcher Joe McGinnity and Cubs shortstop Joe Tinker. McGinnity won the scuffle and tossed the ball into the stands, where Cub pitcher Rube Kroh slugged a fan in order to get it back, ran it over to second, and gave it to Evers, who tagged second base, forc-

Future Hall of Famers Joe McGinnity and Joe Tinker wrestled for the Merkle ball, with McGinnity heaving it into the stands.

ing Merkle.[7] In Evers's mind, it was three outs, still 1–1, and time for the tenth inning.

While neither umpire had the courage (or the stupidity) to make "the correct call" in the middle of an excited mob, the umpires' report submitted that evening called young Merkle out at second, and declared the game a tie, which would be replayed at the end of the season, if it affected the standings.

After the season's final scheduled day, there sat the New York Giants and Chicago Cubs, with identical 98–55 records, still tied. The game was replayed in New York with 35,000–40,000 people in attendance—a huge crowd for a baseball game in those days, and, by some press estimates, a couple of hundred thousand more folks on the roof, climbing telephone poles, on Coogan's Bluff, and on high spots in the general neighborhood, trying to see in. The Giant Killer was on the mound again, against Mathewson. The Giants took a first-inning lead of 1–0, and Frank Chance replaced Pfiester with his ace, Three-Finger Brown, so named because his throwing hand was mangled in a farm accident as a youth.

The Cubs scored four runs against Mathewson in the third, and went on to win the game, 4–2, on their way to a second consecutive World Series win against the Tigers. Was there ever a baseball game more controversial than that one on September 23, 1908? Fred Merkle, who went on to play sixteen seasons in the major leagues, might not think so. Our own Albert Von Tilzer wrote a song about the incident, "Did He Run," in 1909, and "Merkle's Boner," as the base running play is known, echoes into our own age and is still being written about today. Folksinger Chuck Brodsky has written a modern song about the play called "Bonehead Merkle," and David Anderson's book on the 1908 season is called *More Than Merkle*. Whether "Merkle's Boner," should be known as "Evers's Technicality" is a question that still hangs in the air, a hundred years hence. One thing we do know for sure, as of this writing, the Cubs haven't won a World Series since 1908, but one of us sure hopes they do.

Frank Sinatra and Gene Kelly pictured on movie-prop baseball cards from the 1949 musical *Take Me Out to the Ball Game*.

TINKERING
WITH MUSIC

JOHNNY EVERS, THE CUBS second baseman responsible for the "Merkle's Boner" baserunning play of 1908, was a fiery, intense competitor, as was his shortstop, Joe Tinker. In fact, the two did not speak for many years during their playing careers, after a dispute over whether one should have held a cab for the other or simply gone ahead to the game.

But the profit motive is powerful, and in an attempt to exploit the popularity of baseball, the world champion Cubs, and their feud, Tinker and Evers published a song they wrote in November of 1908 (or perhaps had ghostwritten–hard to write a song with someone that you are not speaking to, and while other players had written songs, neither of these guys had a musical background). Middle infielders are quick on the draw, and this might have been the first song that attempted to capitalize on the immense popularity of "Take Me Out to the Ball Game."

The song is called "Between You and Me" and tells a story of two lovers, who hand in hand, "both make a play and steal away down the

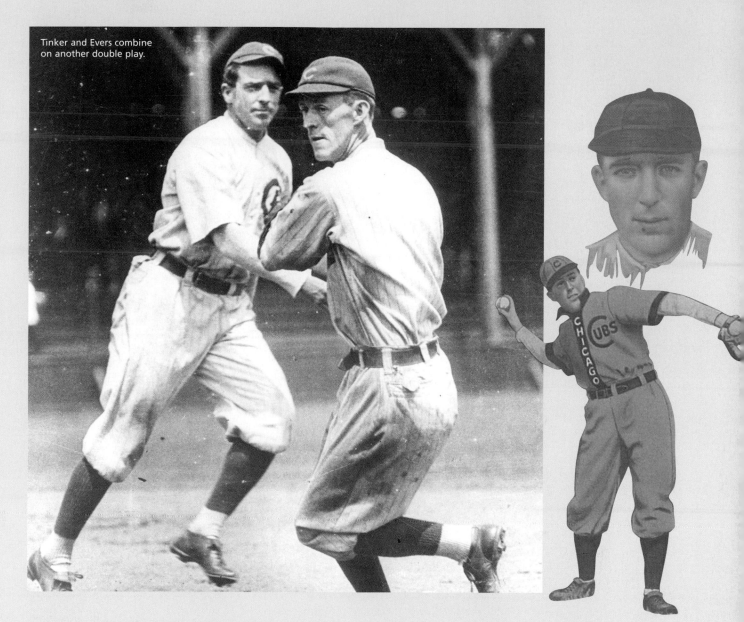

Tinker and Evers combine on another double play.

moonlit strand."[1] The song may even be trying to capital-ize on the "one, two, three strikes" line with this: "She sighs and sighs and then replies: That isn't one-two-three." Tinker and Evers eventually resolved their differences, though one suspects that this song wasn't as big a money-maker as they had hoped.

Tinker and Evers did beat Albert Von Tilzer to the punch. In 1909, he and Junie McCree wrote and pub-lished "Did He Run," a comic song that, among other targets, took aim at poor Fred Merkle:

A ball game was played at the Polo Grounds,
In nineteen hundred and eight,

'Tween the Giants and Cubs one day
And it sealed the Giants' fate, fate, fate.
They had the game in their hands all right
With a man on first and third,
Then a hit brought in the tally to win
But Giant's brain was blurred.

[Chorus]
Did he run? Did he run?
Did he run to second as he should that day
Or did this Mr. Giant semi-circle away
Did he run? Did he run?
A play-wright grabbed his ink and quill
And wrote a play called *The Man That Stood Still*.

A BIT OF
A STRETCH

MANY FANS ARE surprised to learn that "Take Me Out to the Ball Game" has not always been sung or played during the seventh-inning stretch. The custom is so widespread that many will give a double take when they learn of the pivotal role Harry Caray played in linking the song with the venerable stretch in 1976, with the White Sox. (see "Harry Goes Electric").

How about the stretch itself? Where did this charming custom come from? Well, the one thing we know is that it predates 1908, when "Take Me Out to the Ball Game" was written. There are several creation stories surrounding the seventh-inning stretch, and at best, only one of them can be true.

The most unlikely is that President William Howard Taft, attending the Senators' home opener in 1910, grew weary between halves of the seventh and got up to stretch. Fans thought he was getting up to leave and stood out of respect, and thus was a custom born. Why they would stand again at the same time the next day, and every day thereafter, and why fans in other cities would follow suit is never addressed.

Interestingly, the first appearance in print of the phrase "seventh-inning stretch" was that same week, in the *New York Times* of April 17, 1910, in an account of the previous day's Yankees game. To wit: "Seventh inning coming. The spectators stood up, men, women, and children, and took the seventh inning yawn and stretch."[1] It sounds like this wasn't the first time New York fans took the "seventh inning yawn and stretch," but it's a safe bet that those who market baseball today are glad we no longer call it that. Both the Senators and the Yankees (also known as the Highlanders back then) had opened at home on April 14, so if the Taft story is true, which it isn't, then the practice spread quickly up the eastern seaboard.

New Yorkers, who think they invented everything, will quickly tell you that

the stretch originated in 1882, at a game played by the Manhattan College Jaspers. Brother Jasper, the school's athletic director, noticed that the fans were getting restless during the seventh inning due to the heat and humidity. He stopped the game and told the students to stand and stretch for a few minutes.

The stretch was so popular it was repeated game after game, and soon the New York Giants, who allowed Manhattan College to use the Polo Grounds for some games, caught wind of the popular activity and adopted it.[2] And of course, it caught on all around the majors and minors. That last part seems the most unlikely part of the story, but, hey, you never know.

Indeed, by the next year, the stretch was an established custom, even if it didn't necessarily come between halves of the seventh. A note in the newspaper *The Sporting Life* says, "In most of the large cities there is a peculiar practice in vogue at base ball games. At the end of every few innings some tired spectator, who has been wrestling with the hard side of a rough board seat, gets up and yells "Stretch!" A second after, the entire crowd will be going through all the movements of a stretch."[3] Sounds like this custom might also be the start of "the wave," but I digress.

The biggest problem with the Manhattan College story is that an earlier stretch predates it by thirteen years, and it goes back to Hall-of-Famer Harry Wright of the 1869 Cincinnati Red Stockings, baseball's first openly professional team. That year, Wright wrote to a friend, describing Cincinnati fans: "The spectators all arise between halves of the seventh, extend their legs and arms, and sometimes walk about. In so doing they enjoy the relief afforded by relaxation from a long posture on hard benches."[4] Sounds like the seventh-inning stretch to me, Brother Jasper.

The Red Stockings' national tour that year led to a similar stretch during their visit to San Francisco. There the promoter arranged for a ten-minute intermission after the sixth inning to increase revenue from concessions. The Cincinnati papers called it "a dodge to advertise and have the crowd patronize the bar."[5]

However it started, the seventh-inning stretch has become a great platform for "Take Me Out to the Ball Game." And since this book is all about music, we can't resist mentioning Handel's *Messiah*. In the music world's other "seventh-inning stretch," it is customary for patrons at performances to stand during the "Hallelujah" chorus. According to an article by Bruce Anderson in *Sports Illustrated*, this may have started when King George II stood during the London premiere of the work in 1743.[6]

Perhaps we should start a rumor that he was interested in buying some peanuts and Cracker Jack. Oh wait, Cracker Jack wasn't invented yet. Do I hear Harry Caray singing, "Hallelujah . . ."?

GET UP, STAND UP:
HOW THE SEVENTH-INNING STRETCH IS OBSERVED TODAY

THE SEVENTH-INNING STRETCH, once an informal opportunity for fans to stretch and chat while organ music played in the background, has become a programmed entertainment segment, for better or for worse. Here is a survey of what the thirty major league clubs were doing at stretch time as of the printing of this book. Since not all big league clubs answered the survey, we have also relied on the observations of baseball fans who are members of SABR, the Society for American Baseball Research, to complete this survey.

The tragic events of September 11, 2001, caused baseball to put all games on hold for a week. Once the teams returned, they were directed by Major League Baseball to play "God Bless America" during the seventh-inning stretch. MLB scaled this back the following season, directing clubs to play "God Bless America" on Sundays, holidays, and military appreciation days. Since all clubs do that, we have not added that information separately to each club.

Arizona Diamondbacks: Organist Bobby Freeman plays "Take Me Out to the Ball Game" live and fans stand and sing along. After "Take Me Out to the Ball Game," the Diamondbacks play "Brown Eyed Girl," and fans are again encouraged to sing along. Families and individual fans can join Freeman in the booth by requesting the Seventh-Inning Experience certificate through the Community Affairs Department. Fans get special seating for the game, then join Freeman in the booth for the stretch and see themselves on the JumboTron, along with receiving a DVD of their experience. The money raised through this program has totaled over $50,000 per year for charity. Freeman is the former organist for the Padres, who still play a recording of him during the stretch, making him the entertainer for two Major League Baseball seventh-inning stretches.

Atlanta Braves: The Braves' organist plays "Take Me Out to the Ball Game" while the fans stand and sing. The Tomahawk Team, college-age female cheerleaders in short shorts and Braves jerseys, lead the stretch from atop the dugouts, waving rolled-up T-shirts that they will throw into the crowd. After "Take Me Out to the Ball Game," the Braves play John Denver's "Thank God I'm a Country Boy" while the Tomahawk Team square-dances on the dugouts.

Baltimore Orioles: The Orioles play a taped rendition of "Take Me Out to the Ball Game" and fans stand and sing along. They follow "Take Me Out to the Ball Game" with John Denver's "Thank God I'm a Country Boy," which gets the fans singing and clapping.

Boston Red Sox: Organist Josh Kantor plays "Take Me Out to the Ball Game" live while the fans sing along, substituting "Red Sox" for "home team." Cameras follow the mascot, Wally the Green Monster, as he stands atop the Red Sox dugout, leading the song along with a few lucky fans. Cameras also search the audience and some of those shots make the scoreboard. After "Take Me Out to the Ball Game," Kantor plays either "Tequila" by the Champs, Queen's "Bohemian Rhapsody," "Ma Na Ma Na" from Sesame Street, or Chuck Mangione's "Feels So Good."

Chicago Cubs: In a tribute to the late Harry Caray, the Cubs invite a guest conductor to lead the crowd in singing "Take Me Out to the Ball Game" live during the stretch, accompanied by organist Gary Pressey. The guest conductor is often a national or regional celebrity, such as an actor, musician, politician, or Big Ten sports coach. For the tenth anniversary season since Caray's death, the Cubs held a contest for fans to try out to sing the stretch tune. More than 2,700 fans auditioned and ten finalists were chosen by fan balloting on the Cubs Web site. The ten finalists tried out at Wrigley Field in front of a panel of celebrity judges that included Cubs greats Ernie Banks and Billy Williams, along with Dutchie Caray, Harry's widow. The winner was twenty-two-year-old Dustin Eglseder of Guttenberg, Iowa, who had just completed a course of chemotherapy for bone cancer.

 Chicago White Sox: Popular organist Nancy Faust plays "Take Me Out to the Ball Game" live during day games. Fans sing along and the lyrics are posted on the message board. For night games, the White Sox use a recording of Nancy Faust.

 Cincinnati Reds: "Take Me Out to the Ball Game" is played by organist Zach Bonkowski and fans generally sing along.

Cleveland Indians: "Take Me Out to the Ball Game" is played on an organ, followed by an upbeat dance song, which is changed every night.

 Colorado Rockies: Fan David Black reports that "Take Me Out to the Ball Game" is played via an organ recording. People sing along heartily, though "when the Cubs are in town, they sing 'Root, root, root for the Cubbies,' drowning out the Rockies." The scoreboard camera is used extensively to focus on patrons during this time.

Detroit Tigers: Club plays a recording of "Take Me Out to the Ball Game" and fans sing along. On Sundays, the anthem singers sing "God Bless America," followed by "Take Me Out to the Ball Game."

 Florida Marlins: "Take Me Out to the Ball Game" is played live on the organ and the fans sing along. Mascot Billy the Marlin and the Marlins Mermaids dance team lead the crowd from atop the dugouts. After "Take Me Out to the Ball Game," they play a high energy song that our Marlins Mermaids can dance to. Often the song chosen is "R.O.C.K. in the U.S.A." by John Mellencamp. About eight to ten times a year, there is a celebrity guest performer for "Take Me Out to the Ball Game."

 Houston Astros: After "Take Me Out to the Ball Game," they play "Deep in the Heart of Texas."

 Kansas City Royals: "Take Me Out to the Ball Game" is played by an organist, followed by "Kansas City" by Wilbert Harrison, a tradition that started in 2007.

Los Angeles Angels of Anaheim: Organ music is played, and whoever sang the national anthem leads the singing of "Take Me Out to the Ball Game" while standing atop the first-base dugout. Stadium ushers go out on the field and line the warning track from the infield all the way back to the foul poles, demonstratively leading the crowd in singing. When the song mentions peanuts and Cracker Jack, each usher throws a small bag of peanuts into the crowd.

 Los Angeles Dodgers: Organist Nancy Bea Hefley plays "Take Me Out to the Ball Game" while everyone stands, sings, and sways.

 Milwaukee Brewers: "Take Me Out to the Ball Game" is played by an organist, followed by the "Beer Barrel Polka." People sing along to both songs, stretch, and often do the polka, according to club employee Aleta Mercer, who notes, "If you play a polka, people polka." People will polka, Ray, people will most definitely polka. . . .

Minnesota Twins: The club has been doing "Take Me Out to the Ball Game" on the organ for a long time, accompanied by a selected group of people singing along at a mic. In 2007, after "Take Me Out to the Ball Game" they play Glenn Miller's "In the Mood," accompanied by a video tribute to deceased broadcaster Herb Carneal. The previous year, the song was Louis Armstrong's "What a Wonderful World," accompanied by a video tribute to Hall of Famer Kirby Puckett, who had died that year. Prior to the 2006 season, they had been playing Lee Greenwood's "Proud to Be an American" since 2001. Fan Stew Thornley recalls the seventh-inning stretch as a child consisting of the "Mexican Hat Dance," but not "Take Me Out to the Ball Game."

New York Mets: They have been using the Bing Crosby version of "Take Me Out to the Ball Game" since at least the 1980s. They usually follow it with "Lazy Mary" by Lou Monte, which fans refer to as "that Italian clapping song." They have used Mandy Patinkin's Yiddish version of "Take Me Out to the Ball Game" for recent Jewish Heritage Days, and they occasionally have a live celebrity performer, such as George Thorogood recently. Mr. Met leads the crowd in singing from atop the dugout, and the scoreboard video shows fans singing along with the lyrics to "Take Me Out to the Ball Game" running along the bottom of the screen and a bouncing Mr. Met head touching each word as it is sung.

New York Yankees: The Yankees play "Take Me Out to the Ball Game" live. They also play a recording of "God Bless America" first, though they often have that performed live. Some people do sing, but it's not a sing-along.

Oakland Athletics: The A's play a recording of "Take Me Out to the Ball Game," with PA announcer Roy Steele inviting fans to sing along. "Take Me Out to the Ball Game" is followed by a classic rock song, such as "Twist and Shout," "Respect," "Dancing in the Streets," or "Wooly Bully."

Philadelphia Phillies: The Phillies play a recording of late organist Paul Richardson playing "Take Me Out to the Ball Game." Some people sing along, but most do not. Richardson played live until the Phillies moved into Citizens Bank Park.

Pittsburgh Pirates: The stretch begins with the scoreboard showing images of fans, and then an animated pirate comes along and says, "Avast, ye mates. Time to stretch your tired peg legs and join the old Pirate Vince Lascheid (team organist since 1970) in singing "Take Me Out to the Ball Game." The fans stand and sing along. The lyrics are on the screen and a bouncing smiley-faced cookie, the trademark of a local restaurant, bounces along to indicate the tempo.

Saint Louis Cardinals: Organist Ernie Hays plays "Take Me Out to the Ball Game" and the fans sing along. Right after the singing, Hays plays a jaunty instrumental version of "Take Me Out to the Ball Game" while fans talk with one another and continue stretching. After the bottom of the seventh, Hays plays the famous "Budweiser song," actually titled "Here Comes the King."

San Diego Padres: They play a recording of "Take Me Out to the Ball Game" played by Bobby Freeman, formerly the club's organist, and fans sing along.

Sun-soaked San Diego fans relax while watching the Padres and waiting for their cue to sing "Take Me Out to the Ball Game."

Caption

Another song is played afterward, such as "Twist and Shout," "Good Vibrations," or "California Sun."

 San Francisco Giants: They play a recording of "Take Me Out to the Ball Game" and the fans stand and sing.

 Seattle Mariners: They play a recorded organ version of "Take Me Out to the Ball Game," then segue into "Louie, Louie," which was the subject of a light-hearted and unsuccessful movement to become the state song back in the late 1980s. Fans get on their feet and sing along.

 Tampa Bay Rays: They play a live organ version of "Take Me Out to the Ball Game" while selected fans or special guests lead the singing and the crowd joins in. They try to get folks to sing "Root, root, root for the Devil Rays." According to the Rays, "The bigger the celebrity, the less they know the lyrics." After "Take Me Out to the Ball Game," they either play "Cotton Eyed Joe," or "Cha Cha Slide."

 Texas Rangers: They play a recorded organ version of "Take Me Out to the Ball Game" and the fans sing along.

 Toronto Blue Jays: The stretch begins with "OK Blue Jays" and is followed by The Andrews Sisters' version of "Take Me Out to the Ball Game." For decades, only "OK Blue Jays" was played. The fans generally sing along, and the seventh-inning stretch is sponsored by the Ontario Ministry of Health to encourage fans to live healthy lifestyles and exercise more.

 Washington Nationals: The Nationals appear to do "God Bless America" more frequently than most other clubs, who

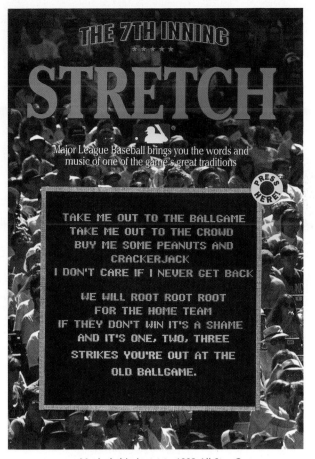

Musical-chip insert to 1992 All-Star Game program.

tend to limit the song to Sundays and holidays. Two fans reported hearing "God Bless America" on a weeknight, making the Nationals and the Yankees the only two teams to do the song regularly more than once a week, in keeping with their status as cities involved in the 2001 terrorist attacks. However, "God Bless America" was not done every night at the Nationals. Following "God Bless America," they play a recorded version of "Take Me Out to the Ball Game" and Screech, the eagle mascot, climbs atop the third-base dugout to lead the crowd. In addition, each dugout has two presidents atop it: the Nationals have a "President's Race" during the middle of the fourth inning, involving costumed mascot Presidents Washington, Jefferson, Lincoln, and Teddy Roosevelt. The Nat Pack, consisting of young men and women cheerleaders, are also atop the dugout shooting T-shirts into the crowd.

THE MOVIE WE
NEVER SAW

THE PHENOMENAL SUCCESS of "Take Me Out to the Ball Game" in 1908 caused a rash of copycat songs designed to capitalize on both the popularity of the song and the surging popularity of the national pastime. But the gold rush wasn't limited to music. Pioneering motion picture actor and director Gilbert "Broncho Billy" Anderson, a baseball fan, was so inspired by the song he used it as the basis of one of his several baseball films.

Little is known about his 1910 silent film *Take Me Out to the Ball Game*, which seems to have suffered the same fate as 90 to 95 percent of early films—it has not survived.[1] The film is known to have been 990 feet in length, or sixteen minutes, and was released in late August 1910.

The film opens with a fan reading the paper to learn of the big game that afternoon. After that, he can't keep his mind on business, only baseball. Finally, he goes home for lunch, where he implores his wife to hurry—he doesn't want to be late. In a nod to Katie Casey's plea in the song, his wife, Fanny, asks to go along. She takes forever to get ready, and then fan, Fanny, and their dog, Jack (Norworth?) board a streetcar. After he secures tickets,

ESSANAY'S BASEBALL COMEDY MADE BIG HIT.

The Essanay Company's baseball comedy picture, "Take Me Out to the Ball Game," has proven one of the most successful comedy pictures that this firm has turned out in many months, and this is saying a great deal for the company whose comedy product is attracting so much favorable attention. Letters from exhibitors all over the country have been received and all speak in a complimentary way about the picture. S. I. Levine, of the Orpheum Theater, one of Chicago's largest motion picture theaters, spoke very highly of the baseball picture. "It is the best comedy we have had in many, many months," he said. "It is pretty hard to wake up a 9 o'clock audience, but we had them laughing all morning. The ladies seemed to like the picture particularly, and during the afternoon, when the house is chiefly composed of ladies and children, the house was in a continuous uproar all through the picture. We have had many requests to show the picture again and will repeat it within the next week or so. We show all the Essanay films and always find them good."

Reviews and notices of the 1910
film in *Moving Picture World*.

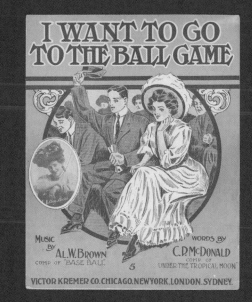

One of the many songs that attempted to ride
the coattails of "Take Me Out to the Ball Game."

"Take Me Out to the Ball Game" (Essanay).—A lively travesty on the passion for baseball which actuates so many devotees of the sport now. Not always, however, will a man become so excited that he forgets to take his wife home, leaving her on the bleachers to find her way home as best she can. Probably the innovation of having bull pups chase umpires all over the grounds will not become popular, particularly with the luckless umpires, but in this instance it adds another feature of fun to a film already overflowing with it. Then comes the finale, which starts with a family row, but ends in peace and happiness at home. Blinks is undoubtedly benefited by his outing, though it must be confessed that his nervous condition borders on collapse at a number of stages of the progress of the story.

our excited fan goes back to where he left his wife waiting and takes the arm of the first woman he sees. Upon entering the stadium, he discovers he's got the wrong woman— this one is large and, as we now say, African American.

There is a lively ball game, and at one point the umpire makes an unpopular decision, prompting Jack the bull pup to attack him—the dog actor playing Jack had made a specialty out of biting pants and hanging on. Fanny joins the melee and brings Jack off the field with a patch of the umpire's pants in his mouth. Tired out and unfamiliar with baseball, Fanny falls asleep. At the game's conclusion, her husband forgets her and goes all the way home, where he realizes his mistake and returns to find her sleeping alone in the stands. Perhaps she didn't care if she never got back. . . .[2]

Anderson had shown an interest in baseball and film starting in 1908, when he filmed portions of a White

Sox–New York Highlanders game at South Side Park, the home of the White Sox. This was also the year he arranged, at the urging of fellow enthusiast Jess Robbins, to film the World Series for the next three seasons.[3] For the movie, Anderson also filmed scenes at the ballpark between games, which allowed him to focus on comedic scenes using actors playing fans. Apparently, filming real fans proved to be difficult because of what was then called "camera consciousness."

SINATRA TO KELLY
TO WILLIAMS

PINCH-HITTING FOR ANDY, BOB, AND TIM:
FILM CRITIC JEFFREY LYONS

*T*AKE ME OUT *to the Ball Game* begins like a Rickey Henderson leadoff home run. Just about right off the bat, we get a terrific rendition of baseball's anthem (written by someone who'd never seen a game at the time, by the way) performed by Gene Kelly and Frank Sinatra. "The Chairman of the Board" (not Whitey Ford) shows surprising skill as a dancer, even alongside Kelly, the greatest dancer of his generation.

Sinatra and Kelly portray two infielders on the defending world champion team called the Wolves. (I suppose they couldn't get the rights to a real team's name and logo.) Spring training is just beginning. They've been moonlighting as vaudeville performers, thinking of switching careers full-time to the one that would surround them with girls all the time. Listen for the name of opposing player Rube Waddell mentioned in the train ride scene and you'll know that it's set at the turn of the twentieth century.

The look of baseball of that era is authentic, though none of the all-white team sports mustaches, a common affectation of those days during baseball's formative years.

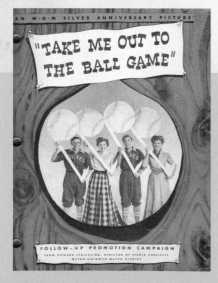

(Were the movie made today, the mediocre number "Yes, Indeedy," about all the girls these two left behind in the off-season, would be surely cut since one verse refers to a girl who turns out to be an eleven-year-old.) Then comes the shocking news that the team's new owner is one K. C. Higgins, who of course turns out to be Esther Williams, who will, of course, eventually land in a modern-looking pool for a number. That was probably part of her contract.

Gene Kelly, while possessing a surprisingly quick bat and one of the most athletic of all movie dancing stars, didn't appear to have held a bat much growing up in Pittsburgh, and by today's standards he and especially Sinatra are about as big as undersized utility infielders. But being a screen immortal helps get them past that.

From a historical perspective, the movie is a curiosity of sorts. There is a reference to one "Charlie Davis of Cincinnati," but no such player existed. This was the dead-ball era of jackets and ties worn for dinner and large sweaters with the team logo. "If she's a dame, she wants romance," says Kelly, immediately dating the movie as well.

Soon second baseman Sinatra and shortstop Kelly, along with first baseman Jules Munchen (who was to star with them in *On the Town* that same year), burst into the movie's most memorable song, "O'Brien-to-Ryan-to-Goldberg," aping the famous "Tinkers-to-Evers-to-Chance" double play.

Later, after Betty Garrett the Broadway star turns up as a fan in love with Sinatra's character, there's a huge number with the entire cast reminiscent of *Seven Brides for Seven Brothers* called "Strictly." Never mind that it has nothing to do with the plot; this is a forties musical, so anything goes.

Surprisingly, there's a subplot involving gamblers, one of whom is portrayed by Edward Arnold, a former head of the Screen Actor's Guild, by the way. His involvement in the story begins to get sinister as he gets the slumping O'Brien, the team's star shortstop, suspended for keeping late hours while rehearsing his vaudeville act.

It all leads up to the climactic game against the Indians, whose uniforms and gloves (like the gloves of the Wolves as well, for that matter) look like 1949 vintage. The baseball skills look a bit clumsy, but that's to be expected.

This was Sinatra's eleventh film, including two uncredited appearances, four years before *From Here to Eternity* would win him the Best Supporting Actor Oscar and revive his screen career. For Kelly, this was his twelfth movie, right before he joined Sinatra in *On the Town*. The DVD, incidentally, includes two deleted numbers. But

thank goodness they kept in a finale number with Sinatra, Kelly, Williams, and Garrett, in which their real names are used in the lyrics along with those of Judy Garland and Fred Astaire. It lets us all in on the fun.

TALKING THE TALK

S O IF YOU DID take yourself or someone else out to the ball game in 1908, here's the lingo you would have heard around the grounds.

base ball—yes, it used to be two words rather than one. Though some occurrences of "baseball" have been found as early as 1858, the term was often two words until the late 1920s.

big smoke—the major leagues

bingle—a clean base hit, with no chance for a play

bug—a fan

bush league, bush, busher—the bush leagues were the minor leagues, a usage that first appeared in 1902. A busher was a minor league player. "Bush league" was also used as an adjective to signify anything cheap or inferior.

chin music—the current meaning of this term is a brushback pitch, thrown at or just below the head. The earlier meaning is much like today's "trash talk," impudent or satirical talk from players to each other or from fans to players.

counting pan or **counting station**–home plate

crank–a baseball fan. The term dates from the late 1880s and was probably still in use in 1908.

crash–a team is crashing when several players in succession get hits

drop–the pitch that is today known as a sinker

fadeaway–a pitch invented by Christy Mathewson, which would later be called the screwball

fast society–the major leagues

gonfalon–a banner or a pennant. See the poem "Baseball's Sad Lexicon" for the line "Ruthlessly pricking our gonfalon bubble."

grounds–the common term for any ball field

Highlander–early nickname for the New York American League club, which would soon be known as the Yankees

hoodoo–(n) an object, person, or player that brings bad luck : (v) to create bad luck or to place a hex

ice wagon–a very slow runner

Jints–New York lingo for the Giants

kick–(n) a protest or complaint : (v) to complain or protest the umpire's decision. This word was extremely common.

meat hand–any player's throwing hand, a reference to the fact the throwing hand is bare as opposed to the gloved hand

Merkle, "To Merkle"–after his infamous baserunning play of 1908, Fred Merkle's surname became both a noun meaning "mistake" and a verb meaning "to make a mistake."

piano legs–legs of a stocky, slow-moving player

pill–a baseball, especially in reference to a pitch thrown at high speed

pinch–key spot in a game, as in the book title *Pitching in a Pinch* by Christy Mathewson

scull–free ticket to a game

slapstick–a baseball bat. Since players choked up on the bat and tried to slap the ball to all fields, the term is more apt than it would be today.

slobber ball–spitball

sou–a coin of low denomination. See the lyrics to the 1908 version of "Take Me Out to the Ball Game" for the line "Every sou Katie blew."

soup bone–the throwing arm, especially of a pitcher

tall grass–low-level minor leagues

warming pan–the bullpen, where relief pitchers warm up

World's Series–an earlier name for "World Series," used in some sources as late as 1930. Contrary to frequent assumption, the name was not a result of sponsorship of the World Series by a newspaper called the *World*.

yannigan–a rookie or young player, also known as a "Rube"

NELLY KELLY

I N 1927, Jack Norworth created a new verse for the song, replacing the heroine Katie Casey with a woman of similar ambition, Nelly Kelly. Why the change? It's not known who Nelly Kelly was, much less Katie Casey—they were most likely fictitious characters whose names fit the rhyme and tenor of the song. However, a clue to the puzzle might be that Norworth divorced in 1927, marrying Dorothy Adelphi in 1928. Perhaps Dorothy was the inspiration for the new lyrics? More plausible perhaps: the reason for the new lyrics may have been nothing more than a shrewd business decision. When Jack Norworth wrote new lyrics in 1927, he effectively created a second version of the song that would garner a second copyright. Whereas the 1908 version is now in the public domain in the United States, the 1927 version is in fact protected under a newer set of copyright laws: in Norworth's case, for a period of ninety-five years after the creation of the new version. In other words, the 1927 version is under copyright protection until 2022!

Sheet music to "The Hinkey Dee" from George M. Cohan's 1923 play *Little Nellie Kelly*, which may have inspired Norworth's 1927 revision of the lyrics that changed Katie Casey to Nelly Kelly.

DAME YANKEES

THE FIRST HEROINE of "Take Me Out to the Ball Game" was Katie Casey, the young woman immortalized in the first verse of the original 1908 version. In 1927, Jack Norworth created a new verse to the song, this time introducing a new heroine, Nelly Kelly:

1908 Version

Verse I

Katie Casey was baseball mad,
Had the fever and had it bad.
Just to root for the home town crew,
Ev'ry sou
Katie blew.
On a Saturday her young beau
Called to see if she'd like to go
To see a show
But Miss Kate said, "No,
I'll tell you what you can do."

Verse II

Katie Casey saw all the games,
Knew the players by their first names.
Told the umpire he was wrong,
All along,
Good and strong.
When the score was just two to two,
Katie Casey knew what to do,
Just to cheer up the boys she knew,
She made the gang sing this song:

1927 Version

Verse I

Nelly Kelly loved baseball games,
Knew the players, knew all their names.
You could see her there ev'ry day,
Shout "Hurray"
When they'd play.
Her boyfriend by the name of Joe
Said, "To Coney Isle, dear, let's go",
Then Nelly started to fret and pout,
And to him, I heard her shout:

The Philadelphia Bobbies—so named for their hairstyles—in the mid-1920s.

The Vassar College Resolutes
baseball team, pictured in 1876.

Postcard circa 1908, which satirizes women's interest in the game.

Verse II

Nelly Kelly was sure some fan,
She would root just like any man,
Told the umpire he was wrong,
All along,
Good and strong.
When the score was just two to two,
Nelly Kelly knew what to do,
Just to cheer up the boys she knew,
She made the gang sing this song:

Why rewrite the song? There are probable copyright reasons (see "Nelly Kelly"). Jean Hastings Ardell, a historian of women and baseball, sees another reason: "In 1927, Jack Norworth revised his lyrics to celebrate the new sort of American girl emerging out of the freedoms of the 1920s." According to Ardell, the "new freedoms women claimed during the Jazz Age are evident in Nelly's demand, stronger now than a plea, to go to the ballpark."[1]

But beyond the two heroines of the song, "Take Me Out to the Ball Game" may owe a debt of gratitude to the legions of female amateur pianists across the country who learned the song, taught it to their children, and carried on the tradition of singing it long before it became a staple at ball parks during the seventh-inning stretch. It worked like this: The touring vaudeville circuit and the music publishing industry worked in tandem. Vaudeville singers would introduce a new song in saloons and theaters.

Enamored with a new song, men would ask their wives or girlfriends to buy the sheet music and learn it so that they could sing it at home. In the early 1900s, it was the domain of women to properly learn piano by buying sheet music and taking lessons. To be sure, men played piano, too, but many did so by rote, never having trained formally. Women taught their children the songs they learned by teaching their children to play and read music. Thus the tradition of parlor songs (as it was known) was passed down from mother to child.

One of the new freedoms of the Jazz Age was suffrage, the freedom to cast votes in national elections, won by crusading suffragettes in 1920, with the Nineteenth Amendment. Baseball played a part in the long quest for women's right to vote. As early as 1869, there was a Women's Suffrage Baseball Club, presumably composed of women, which posted a 19–16 victory over the unfortunately named Invincibles.[2] Though they won the game, the suffragettes didn't win the right to vote in the nineteenth century.

Ironically, on April 14, 1910, the very day he is alleged to have inadvertently started the seventh-inning stretch, President William Howard Taft used the ballpark to escape the suffrage issue. He met with suffragists that morning at the White House and told them he thought it would be a mistake to extend the franchise to women. When they loudly hissed and booed, he ran from the room, grabbing the vice president and suggesting that they go out to the ballpark to see the opening game of the season.[3]

Having perhaps reflected upon Taft's choice of refuge, the strategists of the Votes for Women movement knew that to get their message heard, they would need to take the fight to where the men were—the ballpark. In 1915, activists contracted with John McGraw's New York Giants to hold "Women's Suffrage Day" at the Polo Grounds. They picked a day when the archrival Chicago Cubs were in town and bought nearly 10,000 seats at reduced prices from the club.

The women then resold the seats at full price, netting a profit for their coffers. Part of the sales effort was to canvass local office buildings while dressed in replica Giants and Cubs uniforms—wish we had a picture of that! We can tell you that the larger women dressed as Giants, while the more diminutive dressed as Cubs, a clever touch.[4]

On the day of the big game, the women arranged a "monster suffragette parade" to the ballpark, "attended by a number of bands of music." We can presume that "Take Me Out to the Ball Game" was one number frequently played that day. The women met their immediate goals, to raise funds and publicize their movement at the ballpark, where they could "see to it that their husbands, brothers, lovers, and sons are present to witness their success."[5]

Of course, women have always been drawn to the game, as fans, players, umpires, and sportswriters. As early as 1868, there were calls to encourage more women to attend ball games. Henry Chadwick editorialized that year that "experience has shown that nothing tends so much to elevate the game, to rid it of evil influences, to lead to proper decorum and to gentlemanly contests than the countenance and patronage of the ladies."[6] He went on to note that having ladies present tended to reduce the "profanity, ill-feeling, partisan prejudice, and open gambling" that otherwise would be found at a ball game.

By the 1880s, many professional clubs held "Ladies' Day," offering free admission once a week to encourage ladies to come out to the park. Baltimore, Philadelphia, Chicago, Brooklyn, and minor league New Orleans were early leaders in the practice. In Cincinnati in the late 1880s, women were admitted free when the handsome Tony Mullane pitched. The same was true in Washington in 1897 when George "Win" Mercer pitched. In one such game, Mercer was ejected by the umpire for arguing, and a near riot ensued, causing the club to cease holding Ladies' Days.[7]

In 1909, just a year after "Take Me Out to the Ball Game," the National League banned Ladies' Day because owners assumed that ladies were by now so interested in baseball that they would continue coming to games regardless of whether free admission was offered. In 1914, the Cubs, under new ownership, reestablished the tradition. Ladies' Days continued to be held in the majors until the 1970s, when they were abolished because of concerns they constituted discrimination against both men and women.[8]

The first known women's baseball team was at Vassar College, in 1866. By 1890, women's touring teams were well established. The teams tended to fall into two categories, novelty teams and serious athletic outfits. The former used the novelty of young, often unskilled females playing the game to draw lots of spectators in a sort of sideshow atmosphere.

The latter, often called "bloomer girls" teams, after the pants-like garment popularized by Amelia Jenks Bloomer, played skilled baseball as they toured around the country matching up against local men's teams. Bloomer girls teams often featured one or two men in women's

clothing, playing the high skill positions like pitcher, catcher, and shortstop. Hall of Famer Rogers Hornsby and the great Smoky Joe Wood are two male players who got their start with bloomer girls teams.[9] One could say that they gave new meaning to the term "drag bunt."

Sometimes a girl would want to play ball, but there wasn't a local women's team. In many such cases, she just played with the boys and men. One such young woman was Alta Weiss, of Ragersville, Ohio. She was an athletic young woman, and in 1907, at age seventeen, she signed on to play with a local semipro club, the Vermilion Independents, as a pitcher. After striking out fifteen batters in her debut, she went on to play seven more games for the club, before her father started his own team to showcase her talents, the Weiss All

Stars. So novel and talented was she that special excursion trains would run from Cleveland on her scheduled pitching days.[10] Weiss used the proceeds from ticket sales to fund her education, including medical school.

Another young woman who loved the game was Amanda Clement, the first female umpire, hailing from Hudson, South Dakota. At the age of sixteen, she was a frequent substitute player on the town team. One day a traveling team was in town, and when the umpire failed to show up, Miss Clement stood in. She had a deep knowledge of the rules and that most essential trait of umpires: she could control the game, and thus was a career born. For many years, billed as "South Dakota's Great Woman Umpire," she umpired all over the upper Midwest: The Dakotas, Minnesota, Iowa, and Nebraska. Garnering fees of $25 a game, she used the funds to put herself through college, obtaining a physical education degree in 1909. Amateur umpires today are often paid $40–$50 per game, and according to an Internet calculator, $25 in 1908 would be worth a whopping $521.66 today. Her scrapbook rests today in the archives of the National Baseball Hall of Fame.

So Jack Norworth was really on to something when he had Katie Casey, and later Nelly Kelly, call the shots at the old ball game. Most Americans are not aware of the feminine protagonist of "Take Me Out to the Ball Game," which is oddly fitting, since most Americans are also unaware of the rich history of women and girls in baseball.

FLORENCE AND ANNA

MOVE OVER, Jack Norworth and Albert Von Tilzer. Florence Holbrood and Anna Caldwell followed up on the success of "Take Me Out to the Ball Game" by writing baseball songs the following year in 1909. Ms. Holbrood wrote "He's a Fan, Fan, Fan" and Ms. Caldwell wrote "Stars of Our National Game."

HARRY GOES ELECTRIC

"**A**LL RIGHT, let me hear ya. Ah one, ah two, ah three, *Take me out to the ball game, take me out with the crowd . . . .*"

Just after the last out is recorded in the top half of the seventh inning, the crowd rises as one and an organist begins playing the old familiar tune–"Take Me Out to the Ball Game." It's an experience we've all had, and surely our parents and grandparents and even *their* parents before them have shared this universal, timeless baseball ritual. Heck, it must go all the way back, one hundred years, to 1908, the year the song was written, right?

Wrong. The familiar ritual we share today, from coast to coast–from Fenway Park to Wrigley Field to Dodger Stadium–from the big leagues to the minors, through to college and sometimes even to high school ball–is about thirty years old. That's right, we've been singing the song together for thirty years. That's long enough to be called a ritual, but many baseball fans are surprised to know the ritual is no older than the mid-1970s.

So, from 1869–or possibly earlier, since that was just the first *written* reference to a seventh-inning stretch–to 1908, they must have stretched silently, because our song wasn't written yet. Or there may have been musical interludes between innings. At first, these would have been played by live bands only, as there was neither practical recording technology nor public address systems available in ballparks. The New York Giants were the first club to install a permanent PA system, in 1929. Not long after that,

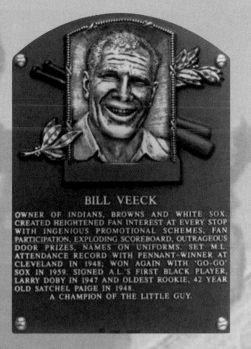

BILL VEECK
OWNER OF INDIANS, BROWNS AND WHITE SOX.
CREATED HEIGHTENED FAN INTEREST AT EVERY STOP
WITH INGENIOUS PROMOTIONAL SCHEMES, FAN
PARTICIPATION, EXPLODING SCOREBOARD, OUTRAGEOUS
DOOR PRIZES, NAMES ON UNIFORMS. SET M.L.
ATTENDANCE RECORD WITH PENNANT-WINNER AT
CLEVELAND IN 1948; WON AGAIN WITH 'GO-GO'
SOX IN 1959. SIGNED A.L.'S FIRST BLACK PLAYER,
LARRY DOBY IN 1947 AND OLDEST ROOKIE, 42 YEAR
OLD SATCHEL PAIGE IN 1948.
A CHAMPION OF THE LITTLE GUY.

the Chicago Cubs installed the first ballpark organ, in 1941. Today, when you attend games at Wrigley, or U.S. Cellular Field across town, and you hear organ music wafting timelessly across the breeze, it seems natural to assume that it was always so—the combination of baseball and the organ is so perfect. But not before 1941.

So "Take Me Out to the Ball Game" was a big hit back when it first came out, selling millions of copies in records, sheet music, and cylinders. But it really wasn't played at ballparks all that much, at least not at first. The first known time that "Take Me Out to the Ball Game" was heard in a ballpark was in 1934, prior to the opening game of the Los Angeles prep baseball season. Later that same year, before the fourth game of the World Series, the song was played on the field by the St. Louis Cardinals band, led by third baseman Pepper Martin.

The first time the song was linked with the seventh-inning stretch was in 1945, when a newspaper piece noted that "'Take Me Out to the Ball Game' booms over the public address system in all Pacific Coast League parks during the seventh-inning stretch." Maybe a young marine named Bill Veeck heard the song that year, just as he was completing his military service in the South Pacific. Whether he saw a PCL game that year or not, he would go on to become, after Norworth and Von Tilzer, the third, or perhaps fourth, most important person in the song's history, along with his partner in crime, the inimitable Harry Caray. It was Veeck who would open the door to Caray's trademark seventh-inning-stretch rendition of the song.

Bill Veeck was baseball's master showman, owner extraordinaire, and champion of working stiffs and other lowly fans. The son of a Chicago Cubs executive, he

planted the famous and sublime ivy at Wrigley Field as a twenty-three-year-old in 1937. Shortly thereafter, he bought the minor league Milwaukee Brewers. He would go on to own the Cleveland Indians, St. Louis Browns, and the Chicago White Sox—twice. Though he won a couple of pennants, in 1948 with the Indians and in 1959 with the White Sox, he was often cursed with bad ball clubs. So when the team wasn't playing well, Veeck was. He was the crown prince of baseball owners, once sending a midget up as a pinch hitter, letting fans in the grandstand manage the game by surveying them on tactical decisions, and installing an exploding scoreboard and a shower in the outfield at Comiskey Park.

In many ways he was destined to work with Harry Caray, the brash, colorful, and fan-centered announcer who began with the Cardinals in 1946. Caray lost his job in 1969, and headed west for one season with the Oakland A's, before becoming the White Sox announcer in 1971. In 1975, Bill Veeck bought the team for the second time. Both men had always loved "Take Me Out to the Ball Game."

Caray used to sing it, unaided by either a microphone or, strictly speaking, any musical talent, in the press box during the seventh-

inning stretch, and Veeck had always wanted to push the song as an essential component of same. "I tried it in Milwaukee, Cleveland, St. Louis, and Chicago the first time, but it never worked. Finally I got the right guy. It does a lot for the game and gets the fans involved even if the Sox are losing."

But how did Veeck get his man? The commonly understood version is that Veeck secretly installed a microphone in the booth, and one day flipped it on, astonishing both Harry and the crowd below. But it's too simple. Caray, an immortal among baseball announcers just for his work with the Cardinals, is often dismissed these days as a bumbling, malaprop-making, shameless self-promoter. But he actually wanted no part of Veeck's scheme to make him a concert performer.

In an interview with Mike Veeck, Bill's son and a true chip off the old block as the owner and promoter of the St. Paul Saints and several other minor league franchises, new details emerge. "The actual truth was we begged Harry for weeks to sing," says Mike Veeck– who worked for his old man's White Sox in the 1970s. Finally, they blackmailed him into singing. "We told him we had a cassette copy of him singing the song, and that we were going to play it whether he wanted us to or not, so he might as well sing live. He had no idea that everyone in the ballpark would stand up and that this would become his signature moment."[1]

In 1981, Harry jumped on the Red Line and moved on up to the North Side, beginning a sixteen-year stint as the Chicago Cubs broadcaster. The Cubs broadcast nearly every game coast to coast on cable superstation WGN, and not only did a thirty-five-year veteran broadcaster become a national figure, but a seventy-three-year-old song gave a 112-year-old stretch new life in the age of electronic ritual. Nowadays, nearly every major and minor league club plays a recording of the song and many fans sing along. The Caray–Veeck act was so smooth that we assume it was handed down from the baseball gods of long ago. And just as the national anthem is thought by baseball fans to end with the words "play ball," Caray's version of "Take Me Out to the Ball Game" often ended with his lagniappe signature flourish: "Let's Get Some Runs!"

Yes, some teams persist in rituals of their own–Harry's own Cardinals played that Budweiser song, "Here Comes the King," as late as 1995–though they've now switched to "Take Me Out to the Ball Game"–the commercial jingle comes a half-inning later. The Baltimore Orioles play John Denver's "Thank God I'm a Country Boy" and the Toronto Blue Jays play a ditty called "OK Blue Jays." But by and large, our national pastime now has its own anthem, "Take Me Out to the Ball Game." (For a complete rundown of seventh-inning-stretch practices at present, see "Get Up, Stand Up.")

That is, it did until September 11, 2001. When the terrorists struck at the heart of our way of life, they inadvertently changed the seventh-inning stretch, and baseball lost a measure of innocence in the process. Baseball games were cancelled for a week after the bombings, and upon their return, "Take Me Out to the Ball Game" was replaced by a Major League Baseball mandate–play "God Bless America." The Cubs did both songs, but many other teams made the switch–temporarily. As life slowly returned to normalcy, many teams switched back to their previous traditions, and now only the New York Yankees–themselves a symbol of America–continue the "God Bless America" tradition at every game–other teams add the classic patriotic tune on Sundays and holidays

But back to the innocence. This is your chapter, Harry and Bill. Back to a summer afternoon at Wrigley Field–built just six years after "Take Me Out to the Ball Game" was written–and served by the same kind of elevated trains on which Jack Norworth scratched out the words. Back to skies of Cubbie blue and dreams deferred since the Cubs last World Series championship–also one hundred years ago, in 1908. Back to Harry Caray and longtime broadcast partner Steve Stone, who once called Harry "the greatest single salesman of the game that ever lived." (Don't tell Bill Veeck, who planted that ivy, that one!)

"Hey, Steve," Caray would exclaim at slow moments. "What Italian has sung to the most people? Frank Sinatra? Luciano Pavarotti? No, it's me! I was born Harry Carabina, and I sing to 30,000 people every afternoon, and countless more on TV and radio."

"Buy me some peanuts and Cracker Jack. I don't care if I never get back . . ."

Statue of legendary broadcaster Harry Caray outside Wrigley Field.

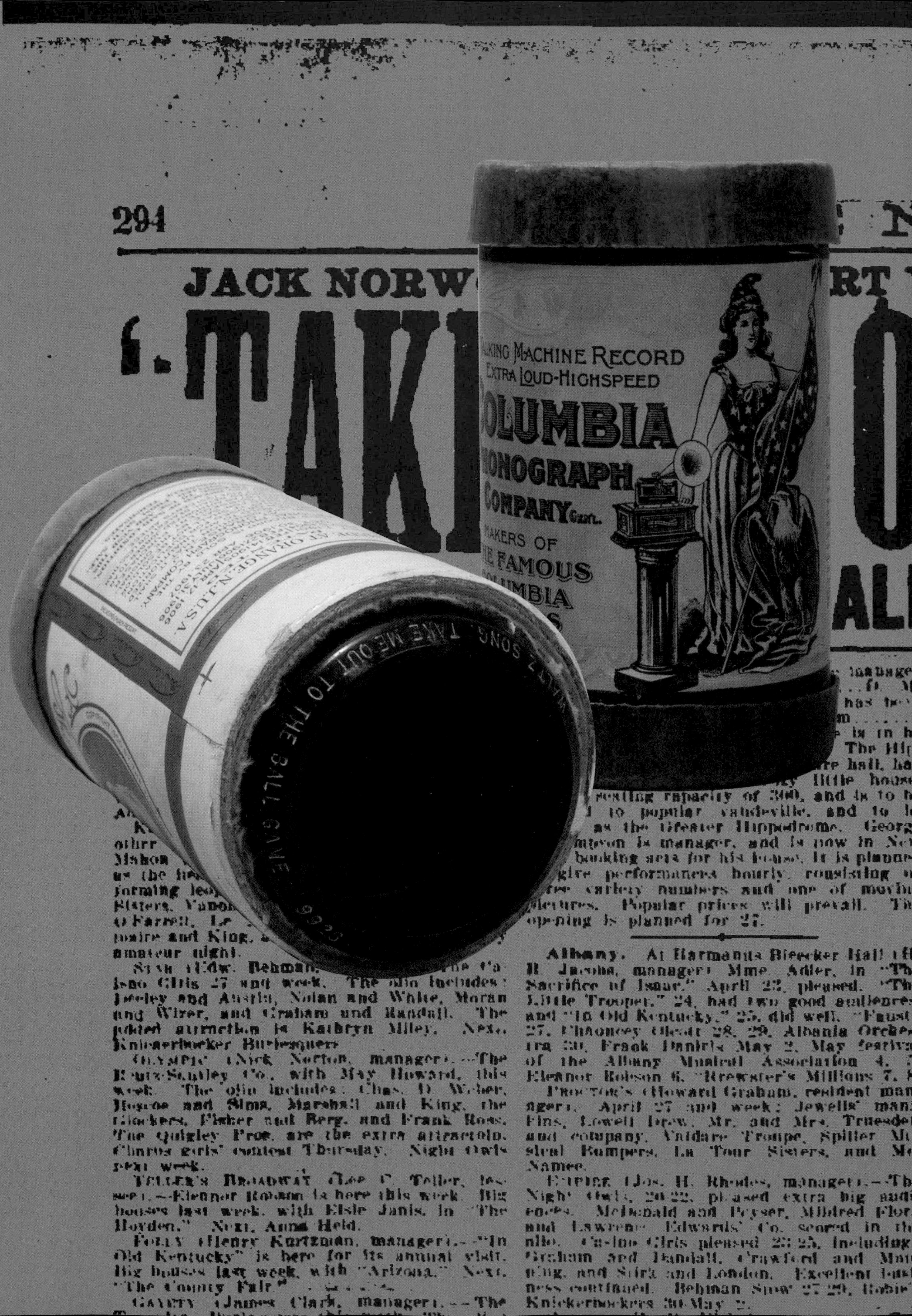

294

JACK NORW

TAK

ALKING MACHINE RECORD
EXTRA LOUD-HIGHSPEED
OLUMBIA
HONOGRAPH
COMPANY Ltd.
MAKERS OF
HE FAMOUS
OLUMBIA

TIME LINE

THE EARLIEST KNOWN reference to the seventh-inning stretch is in a letter from Hall of Fame player Harry Wright written in 1869: "The spectators all arise between halves of the seventh, extend their legs and arms, and sometimes walk about. In so doing they enjoy the relief afforded by relaxation from a long posture on hard benches."[1]

1877 (December 24)–Thomas Edison files a patent for the phonograph, designed at first for office dictation. It consists of a metal cylinder with a fine spiral groove, two diaphragm and needle units (one for recording and one for playback), and a small horn.

1887 (September 26)–Emile Berliner files a patent for the gramophone, which utilizes zinc discs instead of cylinders. In November of the same year, Edison records his first solid-wax cylinders to replace the primitive tinfoil recordings.

1892 (January 9)–"Slide, Kelly, Slide" reaches the number one spot in the Top Ten charts, staying there for three weeks. It is the first hit among baseball songs.

1907 (November)–Ada Jones and Billy Murray, the most popular of all female-male vocal pairings, have their first number-one record. Up until now, nearly all vocal records have been in one of two styles: minstrel-styled comedy (such as Collins and Harlan) or formal European-influenced ballad singing (led by Henry Burr). Ada and Billy introduce a more casual, natural style of singing, which set the stage for tunes like "Take Me Out to the Ball Game."

1908–Jack Norworth purportedly boards the New York City subway and writes lyrics to "Take Me Out to the Ball Game." The song was written sometime before May 2, 1908, when an ad for the sheet music appeared in the *New York Clipper*, a newspaper devoted to sports and entertainment. That same day, the song was registered with the copyright office.

1908 (September)–First recording of "Take Me Out to the Ball Game," by the Haydn Quartet, is released.

1908 (October)–Columbia advertises America's first two-sided records and the appeal of "two songs for the price of one" is a key marketing tool.

1908 (October 17)–Edward Meeker's recording of "Take Me Out to the Ball Game" (Edison 9926) reaches the Top 10 charts for the first time, peaking at the number-five position for one week before dropping off the charts.

1908 (October 24)–Exactly one week after the Meeker recording, a new recording by the Haydn Quartet with Billy Murray (Victor 5570) charts, peaking at number one for

Edison wax cylinders—the precursors of flat records—included several renditions of "Take Me Out to the Ball Game."

seven weeks and lasting sixteen weeks total on the Top 10 charts (through winter!) before dropping off the charts on January 30, 1909. Ironically, although Billy Murray is credited on the recording, he never sang on it, and Victor corrected the "error" in subsequent catalogs. But Murray's billing on the recording, whether marketing ploy or error, certainly helped spur sales

1908 (November)–Edison begins producing four-minute wax Amberol cylinders, nearly doubling the previous maximum length.

1908 (November 21)–At the same time Billy Murray's recordings was charting, Harvey Hindermeyer's recording (Columbia 586) reaches the charts, peaking at the number three spot and staying on the Top 10 chart for four weeks. Eight baseball songs were published in 1908, but after the great success of "Take Me Out to the Ball Game," there was a rush to capitalize on the song's success–twenty-two baseball songs were published in 1909. There were also other spin-offs. Albert Von Tilzer and Junie McCree published "Let's Go into the Picture Show," perhaps on the theory that "Take Me Out to the Ball Game" was popular not just because of baseball but also because of the dating scenario that plays out in the song.

1910–In a further attempt to capitalize on the song's success, legendary silent film director Gilbert "Broncho Billy" Anderson directs a sixteen-minute theatrical release also named "Take Me Out to the Ball Game."

1929–The New York Giants install the first public address system in Major League Baseball.

1932–At a testimonial dinner for George M. Cohan, Albert Von Tilzer sang his famous old song "Take Me Out to the Ball Game," and Louise Fazenda exclaimed, "Why you could really tell what the tunes were in those days! They weren't all gummed up with a drum boom-boom here, a sliding trombone blare there, and some jazz from the rest of the boys."[2]

1933–According to the *Detroit News*, "Take Me Out to the Ball Game" is adopted as "the official base ball song" by both the American and National Leagues.[3]

1934–Albert Von Tilzer, billed as the composer of "Take Me Out to the Ball Game," appears at the Biltmore Hotel in Los Angeles at a banquet celebrating the opening of the baseball season. The evening features more than 200 players from the Chicago Cubs, Chicago White Sox, Pittsburgh Pirates, Los Angeles Angels, Hollywood Stars, and Portland Beavers. Celebrities set to speak or sing include Will Rogers, "stage favorite" Fred Stone, motion picture star Dick

Powell, Harold Grayson's orchestra, and Johnnie Murray and his Hi-Jinks radio crew.[4]

1934–"Take Me Out to the Ball Game" is played at the annual Gridiron Club dinner in Washington, D.C., as part of a spring training skit.[5]

1934–Los Angeles prep baseball season opens with a band playing "Take Me Out to the Ball Game," the first known time the song is played in a ballpark.[6]

1934–Before Game 4 of the World Series the Cardinal Band, led by third baseman Pepper Martin, plays "Take Me Out to the Ball Game." The *Los Angeles Times* quips, "The way the Cardinal pitchers came and left, they should have played 'Take Me Out of the Ball Game.'" The Cardinals had used five pitchers (Carleton, Vance, Walker, Haines, and Mooney) in a 10–4 home loss to the Tigers.[7]

1935–The S.S. *Manhattan* docks in New York to the strains of "Take Me Out to the Ball Game," described as "Baseball's theme song," as Babe Ruth, his wife, Claire, and her eighteen-year-old daughter return from a four-month trip around the world, with stops in Vancouver, Honolulu, Japan, Bali, Java, the Suez Canal, Paris, Switzerland, and London.[8]

1935–A group of musical Chicago Cubs ballplayers sings "Take Me Out to the Ball Game," "Sweet Adeline," and other "old songs" during a stage appearance at Los Angeles Theatre Mart. The group includes Chuck Klein, Augie Galan, Tex Carlton, Freddie Lindstrom, Stan Hack, and Billy Jurges.[9]

1935–The Marx Brothers release "A Night at the Opera," with a scene in which the orchestra members get their music mixed up and begin playing "Take Me Out to the Ball Game." *The Los Angeles Times* reports that this sequence inspired the Marx Brothers to begin developing a film called "Take Me Out to the Ball Game," with a burlesque old-time baseball game setting. Alas, the film was never made.[10]

1936–Jerry Vogel purchases a share of the copyright to "Take Me Out to the Ball Game" from Albert Von Tilzer's company, Broadway music. Vogel's relentless marketing of the song over the next several decades is undoubtedly a factor in its continued popularity.

1936–The American League releases *Take Me Out to the Ball Game*, an educational and promotional film that will be shown at countless YMCAs, Elks Clubs, Church basements, etc., over the off-season. The film is directed by George Moriarty, a former player and umpire turned songwriter, columnist, and director, whose grandson, actor Michael Moriarty, appeared in the classic 1973 baseball film *Bang the Drum Slowly*.[11] In June, the American League releases final attendance figures for the film–which was viewed by 687,592 people between February 8 and May 1.[12]

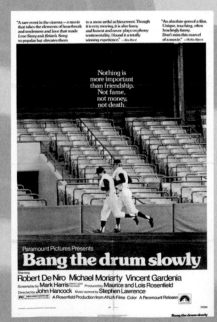

1936–As the Chicago Cubs arrive for spring training on Catalina Island off the California Coast, the island's carillon plays "Take Me Out to the Ball Game."[13]

1936–To the Strains of "Take Me Out to the Ball Game," San Diego Padres shortstop George Myatt marries Miss Georgia Smith at home plate at San Diego's Lane Field, in the first known wedding to feature the song.[14]

1936–In a profile of Albert Von Tilzer, the *Los Angeles Times* reports that he wrote twenty-one songs that sold a million or more copies and implies that "Take Me Out to the Ball Game" was even more popular, calling it "the one tremendously popular song which has never died." The profile indicates that the young Von Tilzer was a musical prodigy and that his parents insisted that he study music every day. "Hundreds of millions of hearts have beaten more gaily or more tenderly because of what Von Tilzer has composed, and that is the kind of music he still writes."[15]

1937–"It was thirty years ago that Alfred [sic] Von Tilzer wrote "Take Me Out to the Ball Game" but he never took it seriously until seven years ago. That is doubtless because he suddenly discovered it was still selling."[16]

1939–"Jack Norworth, whose song "Take Me Out to the Ball Game" was a hit a quarter of a century ago and still stirs the blood of audiences, never saw a ball game until last fall."[17] That would be the fall of 1938, though there is no separate documentation that he saw a game in 1938. The first game we know he attended was on June 27, 1940 (see later).

1939–In a review of the first televised baseball game, the *New York Times* opines: "Television is too safe; there is no ducking the foul ball, no reaching for the 'souvenir' sphere to take home to Sonny if the catch is made when it sails into the grandstand. In fact, after an inning or two, the viewer may feel like singing that old refrain, 'Take Me Out to the Ball Game.'"[18]

1939–As the National Baseball Hall of Fame and Museum in Cooperstown, New York celebrates its grand opening and the "centennial of baseball," ten of the eleven living inductees are introduced to the crowd while a band serenades them with "Take Me Out to the Ball Game."[19]

1939–At a gala parade to welcome the Cincinnati Reds back home after losing the first two games of the World Series to the Yankees in New York, a band plays "Take Me Out to the Ball Game," along with other "current favorites and some of the old ones."[20]

1940–"Take Me Out to the Ball Game" is played at the Democratic National Convention in Chicago, amid reports that DNC Chairman (and Postmaster General) James A. Farley plans to buy the New York Yankees from the estate of Jacob Ruppert.[21]

1940 (June 27)–According to *The Sporting News*, to honor the lyricist of "Take Me Out to the Ballgame," Jack Norworth Day is celebrated at Ebbets Field in Brooklyn. Neither Norworth nor his partner, Albert Von Tilzer, who wrote the music, had ever seen a game when they created the song in 1908. The Dodgers host the Cubs that day. In the evening, a testimonial dinner

Ann Sheridan as Nora Bayes and Dennis Morgan as Jack Norworth, pictured on sheet-music cover of "Time Waits for No One," from the 1944 Norworth biopic *Shine On Harvest Moon*.

is given for Norworth at the St. George Hotel in Brooklyn. Former NYC mayor Jimmy Walker is toastmaster for the dinner. Sam Hellman of Hollywood and Tommy Lyman, night club vocalist, will lead the singing both before the game and after the dinner.[22] In a later article, Norworth will say, "I lived in New York and Brooklyn, but it never occurred to me to go out and see a ball game until 1940. How did I know about peanuts and Cracker Jack? From listening. I saw bush games as a boy and got the 'feel' of the game."[23]

1941–The Chicago Cubs install the first ballpark organ. The Brooklyn Dodgers follow suit the next year.

1941–Jack Norworth gives an impromptu concert of old songs at Chicago's Great Northern Theatre, including "Take Me Out to the Ball Game." He had intended to speak, but the audience insisted that he sing. With a twinkle in his eye, Norworth said, "I have written 2,000 popular songs. Seven of them were successful."[24]

1944–Albert Von Tilzer plays "Take Me Out to the Ball Game" at the Shrine Auditorium in Los Angeles as part of a two-night benefit concert called "America's Music," which raised funds to supply records to Americans serving abroad. According to the article, Jack Norworth played "Shine On Harvest Moon." It is not clear why they didn't perform together.[25]

1944–Jack Norworth is on hand for the opening-day celebrations of the Hollywood Stars baseball team and leads the singing of "Take Me Out to the Ball Game."[26] Actors Jack Carson, George Tobias, Dennis Morgan, and

"I lived in New York and Brooklyn, but it never occurred to me to go out and see a ball game until 1940."—JACK NORWORTH

Alan Hale harmonize on "Take Me Out to the Ball Game," called "the game's theme song." Morgan played Norworth in *Shine On Harvest Moon*, the biopic based on his life and released earlier that month. Carson was also in the film. Jack throws out the first pitch to Sheriff Gene Biscalluz, with baseball-obsessed comedian Joe E. Brown wielding the bat.[27]

1945—In the first known linking of "Take Me Out to the Ball Game" with the seventh-inning stretch, the *Chicago Tribune* reports that "Take Me Out to the Ball Game" booms over the public address system in all Pacific Coast League parks during the seventh-inning stretch.[28]

1949—*Take Me Out to the Ball Game*, a Busby Berkeley movie musical starring Gene Kelly, Frank Sinatra, and Esther Williams, is released.

1950—Renowned behavioral psychologist B. F. Skinner of Harvard University teaches pigeons to play "Take Me Out to the Ball Game" on a special seven-key piano. The experiment is part of his larger work on behavior and rewards—if the pigeons can repeat patterns, they are rewarded with food.[29]

1951—In perhaps the strangest musical performance ever of "Take Me Out to the Ball Game," the song is played by 2,426 "musicians" on Music Depreciation Night at Ebbets Field in Brooklyn. Seems the house band, the Dodger Sym-Phony, had ruffled feathers over at

Local 802 of the American Federation of Musicians. After working out a deal with the union, Dodger owner Walter O'Malley celebrated peace by disturbing it, allowing everyone carrying an instrument in free of charge. Trumpets, tubas, saxophones, violins, cymbals, drums, guitars, even a glockenspiel were wielded by the happy crowd in a cacophony of joy, much of it untrained. Prior to the game, three official numbers were played, "Hail, Hail, the Gang's All Here," "Take Me Out to the Ball Game," and "Roll Out the Barrel." The rest of the evening proved a musicologist's nightmare as strains of "La Traviata" mixed with "My Wild Irish Rose" over "The Sheik of Araby."[30]

1952—Jack Norworth helps to found Little League Baseball chapter in Laguna Beach, California, calling together Laguna Service Club leaders at a dinner and showing baseball films. He is named honorary president of the Laguna Little League.[31]

1952—Ed Sullivan devotes successive Sunday evenings to a tribute to ASCAP, the American Society of Composers, Authors, and Publishers. The bulk of the show consists of composers singing their own songs, including Jack Norworth singing "Take Me Out to the Ball Game" and "Shine On Harvest Moon."[32]

Top, Ed Sullivan.
Bottom, Joe E. Brown.

1953–Jack Norworth sings "Take Me Out to the Ball Game" at the annual Masquer's Club baseball dinner in Hollywood. He is seated at the head table full of luminaries of the baseball and entertainment worlds, including Groucho Marx, Vern Stephens, Del Webb, Joe E. Brown, Chuck Dressen, Leo Durocher, Casey Stengel, Ty Cobb, Fred Haney, Duke Snider, Hank Sauer, Johnny Lindell, and Bob Lemon. Norworth was probably an annual attendee, as another press report has him at the same dinner in 1958, where he quipped "this song has done all right by me. How else do you think I got that Mercedes-Benz I'm driving?"[33]

1954–Bob Cobb, president of the Hollywood Stars baseball team, dreams up a contest to find a new baseball anthem to take its place alongside "Take Me Out to the Ball Game." The contest lasts three months and draws over 1,000 entries from thirteen western states. Mason Mallory of Pasadena was the winner with

"Batter Up, Batter Up, Batter Up." The song has left no trace on the American musical landscape.[34]

1955 (May 9)–Harpo Marx appears on *I Love Lucy*, playing "Take Me Out to the Ball Game" on his harp.

1956–A baseball signed by Jack Norworth and Albert Von Tilzer, the only such ball we've heard of, was thrown out as the ceremonial first pitch for the opening of the Virginia Amateur League in Bedford, Virginia, on May 12. Wonder where that ball is today. . . .

1956–Albert Von Tilzer, composer of the music to "Take Me Out to the Ball Game," dies at age seventy-eight in Los Angeles, on October 1. He had been ill since suffering a stroke several years earlier. His *Los Angeles Times* obituary noted in its headline what he would be remembered for: "Von Tilzer Dies at 78; Wrote Ball Game Song." The first sentence continued the theme:

"Songwriter Albert Von Tilzer, whose song "Take Me Out to the Ball Game" has become the theme of organized baseball, died yesterday at his Park La Brea apartment." The article notes that twenty-four of his songs sold more than a million copies in sheet music sales. Von Tilzer's wife died several years earlier, and they had no children. His *New York Times* obituary calls "Take Me Out to the Ball Game" "baseball's theme song" and notes that it was among his million-sellers. It also states that he moved to California in 1930. In an article announcing his funeral the next day, the *Los Angeles Times* notes that he "will be laid to rest here today while in Brooklyn, players start the first game of the World Series." The song will be heard at his funeral.[35]

1958–In an article on the song's fiftieth anniversary, the *Sporting News* notes: "There isn't a ball park in the country where it hasn't been played dozens of times. The Yankees play it before every home game."[36] This quote shows in two ways that by that time it was not standard practice to play the song during the seventh-inning stretch. Had they used the word "hundreds" instead of "dozens," it might be because the song was being played every day, which it apparently was not.

1958 (April 13)–Mickey Mantle, Yogi Berra, Whitey Ford, and Bill "Moose" Skowron sing "Take Me Out to the Ball Game" on *The Ed Sullivan Show*.[37]

1958–On the eve of the first San Francisco Giants game, a band plays "California, Here I Come" and "Take Me Out to the Ball Game" as the Giants arrive by airplane after completing spring training.

1958–The Los Angeles Dodgers invite Jack Norworth to his own tribute, Jack Norworth Day, at the Los Angeles Coliseum.

1959 (April 13)–A *Los Angeles Times* article, calls "Take Me Out to the Ball Game" "the refrain that has become synonymous with the national sport." Later the same article says it "has become the national anthem of base-

ball" and "the lilting old melody is heard with ever-increasing frequency."[38]

1959 (September 1)–Jack Norworth dies of a heart attack at age seventy-nine at his home in Laguna Beach, California. He is survived by his fifth wife, Amy, and a sister, Mrs. Loren Blodgett of Philadelphia. Episcopal funeral services are held for Norworth and George Jessel gives the eulogy.[39]

1959–In a letter to the editor of the *Los Angeles Times*, a Mae Newman of North Hollywood points out that Albert Von Tilzer should be mentioned along with Jack Norworth as the composer of the song, pointing out that Von Tilzer wrote the music. As she put it: "I wish to point out that it is the music, not the words, that is usually heard at ball games."[40] (Until Harry Caray comes along later, that is.)

1968–Music publisher Jerry Vogel issues a press release announcing the first ten pop songs named to the American Music Hall of Fame, a nascent effort by "a steering committee of music industry notables, who have worked to develop the project since 1965."[41] "Take Me Out to the Ball Game" is one of the ten songs.

1968–In an event staged by United Airlines to promote travel to Hawaii, a Hawaiian revue takes place at a night game at Dodger Stadium. A bevy of grass-skirted dancers perform native songs and dances and do a version of "Take Me Out to the Ball Game" in their native language. The first line: "E la we iau ike Kini popo . . . ."[42]

1969–Major League Baseball, marking its centennial, commissions a new song meant in part to replace "Take Me Out to the Ball Game." "Baseball Is More Than a Game" is dreamed up by the newly formed Major League Baseball Promotion Corporation and debuts at the centennial dinner preceding the All-Star Game. Music is by George Romanis and lyrics are by Floyd Huddleston. Copies are sent to radio stations and teams in hopes that it will catch on. The song is described as

"upbeat," and a baseball executive says, "We don't mean for it necessarily to replace 'Take Me Out to the Ball Game,' but it's more in line with what today's youth might like." The executive, Tom Villante, goes on to say, "What we're hoping for is to get a pop group, such as the Fifth Dimension, to record it and maybe it'll become a big hit." The Fifth Dimension never did show up, but the song was recorded by the John Bahler Singers and released on the Composition label. We've never heard it, have you?

1971–Harry Ruby, the composer of many hit songs, including "Who's Sorry Now?," " I Wanna Be Loved By You," "Three Little Words," and "A Kiss to Build a Dream On," is quoted as saying, "I wrote a letter to God the other day and I said, 'Dear God, why did you let somebody else write 'Take Me Out to the Ball Game'?" [43]

1975–ASCAP, the American Society of Composers and Performers, receives a bequest from the estate of Jack Norworth that all future royalties from "Take Me Out to the Ball Game" should be used to fund a program to support and honor young composers in every genre.

1975–A recording of "Take Me Out to the Ball Game" replaces "Thank God I'm a Country Boy" as the seventh-inning-stretch song at Texas Rangers games. They had started playing "Country Boy" early in the season at the suggestion of manager Billy Martin. When Martin was fired in July, "Take Me Out to the Ball Game" came in. [44]

1976–It's a bit of a mystery, but in a *Washington Post* article, titled "It's Hard to Escape the Rare Charm That Is Wrigley," recollecting a visit to Wrigley Field on August 12, 1970, John Schulian writes: "The crowd was singing 'Take Me Out to the Ball Game,' and someone accidentally turned on Pat Pieper's microphone. [Pieper was the Cubs 'antique PA man,' according to Schulian] He was singing, too, in his beautiful little old man's voice." [45] The incident almost eerily prefigures Harry Caray becoming a public singer of "Take Me Out to the Ball Game" in 1976, when White Sox owner Bill Veeck may or may not have secretly installed a mike in Harry Caray's booth.

1976 (September 26)–The White Sox plan to give away a premium for the Sunday game, but the game is rained out. The team had planned to give away a flexible, lightweight recording of Harry Caray singing "Take Me Out to the Ball Game." The article says fans will have to wait until spring to get their records. [46]

1977–In an article on White Sox fans and the Comiskey Park neighborhood, Sox owner Bill Veeck says: "The way they sing 'Take Me Out to the Ball Game' with Harry Caray is terrific! Why, we tried that in Milwaukee with Charlie Grimm in 1941, and not even the Milwaukee people would sing like fans are singing now. This is typical of the kind of fun atmosphere we're trying to create here." [47]

1978 (August 19)–In an editorial, the *Sporting News* editor and publisher C. C. Johnson Spink writes: "On the occasion of this year's Hall of Fame inductions at Cooperstown, we believe the trustees ought to consider

Shipstad and Johnson's Ice Follies did a tribute to "Take Me Out to the Ball Game" in its 1962 revue.

In response to the baseball players' strike, sports radio station WJMP-AM played 25,000 consecutive versions of "Take Me Out to the Ball Game."

immortalizing composer Albert Von Tilzer and lyricist Jack Norworth, who teamed up to produce the baseball classic in 1908. They have done as much for the game with their words and music as many of the Hall of Fame players have done with their pitching and batting."[48]

1980–Jerry Vogel, founder of the Jerry Vogel Publishing Company, dies at age eighty-four. His company is the publisher of "Take Me Out to the Ball Game" and also "Shine On Harvest Moon," two of Jack Norworth's biggest songs. Sadly, Vogel's *New York Times* obituary referred to him as "Larry" Vogel, both in the headline and in the text. The obit shows "Larry" Vogel's offices on West 44th Street, and later W. 45th Street.[49]

1980–An article on the seventh-inning stretch at Shea Stadium indicates that the Mets have not yet joined any bandwagon created by Harry Caray. They play "Thank God I'm a Country Boy"–imported by GM Frank Cashen from Baltimore, and he is also said to be experimenting with Bill Haley's "Rock Around the Clock." The article indicates that "Cashen is planning to ask the fans to sing along with 'Take Me Out to the Ball Game' one of these nights."[50]

1981–In an article speculating whether the new owners of the White Sox will rehire Caray, he goes on a rant against his critics and against team management that has generally fielded a poor product: "When the talent isn't there, that's when you start singing 'Take Me Out to the Ball Game.'"[51]

1984 (April)–Two fans, Dennis Dembek and Joseph Turnbull, are arrested for expressing themselves at

Yankee Stadium. During the seventh-inning stretch, the two placed paper bags over their heads and sang "Take Me Out to the Ball Game." When asked to stop, the pair refused and a melee occurred, which led to their being charged with assault and disorderly conduct.[52]

1985 (September)–After leaving the Cubs broadcast team–where he was once the heir apparent to Jack Brickhouse–Astros broadcaster Milo Hamilton airs his personal feelings about his rival Harry Caray: "I don't like what he does in the booth. I don't like his singing– if it's so great, why doesn't anyone else do it? I don't like his effrontery in showing up his fellow workers."[53]

1988 (June 9)–A first printing of the sheet music to "Take Me Out to the Ball Game," signed by Jack Norworth and Albert Von Tilzer, fetches $2,750 at auction in New York City.[54]

1991–Bill Veeck is elected to the Baseball Hall of Fame. In his Sports of the Times column in the *New York Times*, George Vecsey writes: "His name is synonymous with exploding scoreboards and goofy productions and he was also the man who persuaded Harry Caray to sing "Take Me Out to the Ball Game" during the seventh-inning stretch, if you want to know whom to blame."[55]

1991–As the Minnesota Twins battle the Atlanta Braves for the World Series championship–which the Twins won–congregants at St. Olaf's Roman Catholic Church sing "Take Me Out to the Ball Game" after all masses throughout the seven-game series.

1991–In a series of concerts at Carnegie Hall, musicologist

Buck O'Neil.

and humorist Peter Schickele, performing as P.D.Q. Bach, includes "Eine Kleine Nichtmusik," a composition that samples snippets from "Take Me Out to the Ball Game," the last movement of Brahms's *Third Symphony*, "The Mexican Hat Dance" (which interestingly has also been used as a seventh-inning-stretch song), Handel's *Messiah*, "Dixie," and symphonies by Franck and Mozart.[56]

1992–San Francisco Giants fans at Candlestick Park stand and sing "Take Me Out to the Ball Game" in the seventh-inning stretch of what could be the final game for the San Francisco Giants, who are considering a move to St. Petersburg, Florida.[57]

1992–"Connecticut's Secretary of the State, Pauline R. Kezer, wants people to be excited about things like civic duty and voting. To that end she was seen at a recent charity event belting out the lyrics to 'Take Me Out to the Polling Place,' to the tune of 'Take Me Out to the Ball Game.'"[58]

1993–The opening television segment for the All-Star Game in Baltimore's new Camden Yards ballpark featured a "supergroup" rendition of "Take Me Out to the Ball Game," including Glenn Frey,

The Allman Brothers, Aaron Neville, Melissa Etheridge, Vince Gill, MC Hammer, Nils Lofgren, James Brown, Clarence Clemons, The Moody Blues, Alice Cooper, and Southside Johnny.[59]

1994–First Lady Hillary Rodham Clinton, a longtime Cubs fan, throws out the first pitch on opening day at Chicago's Wrigley Field. She also teams with Harry Caray to sing "Take Me Out to the Ball Game" during the seventh-inning stretch. The game is made exciting by Cub center fielder Tuffy Rhodes, who homers three times off Dwight Gooden of the Mets. Gooden gets the win, however, as the Mets prevail, 12–8.[60]

1994–In response to the baseball players' strike, sports radio station WJMP-AM played 25,000 consecutive versions of "Take Me Out to the Ball Game." "We've gotten tremendous response. People seem to want to stay tuned to it like it's a mantra," said Bob Klaus, the station's vice president.[61]

1994–Ken Burns's eighteen-hour *Baseball* documentary premieres on PBS. The *New York Times* notes that Burns collected nearly 250 versions of "Take Me Out to the Ball Game" for possible use in the documentary. One such version was recorded by nonagenarian Senator Albert "Happy" Chandler, just months before his death. Some reports have Burns asking all interview subjects to sing the song, meaning that somewhere out there are wonderful versions of the song as recorded by Ted Williams, Billy Crystal, Buck O'Neil, Mario Cuomo, and many others. The CD sound track features excellent recordings of the song by Dr. John, Carly Simon, and others.[62]

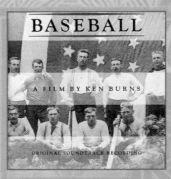

BASEBALL

A FILM BY KEN BURNS

ORIGINAL SOUNDTRACK RECORDING

Stan Musial on the harmonica and Bob Wolff on the ukulele at the Baseball Hall of Fame induction ceremonies.

1995—At the Baseball Hall of Fame induction ceremony, Bob Woolf, longtime broadcaster for the Washington Senators and the Minnesota Twins, receives the Ford C. Frick Award, given annually to a broadcaster for lifetime achievement. After giving his speech, Woolf pulls out his ukulele and sings "Take Me Out to the Ball Game." In recent years, it has not been unusual for Hall of Famer Stan Musial to play the song on his harmonica at the induction ceremony.

1996—In a marketing campaign designed to broaden the appeal of baseball, especially to younger audiences, Major League Baseball airs commercials featuring LL

LL Cool J

Cool J and Aretha Franklin doing their versions of "Take Me Out to the Ball Game." Ms. Franklin's commercial shows her singing while on the mound, at bat, and promenading under crossed bats with Cecil Fielder. LL Cool J's version includes him rapping with Ken Griffey, Jr., and Sammy

The Goo Goo Dolls

Sosa. Executive Lee Garfinkel, whose company put the campaign together, said "We thought, what if we made 'Take Me Out to the Ball Game' hip and contemporary? There are a lot of different target audiences that we are trying to reach and satisfy. That's why were going to have a range of artists. But we are concentrating a lot on younger fans." The Goo Goo Dolls also record the song during this campaign, and the article notes that future artists slated to participate include Mary Chapin Carpenter, Hootie and the Blowfish, and Eddie Vedder. LL Cool J adds a verse:

> Me and you could drive to the stadium
> Eat hot dogs in the stands
> Girl, I'll even steal home base for you
> Girl, I'll place it right inside your hand.[63]

1997—Frito-Lay buys Cracker Jack from Borden. In a business brief, the *New York Times* says, "Cracker Jack, a candy-coated mix of popcorn and peanuts, is a 104-year-old brand best known for the song 'Take Me Out to the Ball Game,' and for the toy in each box." Terms of the sale were not disclosed, though the Times mentions that in 1996, Cracker Jack had sales of $60 million.[64]

1998—Harry Caray, the most important figure in the song's history besides its co-writers, dies on February 18, 1998, after collapsing during a Valentine's Day dinner with his wife. The Cubs shortly announce that their tributes to Caray will include holding Harry Caray Day on August 2, a statue of Caray outside the ballpark, and a commemorative patch of his visage to be worn by

EDDIE VEDDER

players on their sleeves all season. They also announce that they will continue Caray's tradition of singing "Take Me Out to the Ball Game" live during the seventh-inning stretch, forming a roster of "guest conductors" who still lead the crowd in singing the song every home game. The first guest conductor, on opening day 1998, was Harry's widow, Dutchie Caray. As her rendition concluded, balloons were released over the field and "Amazing Grace" was played over the PA system. Notable guest conductors have included Cubs alumni such as Ernie Banks, Billy Williams, Ron Santo, Andy Pafko, Andre Dawson, Mark Grace, Bill Buckner, and Glenn Beckert; players and alumni from the Bears, Bulls, and Blackhawks, and other notables such as Jay Leno, Chuck Berry, Kenny Rogers, Eddie Vedder, Ozzie Osbourne, Dennis Miller, John Fogerty, Julia Louis-Dreyfus, John Cusack, Tim Robbins, Lou Rawls, Cyndi Lauper, Muhammad Ali, Bonnie Blair, and George Will.

2000–The Game Time Schedule wristwatch is released. Each day at the starting time of your favorite team's game, the watch alerts you by playing "Take Me Out to the Ball Game." The watch is also loaded with the season schedule and past World Series results. It can be updated each year via a USB connection.[65]

2001–Billy Murray's recording of "Take Me Out to the Ball Game" comes in eighth on the list of the top 365 songs of the last hundred years, in a survey of Americans conducted by the Recording Industry Association of America and the National Endowment for the Arts. The songs that finish ahead of "Take Me Out to the Ball Game" are certainly reasonable; number one was "Over the Rainbow" by Judy Garland, followed by Bing Crosby's "White Christmas," Woody Guthrie's "This Land Is Your Land," "Respect" by Aretha Franklin, "Boogie Woogie Bugle Boy" by the Andrews Sisters, and the *West Side Story* cast album. The baseball anthem finished just ahead of Scott Joplin's "The Entertainer," "In the Mood" by the Glenn Miller Orchestra, and "Rock Around the Clock" by Bill Haley and the Comets. Baseball writer Jayson Stark of ESPN.com noted that the song finished twenty spots higher than the Beatles, fifty-one spots ahead of Bruce Springsteen, sixty slots ahead of Elvis Presley, and eighty-four places higher than Bob Dylan. Brainy outfielder Doug Glanville of the Phillies thought the song should have done better: "It should be seventh–for seventh inning. The ranking should go with the number, like 'Take Five' by Dave Brubeck–that should be number five."[66]

2001–As baseball returns from a week-long hiatus following the attacks of September 11, "God Bless America" is played instead of or preceding "Take Me Out to the Ball Game" in moving ceremonies at all major league parks during the seventh-inning stretch. Over the next two seasons, most clubs return to their normal seventh-inning-stretch practices, though as of writing time, the New York Yankees are continuing the new "God Bless America" tradition.[67]

2003–After complaints from the American League Division Series opponents the Minnesota Twins, *New York Times* writer William C. Rhoden criticizes the Yankees' postseason treatment of the seventh-inning stretch, which includes a long version of "God Bless America" sung by Irish tenor Ronan Tynan. The games are delayed by over six minutes for the emotional, patriotic ceremony, but according to Rhoden, "A six-minute break at night in the fall in New York is too long." Rhoden argues that the visiting pitcher, who cannot throw during the song, might tighten up. "As temperatures plunge and the stakes of postseason competition rise," says Rhoden, "the live rendition should be shortened, sung before the game, or shifted to the end of the sixth inning so the Yankees can stand around before they resume playing defense."[68]

2007–The Hold Steady, an indie rock band, records a modern, Twins-centric version of "Take Me Out to the Ball Game" for use at Minnesota Twins home games during the seventh-inning stretch. The song was recorded at the request of Twins musical director Kevin Dutcher, a fan of the band.

2007–*The Empress of the North*, a cruise ship, runs aground in the middle of the night in frigid waters off Alaska. With visions of the *Titanic* running through her head, the ship's entertainment director did what she was assigned to do in the event of an emergency–she entertained, leading the passengers in songs including "Take Me Out to the Ball Game."[69]

2007–Major League Baseball announces that the 2008 season will begin with a celebration of the centennial of "Take Me Out to the Ball Game," featuring singing contests at each ballpark, sponsored by the makers of Baby Ruth candy bars. The best singer will perform the song at the All-Star Game in Yankee Stadium.

2008–The United States Postal Service issues a stamp to commemorate the centennial of "Take Me Out to the Ball Game."

2008–New ground is broken in the study, appreciation, and celebration of "Take Me Out to the Ball Game" when Andy Strasberg, Bob Thompson, and Tim Wiles write the book you are holding in your hand. Godspeed to baseball's anthem as it enters its second century.

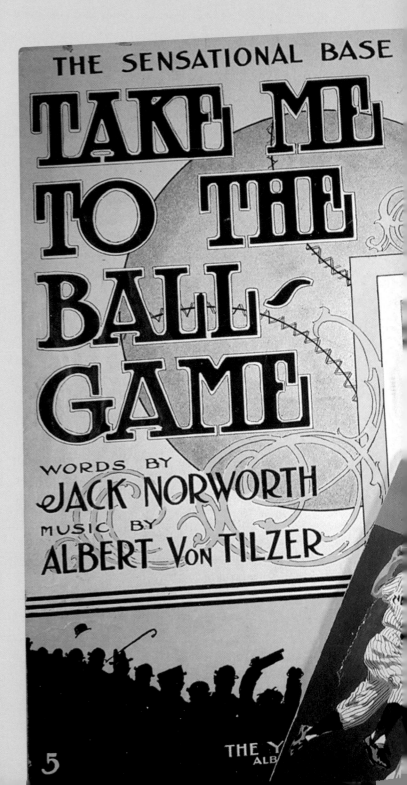

peaches and cream and roses and violets compared to the job of managing a big league club. An umpire works two hours a day. A manager worries twenty-four hours a day. An umpire takes each play as it ... what happened ... month." ... speech, it so hap- ... Moriarty led a ... adium an umpire ... sure of spiking a ... ent, but from an ... ccident. Usually ... and not entirely ... the wrong time. ... lly ...

STAMP SERVICES

UNITED STATES
POSTAL SERVICE

August 5, 2004

Mr. Andy Strasberg
ACME Marketing
3104 Fourth Avenue
San Diego, CA 92103-5803

Dear Mr. Strasberg:

Thank you for your July 30 letter to the Citizens' Stamp Advisory Committee expressing your support for a stamp commemorating the baseball song *Take Me Out to the Ball Game*.

You will be pleased to know that this proposal will be placed before the Citizens' Stamp Advisory Committee. The Committee is responsible for reviewing stamp proposals and making subject and design recommendations to the Postmaster General.

As information, the Committee decides on new stamp subject recommendations far in advance of the issue date in order to provide time for planning, design, production, and distribution. Currently, the 2005 and 2006 stamp programs are completed, and stamp subjects for the 2007 program and subsequent years are being selected. Although many of the subjects for upcoming new stamps have been identified, no public announcement of individual new stamps is made until the entire stamp program for that year has been approved. This occurs in the fall preceding the year of issuance. Enclosed for your reference is the *Creating U.S. Postal Stamps* brochure.

We appreciate your interest in our stamp program.

Sincerely,

Terrence McCaffrey

Terrence W. McCaffrey
Manager
Stamp Development

Enclosure

1735 N LYNN ST, SUITE 5013
ARLINGTON, VA 22209-6432
WWW.USPS.COM

July 30, 2004

United States Postal Service
Citizen Stamp Advisory Committee
1735 N Lynn St
Arlington VA 22209-6432

Dear Citizen Stamp Advisory Committee,

As members of Baseball's Hall of Fame, we respectfully submit for your consideration, that the USPS produce a stamp in 2008 to commemorate the 100th birthday of the unofficial anthem of America's Favorite pastime – baseball – *"Take Me Out to the Ball Game"*.

The song, *"Take Me Out to the Ball Game"* is one of the three most often sung songs (Happy Birthday and the Star Spangled Banner) in our country. This is a testament to its popularity and how it has woven itself into the fabric of American culture.

The song's origin – written on a subway by Jack Norworth in NYC is part of the folklore of America. The fact that the song has been recorded by over 350 artists on Edison Cylinders, 78-45- 33 RPM records, music rolls, cassettes, CD's and even 8-tracks ranging from The Boston Pops, Liberace, Mitch Miller, Count Basie, Mary Chapin, Goo Goo Dolls, Frank Sinatra, Bruce Springstone, Harpo Marx, Cool J, Bing Crosby, Aretha Franklin, Carly Simon, Jerry Lee Lewis, and The Ink Spots, is another indication of its timelessness and generational attraction.

The musical genre it has been recorded in is as varied as the artist who recorded them – Dixie, Jazz, Blues, Rick, Folk, Rap, Country, and Square Dance.

Needless to say, the instruments used to record this classic song match the genre and artists listed above.

We are confident that the 100th birthday of the song will be celebrated by millions of fans who on a daily basis sing the song. The experience of singing this plea to see a baseball game is not only done exclusively in the Major Leagues, but can be heard in neighborhood little league games, school games and throughout the minor league teams (over 160 teams) around the United States. But perhaps the most notable of teams that participates in this timeless tradition is the Chicago Cubs as they invite a celebrity to lead the fans in the song at Wrigley Field during every 7th inning stretch.

We are hoping that you will lead the celebration of *"Take Me Out to the Ball Game"* with a commemorative stamp.

Thank you for your consideration.

[multiple signatures]

... season the ... r grade and the Tiger infield ... record for double plays

CAN PIGEONS
CARRY A TUNE?

"TAKE ME OUT to the Ball Game" is indeed ubiquitous in our culture. So much so that famed psychologist B. F. Skinner chose to use the tune in some experiments he conducted at Harvard in 1950.[1] As part of the much larger work of studying the role of reward and punishment, Skinner and his graduate students taught pigeons to "peck out such simple tunes as 'Over the Fence Is Out, Boys,' and 'Take Me Out to the Ball Game' on a simplified, seven-key piano."[2] As they learned to repeat the musical sequence, those who succeeded were rewarded with food.

In an effort to locate a recording of the musical pigeons for the CD that accompanies this book, we contacted the B. F. Skinner Foundation in Cambridge, Massachusetts. They did not have a recording of pigeon music, but did let us know that Skinner was a Red Sox fan. He and his graduate students would go to home games at Fenway Park, and Skinner followed the Sox on TV until he died in 1990. While we are sorry that he had to watch the Red Sox lose the 1986 World Series to the Mets, we do note the irony that a man so closely associated with behaviorism and operant conditioning would not learn over time that his watching the Red Sox was unlikely to produce a reward.

If your dealer cannot supply you with this instru-
mental, we will, on receipt of
25 cts., send you a copy post-
paid, to any part of the world.

The York Music Co.
Albert Von Tilzer, Mgr.
1367 Broadway
NEW YORK

WHAT'S IN
A SONG?

ON SEPTEMBER 11, 2001, shortly after the attacks, I [Bob] was riding a subway to upper Manhattan, trying to get home. For those of you who've yet to ride the New York City subway, singing and panhandling often go together, and this day was no exception—a middle-aged woman boarded the train, cup in hand, singing for spare change. But as the first strains of "Amazing Grace" filled the car, a strange thing happened.

The woman seated next to me joined in.

Others followed. So did I.

And suddenly all of us, heads bowed, were singing "Amazing Grace." Those who didn't know all the words hummed—it didn't matter. What mattered was that we were all singing—together.

I don't know what prompted our collective subconscious to join in unison with this woman that morning, but I do know that the act of doing so brought us together on a day when others were trying to tear us apart.

The experience of large masses of human beings singing together is predawn. We experience it in our religious ceremonies, at birthday parties and other rites of passage, in cultural and artistic celebrations, at mealtimes and other family gatherings, and of course, at the ballpark. But while many of us grope at the words and pitches to our national anthem (admit it—you've heard many a voice crack straining for those *rockets red glare* high notes), "Take Me Out to the Ball Game" offers something a bit more down to earth and accessible: a song that can easily be sung, not just alone but by tens of thousands of fans simultaneously. Writing a song that can be sung by so many is no easy task. But that's the business Jack and Albert were in—writing songs that America could sing.

To understand the genius of "Take Me Out to the Ball Game," we'll need to call in a specialist—a reliever of sorts. Baseball has its statisticians: music has its theorists—

those rare souls who can dissect a song into a thousand elements, much like analyzing all the motions of a pitcher hurling a fastball. Enter Dave Headlam, professor of music theory at the prestigious Eastman School of Music, University of Rochester, to teach us why "Take Me Out to the Ball Game" is baseball's greatest hit.

"Professor Headlam! In layman's terms please!"

"Thank you. Okay–layman's terms! Hmmm. Let me ask you this–why does a song become popular, sticking in our heads and enticing us to sing it over and over? Well, the song "Take Me Out to the Ball Game" has this quality. First, it's a waltz in 3/4 time; even those of us with two left feet can manage the one-two-three lilting motion of a waltz and we all know the Tchaikovsky waltzes, such as "Waltz of the Flowers" from *The Nutcracker*.

"Second, the song is easy to sing: the chorus stays mostly within an octave. If you don't know what an octave is, sing the first two notes of the song–*take me*. They're the same notes, but to sing the second word *me*, you ascend: it's an octave higher than the first word *take*. So, 'Take Me Out to the Ball Game' starts with an octave leap, and not coincidentally two of our most beloved songs, "Over the Rainbow" and "The Christmas Song" (you know–*chestnuts roasting on an open fire . . .*), start the same way. It's a satisfying musical 'interval' to sing.

"I should add, those opening octave leaps (*Take ME out*) are musically very visual–imagine an outfielder leaping to snag a potential home run at the warning track while those notes are being sung and you'll get the picture.

"Third, one of the most important elements that draws us into the song is its use of repetition. Repetition helps us to remember songs, but if the repetition is always the same, the song quickly loses our interest. Imagine a pitcher who only threw fastballs as opposed to a pitcher

who throws curves, sliders, and changeups. That's what Norworth and Von Tilzer do–they throw us a fastball (an exact repetition), a curve (a repetition that's varied), and just when we think we'll get a fastball again, they throw a slider (in this case, it's something called a *sequence*).

"A sequence is where a group of notes get repeated at higher or lower pitches (think of the organist's rallying cry of *Da da da Da–da Da! Charge!* The organist keeps repeating the notes at higher and higher pitches, rallying us all into a frenzy). A good example of a sequence in 'Take Me Out to the Ball Game' is the words *I don't care if I never get back*, which is a sequence (somewhat varied) of the previous line, *Buy me some peanuts and Cracker Jack*. It's the same phrase but sung at a higher pitch. As with the organist's sequence, the higher pitch level on the second step of the sequence raises the excitement and sets us up for the following music. Norworth and Von Tilzer used an arsenal of pitches (pun intended) to create a song that's enjoyable

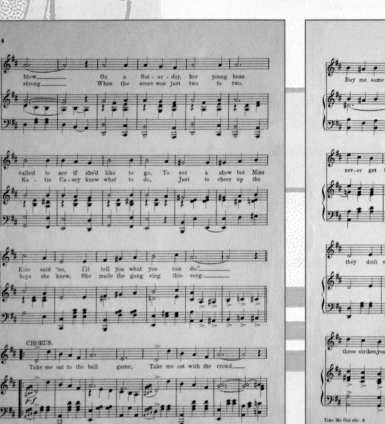

to sing, keeps our interest, and makes us want to sing it again the next time we're at the ballpark.

"Finally, 'Take Me Out to the Ball Game' memorably sets the *three strikes* aspect of baseball with its final line of *and it's ONE, TWO, THREE strikes you're out*. This is the part of the song where you get to shout! It's also the part of the song that is melodically disruptive. Think about it: you're singing along like a nightingale and all of a sudden you're not singing a song anymore— you're shouting out strikes! The *ONE, TWO, THREE* is the high point of the song, the part where we're all singing at full throttle. But it's also the song's *hook*—the part that becomes most ingrained in our brains. Everything in "Take Me Out to the Ball Game" is leading us to this *ONE, TWO, THREE*. If Norworth and Von Tilzer hadn't put the *ONE, TWO, THREE* punch into their song, 'Take Me Out to the Ball Game' might have left the game long before the seventh-inning stretch!

"There are many other features of the song that make it memorable. For those interested in barber shop singing, it has the requisite sliding motions—think of sliding into second base on a steal—that made such singing very popular at the time 'Take Me Out to the Ball Game' was composed. Such slides (think of *buy me some*) are called *chromaticism* in music theory. And I'm sure that you'd like to hear about each of the chords and the musical structure, so without further ado . . ."

"Yes, yes, [one of the authors interrupting], thank you, Dr. Headlam! Regrettably we're out of time—but please give me your notes on the many pitches in this song. So there you have it–'Take Me Out to the Ball Game' is an easily singable waltz—it's got some nice leaps to wake up our vocal cords and has a system of repetition that keeps the song in our heads. And like a good pitcher, Jack and Albert varied their pitches to make it interesting. And that helped make it baseball's greatest hit!"

(For more of Professor Headlam's analysis, see the addendum.)

MUSIC CO
TILZER, M'gr.

WEDDINGS, FUNERALS, AND LL COOL J

FOR ONE HUNDRED years, "Take Me Out to the Ball Game" has been a popular and enduring crossover hit. Why?

First, the popularity of the song results from the ease with which the audience can participate in singing the chorus and gesture the three-strike count while singing. The audience becomes an integral part of the performance.

While initially sung in movie houses, the song eventually migrated to the ball park, where fans would frequently and spontaneously break out into singing the song, much like the "wave" phenomenon we experience today.

Like the wave, the participant moves from watching the experience to playing a starring role in it. The observer instantly becomes an involved contributor to the enjoyable goings-on. And when people enjoy things, they'll do them again. It's fun. It's a bit thrilling to be a part of the action, and it takes little effort on anyone's part.

Dr. William Gay, professor emeritus of sociology at San Diego State University, noted that not all fans are fans. He explained, "Not everybody goes there for the game. People want to be part of the scene. Plus we live in an interactive era where the audience becomes more and more part of the show. People go to perform and be part of the performance."[1]

Second, the popularity of "Take Me Out to the Ball Game" was measured not only by the throngs of people singing it but by the vast number of copies of sheet music sold. In fact, by 1956, the *New York Times* reported that record sales had surpassed the 8 million mark![2] "Take Me Out to the Ball Game" hit the scene at a time when the

home entertainment center was a piano, banjo, or other instrument, any of which provide a natural accompaniment to the breezy little song. Over the years, artists have recorded "Take Me Out to the Ball Game" in genres as disparate as waltz, disco, calypso, square dance, and, of course, rap, which speaks volumes about the song's enduring popularity and flexibility.

The list of musicians who recorded the song and made it a crossover hit is impressive, varied, and long. "It's an amazingly flexible tune," said Ken Burns, the documentarian of the series *Baseball*, who used many different recorded versions of the song to "denote whatever mood we felt was pertinent to the moment."[3]

Many movies use the song "Take Me Out to the Ball Game" for creative purposes. It would be obvious for a baseball movie to incorporate the song into the film, but "Take Me Out to the Ball Game" is often used as background scoring in films that have no baseball theme whatsoever. In the classic 1935 Marx Brothers' film *A Night at the Opera*, at one point, the orchestra's music is all mixed up and they suddenly begin playing the song. And in 1941's *Meet John Doe* with Gary Cooper, the audience may not be aware that the song is being sung. It is the scene where the citizens are in a rally hall waiting for Gary Cooper (John Doe),

The 1936 wedding of Padres player George Myatt at San Diego's Lane Field featured "Take Me Out to the Ball Game."

and they begin singing "Take Me Out to the Ball Game" for no apparent reason. You have to listen closely to hear it.

Movies and entertainers have always had a major influence on popular culture, and at the same time they are reflections of the reigning public interest. In 1949, forty-one years after the song was written, Hollywood turned its attention to the popular tune and produced *Take Me Out to the Ball Game* the movie.

The movie's stars were some of the most popular box-office attractions of the time. The formula for the movie's success was to combine the beloved national pastime with the athletic dancing style of Gene Kelly (who had the childhood dream of being the shortstop for the Pittsburgh Pirates)[4], add to that bathing beauty Esther Williams, then top it all off with Frank Sinatra's crooning. Sinatra had a deep love and admiration for baseball, as did many in the entertainment business. Not much has changed. In the 1950s, Bob Hope and Bing Crosby became part owners of the Cleveland Indians and Pittsburgh Pirates, respectively. Now Bill Murray and Billy Crystal are minority baseball team owners. The bond between teams and players on the one hand, and the entertainment industry on the other, is as strong today—or stronger—than ever. Sixty years after the song was published, the American Music Hall of Fame selected "Take Me Out to the Ball Game" as one of its ten charter songs.

It seemed that "Take Me Out to the Ball Game" was recorded

on every children's record label. In July 1954, Wheaties decided to include an actual record on the back of its cereal box, such that kids could cut out the record from the box and play it on their record player. You could get a box of Wheaties and a record for only twenty-five cents.

Television also contributed to "Take Me Out to the Ball Game"'s popularity. The continued support the song received and the evolution of the electronic age can be traced back to Philo Farnsworth's invention of the television. It is now acknowledged that the earliest baby boomers had television as their babysitter. This new invention, radio with pictures, could keep a child entertained for hours. The major concern at that time was the potential damage to young eyes that sitting too close to the tube might cause. Apparently it was not enough of a concern to turn off those sets. And television exposed the song to millions of viewers. Television's evolution from radio, which was known as "theater of the mind," now made mental images identical for everyone and almost instantaneously popularized what was broadcast.

As is common with most new technologies, people feared the potential for change and predicted economic and cultural disasters of one type or another. Baseball owners feared television (much as they had feared radio in an earlier era), believing that their fan base would dwindle and not want to buy a ticket to a baseball game if they could see it on TV. The effect was just the opposite. The baseball game broadcast sometimes seemed like a long commercial and would drive home to the watching fan the idea that the *excitement* of the game could only be experienced live, in the ballpark. So every play-by-play broadcast was unconsciously saying: "Take Me Out to the Ball Game."

The early days of TV made household names of stars like Lucille Ball, Liberace, Perry Como, Superman, The Lone Ranger, Mickey Mouse, and Miss Francis' Ding Dong School. One of the most popular TV shows of its time was *I Love Lucy*, starring Lucille Ball and Desi Arnaz.

Liberace performing "Take Me Out to the Ball Game."

The Ink Spots.

The Ink Spots

When Lucy gave birth to Little Ricky as part of an episode, it was a watershed event in television as 117 million people watched (A. C. Nielsen Co. published a report that 71.7 percent of the potential TV audience in the nation watched the show).[5] Longtime movie stars recognized the power of television and made the transition from big screen to small, as either TV stars in their own right or as guest performers. While former movie star Groucho Marx was working his double entendres for his new TV audience on *You Bet Your Life* in 1955, his brother Harpo Marx made a guest appearance on *I Love Lucy*. Families watched as Lucy's neighbor, Ethel Mertz, asked Harpo to play a song on his harp. The mute character whistles his selection of the 1908 classic that everyone knows and loves—"Take Me Out to the Ball Game"—and then sits down to play it ever so softly on his harp.

Parents watching at home were touched and waxed nostalgic, while their kids were enlightened by an artist and instrument that normally was not a mainstay of their tastes. Other TV programs that showcased the song included *The Ed Sullivan Show*, *The Tonight Show*, *The Perry Como Show*, and even *Shindig*, the very groovy 60s version of *American Bandstand*. TV executives knew that the song was not a risk but a crowd pleaser, regardless of the era, the age of the audience, or the political climate. "Take Me Out to the Ball Game" is pure entertainment.

The song was originally a pre-game form of entertainment in the ballpark, not the staple of the seventh-inning stretch. At first the song was played by a band, either one that had been invited or a spontaneous serenade from fans that had brought along their own instruments. It was not until the 1940s and 1950s that the organ started to appear in ballparks across the country. Once again, this evolution helped to make the song even more accessible and popular.

Berlin, the Beatles, Elvis, Gershwin, Kern, Porter, Rodgers—these are songwriting greats who have in their individual style come close to creating *the* formula for a hit song. On the other hand, "Take Me Out to the Ball Game" became a crossover hit because of . . . money. Musicians universally need to eat and they are betting on a sure thing when they record the song that has been in public domain for the past twenty-five years. When asked why he wrote the song, Jack Norworth replied: "We were commercial writers. I decided that there hadn't been a moon song in a long time and wrote 'Shine On Harvest Moon.' Same way with baseball. I had an idea that we needed that type of song. Neither took more than fifteen minutes."[6] The song has held its own for one hundred years, never losing its originality even while being endlessly tinkered with by a huge and dissimilar constellation of artists. A small sampling of those artists includes Liberace, who plays the song quickly and feverishly; the Ink Spots, who sing it slowly and caress it; and Bob Dylan, who sings it like, well, Bob Dylan.

Perhaps the greatest testament to the song being a "crossover hit" would be that it is not unusual for ardent baseball fans to have a rendition played at weddings *and* funerals.

When a popular song can be transformed easily into almost any musical style and gains a mass audience while managing to maintain its original appeal, the song will thrive and continue to be recorded for one hundred years and more. LL Cool J proved this in 1996 when he recorded the song at the request of Major League Baseball, along with the Goo Goo Dolls, Mary Chapin Carpenter, and Aretha Franklin.

SHOW ME THE MONEY

IT'S IMPOSSIBLE TO know how much "Take Me Out to the Ball Game" earned for Albert Von Tilzer and Jack Norworth, but it was substantial. Although there is no hard data, the best estimate is that it sold at least 6 million copies of sheet music and over 8 million recordings. According to the American Society of Composers and Publishers (ASCAP), "Take Me Out to the Ball Game" has earned "many millions of dollars in royalties." Some further facts from ASCAP[1]:

Over 160 arrangements of the song have been made.

The song has been heard in over 1,200 films and TV programs from *Arsenic and Old Lace* and *Bad News Bears* to *The X-Files*.

It is heard on the air on radio and/or television somewhere in the world every single day of the year (including Christmas and New Year's!).

It is performed about 2,500 times each year in major league games during the seventh-inning stretch.

The original 1908 version of the song entered the public domain in 1983 in the United States and thus ceased to earn income within the country; however, it continued to earn income in countries outside the United States (such as Japan) due to different copyright laws that allowed the song continued copyright protection.

How did "Take Me Out to the Ball Game" earn its money for Jack Norworth and Albert Von Tilzer? Royalties! And plenty of them. First, there was the sheet music. For songwriters, the standard royalties were about 10 percent based on the retail price of copies sold, with the

Singer Misty Castleberry with
the Baseball Music Project.

remainder going to the publisher to pay for the production and marketing of the song. Publishers would earn a profit once they broke even on a song, having earned back their production and marketing expenses.

Then there were the sound recordings, for which both the publisher and the record company would profit, with a share of those profits being returned to the songwriters. Mechanical royalties, as these sound recording royalties came to be known (with the advent of mechanical piano rolls), were paid to songwriters whenever their songs were "mechanically" reproduced (including piano rolls, LPs, CDs, and, yes, digital downloads). Jack and Albert earned a hefty sum from the 8 million recordings sold.

Additionally, there were "synchronization" royalties (the term is derived from the synchronization of music to visual media) paid any time "Take Me Out to the Ball Game" was used as part of a film or television program. Since the song appeared in over 1,200 TV shows, commercials, and movies, Norworth and Von Tilzer profited handsomely.

Finally, and perhaps most importantly, there were the performance royalties: every time the song was sung in public, whether it was in a ballpark, a theater, on the radio, or in a saloon, ASCAP would pay a proportional share of the income it received to both Jack and Albert as well as the publisher (in this case, York Music Company, which Albert Von Tilzer owned!).

The music publisher was instrumental to a song's success, and there have been, in effect, three publishers of "Take Me Out to the Ball Game." The song was first published by York Music Company, run by Albert Von Tilzer and his brother Jack. Albert later changed the name to Broadway Music in 1915, which in effect became the second publisher of the song. Years later, in 1936, Jerry Vogel Music became the publisher.

In 1908, Jack and Albert could reasonably expect to earn royalties for twenty-eight years, through to 1936, after which the song would enter the public domain and cease to earn further royalties. But to their

advantage, in 1909, the United States amended the law, allowing works to be protected for twice the original duration: an initial term of twenty-eight years, after which it could be renewed for an additional twenty-eight years of copyright protection, for a total of fifty-six years of copyright protection. The law was subsequently amended to include an additional nineteen years of protection beyond fifty-six years, such that the song would be protected for a total of seventy-five years (28 + 28 + 19). For the sake of "Take Me Out to the Ball Game," this meant the song would be under copyright until 1983 (1908 + 75).

After the first twenty-eight years of copyright, it was possible for someone to "purchase" the renewal rights for the subsequent forty-seven-(28 + 19)–year term of protection. In 1936, twenty-eight years after the song was first published in 1908, a man by the name of Jerry Vogel did just that. He purchased the copyright to "Take Me Out to the Ball Game" from Von Tilzer's company, Broadway Music. It's not known exactly why Von Tilzer sold the copyright, but the publishing industry in the wake of Tin Pan Alley's demise was consolidating, unable to keep up with the trends of talking pictures and consumer tastes.

Jerry Vogel relentlessly promoted "Take Me Out to the Ball Game," sending out numerous flyers to radio stations, television networks, movie studios, and even ballparks, encouraging them to use the song.

The fact that "Take Me Out to the Ball Game" appeared in over 1,200 TV shows, commercials, and movies was no accident: Jerry Vogel tirelessly marketed the song, insuring its continued dominance in American popular song.

Today, the original song, in its 1908 version, is in the public domain in the United States. It's entirely free to be heard on radio, in movies, and on television, free to be arranged, sung off-key, and even parodied. Whereas the song once belonged to a music publisher, today it belongs to everyone. There may not be such a thing as a free lunch, but there indeed is such a thing as a free baseball song.

THE SONG THAT
KEEPS ON GIVING

IN JUNE 1975, the month in which Nolan Ryan pitched his fourth career no-hitter to tie the record set by Sandy Koufax, "Take Me Out to the Ball Game"'s influence was about to be felt far beyond any ballpark. The American Society of Composers and Publishers (ASCAP) received a bequest from the estate of Jack Norworth with instructions to create a program to honor and support young composers and to use the royalties from "Take Me Out to the Ball Game" to fund it.

It was a remarkable moment. In effect, Jack Norworth, who passed away nearly sixteen years earlier, had posthumously gifted the royalties of "Take Me Out to the Ball Game" to future generations of songwriters, entrusting them to carry on the grand songwriting tradition borne out of Tin Pan Alley. After 1975, every penny earned from seventh-inning stretches at ballparks would help the careers of burgeoning composers and songwriters of every genre. The ASCAP Foundation, as it has come to be known, is now one of the largest music foundations "dedicated to nurturing the music talent of tomorrow, preserving the legacy of the past, and sustaining the creative incentive for today's creators through a variety of educational, professional, and humanitarian programs and activities which serve the entire music community."

Dizzy Dean on the sousaphone.

THE TIMES THEY
ARE A-CHANGIN'

IN 1969, THE year of the Woodstock festival, at the height of the Vietnam War, and the year the Amazin' Mets would win the World Series, Major League Baseball did something it had never done before. It wrote a song. Actually it commissioned a couple of songwriters to write the song for them. MLB can do that sort of thing. Unlike "Take Me Out to the Ball Game," which claimed inspiration from a subway ride and was adopted as the sport's anthem, this new song was dreamt up by boardroom marketers and promoters. The thought was that if Major League Baseball could introduce a new song, the song could better unify and promote major league ball. There was an added bonus, too: Major League Baseball would own the copyright, and every time the song was played, well, Major League Baseball would earn money (remember, "Take Me Out to the Ball Game" earned millions of dollars in royalties. This new song could be a cash cow!)

The idea was the brainchild of Tom Villante, then the executive director for Major League Baseball Promotion Corporation, who commissioned the song. Villante hired composer George Romanis and lyricist Floyd Huddleston, two veteran television composers, to write a song about baseball that would hopefully catch on as much as "Take Me Out to the Ball Game" had.

"We don't mean for it necessarily to replace 'Take Me Out to the Ball Game,'" Villante said. Of course, if it were to replace "Take Me Out to the Ball Game," no one in the boardroom would object to cashing those royalty checks.

The song was called "Baseball Is More Than a Game" and was recorded by the John Bahler Singers with copies sent to each of the twenty-four teams in the majors, radio stations throughout the country, and television stations that handled telecasts of the teams' games.

Shortly after the song's release, Villante said, "We don't know exactly how well it's doing, but we've had some good reaction. The instrumental [on the other side of the vocal] is really great, and we're going to make great use of it as background music for our films."

Villante once said that the song was "more in line with what today's youth might like." However true that statement might have been in 1969, "Baseball Is More Than a Game" spent a short time in the major leagues before being sent down to the minors, where it vanished into obscurity (if you don't believe us, stop reading right now and sing the song for us . . .).

Major League Baseball put in a good effort, to be sure, but not even they could kick "Take Me Out to the Ball Game" out of the park.[1]

There were other attempts to unseat "Take Me Out to the Ball Game." One of the most interesting was a contest sponsored by the Pacific Coast League team the Hollywood Stars, who sponsored a three-month songwriting contest in 1954. There were over 1,000 entries submitted from thirteen states. The winning entry, "Batter Up," was composed by Mason Mallory of Pasadena, but it failed to find a permanent home in any ballpark.[2]

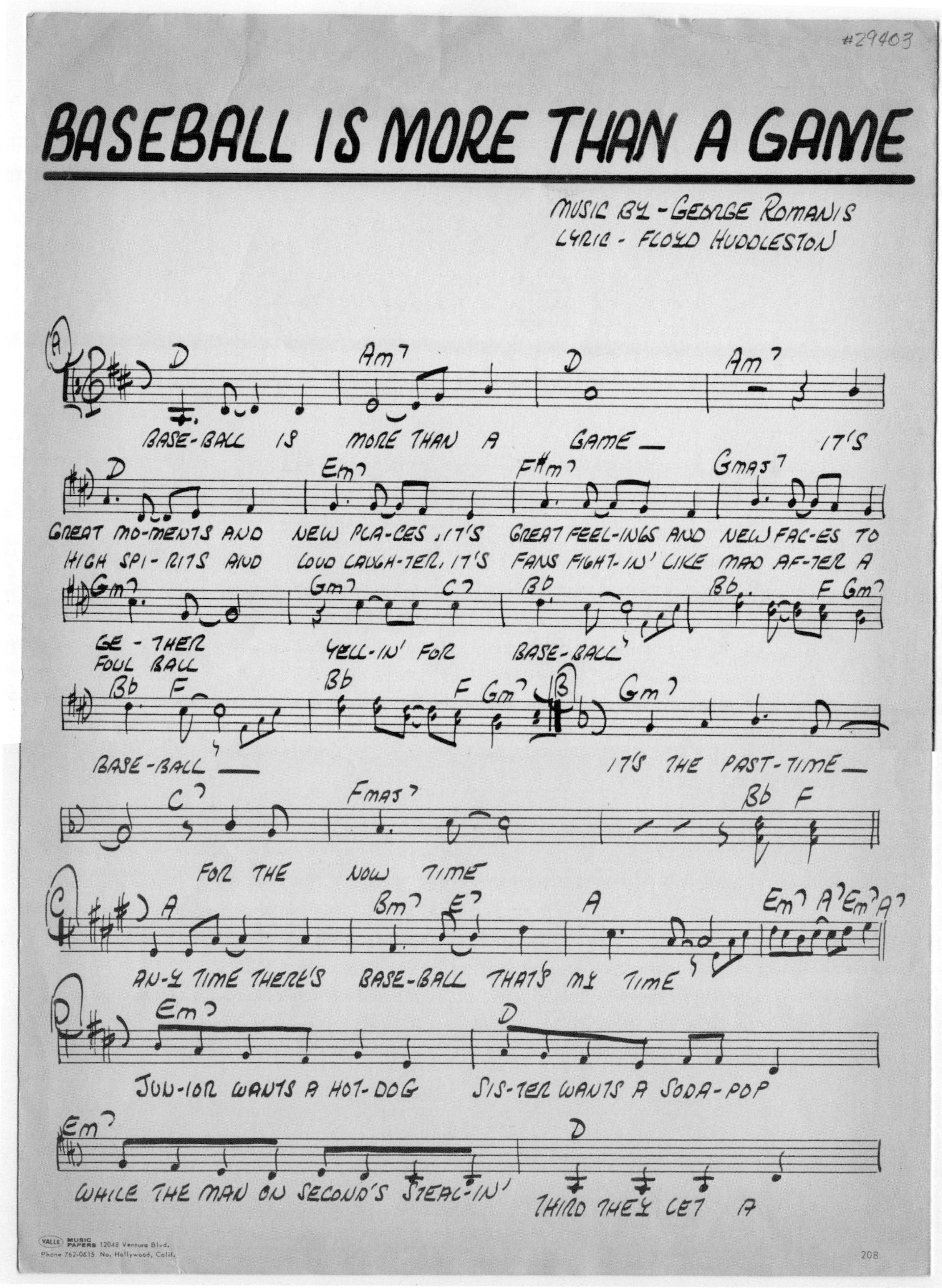

#29403

BASEBALL IS MORE THAN A GAME

MUSIC BY - GEORGE ROMANIS
LYRIC - FLOYD HUDDLESTON

BASE-BALL IS MORE THAN A GAME — IT'S

GREAT MO-MENTS AND NEW PLA-CES ,IT'S GREAT FEEL-INGS AND NEW FAC-ES TO
HIGH SPI-RITS AND LOUD LAUGH-TER, IT'S FANS FIGHT-IN' LIKE MAD AF-TER A

GE - THER YELL-IN' FOR BASE-BALL,
FOUL BALL

BASE-BALL' — IT'S THE PAST-TIME —

FOR THE NOW TIME

AN-Y TIME THERE'S BASE-BALL THAT'S MY TIME

JUN-IOR WANTS A HOT-DOG SIS-TER WANTS A SODA-POP

WHILE THE MAN ON SECOND'S STEAL-IN' THIRD THEY GET A

VALLE MUSIC PAPERS 12048 Ventura Blvd.
Phone 762-0615 No. Hollywood, Calif.

208

GOING, GOING, GONE...

WALKING INTO A ballpark an hour or two early on a sunny day, hearing live organ music waft lazily on the breeze, punctuated by the crack of the bat at batting practice—the soundscape is so perfect, pleasant, and timeless that you think it was always exactly like this. But while music has been a part of baseball since the very beginning, the first ballpark organ was installed relatively recently, at Chicago's Wrigley Field in 1941, with Brooklyn's Ebbets Field quickly following suit in 1942.

For the next several decades, nearly all clubs employed a full-time organist, many of whom became local celebrities, releasing albums of their music and making public appearances outside the ballpark. Organists were often witty and clever, playing snippets of songs that were perfect for the player and/or the moment. Once at the end of a sixteen-inning Cubs victory at Wrigley Field, Gary Pressey played "You're Sixteen (You're Beautiful and You're Mine)." When Carlton Fisk hit his dramatic twelfth-inning home run in Game Six of the 1975 World Series, giving victory to the Red Sox, organist John Kiley played the opening notes of Handel's "Hallelujah Chorus."[1] As Mark Grudzielanek stepped up to the plate late in the 1996 All-Star Game, organist Paul Richardson played Jim Croce's "I Got a Name." Longtime Chicago White Sox organist Nancy Faust (1970–present) liked to play "I'm in the Money" when Reggie Jackson came to bat, and brilliantly played "Jesus Christ, Superstar" for Dick Allen.

"You had to be extemporaneous," says Jane Jarvis, longtime organist for the Milwaukee Braves and then the New York Mets. "The game belongs to itself, and I played what I thought was appropriate. One day Louis Armstrong was in the house, so I played "Hello Dolly." He turned and gave me an enormous bow, which I will never forget. I did that for all the big

Longtime, beloved Yankee Stadium organist Eddie Layton. Page 98, *top*, Helen Dell; *bottom*, Nancy Faust.

musical stars that would come to the games."[2]

A short list of the great ballpark organists would have to include Gladys Goodding, who played for the Brooklyn Dodgers' fans at Ebbets Field from 1942 to 1957. John Kiley played for the Red Sox for more than forty years, and Eddie Layton of the Yankees earned five World Series rings during his decades with the club. He only wore the smallest one (1978), for fear the larger rings would weigh down his fingers, producing a sour note.[3] Paul Richardson was with the Phillies from 1970 to 2006. Vince Lascheid began with the Pirates in 1970 and is still there. Also in 1970, Nancy Faust started with the White Sox. The Cardinals' Ernie Hays started in 1971 and has-

n't left. Shay Torrent started with the White Sox in 1960 and moved to the Angels in 1965, where he played until 1986. Jane Jarvis started with the Milwaukee Braves and played for the Mets from the mid-1960s to 1979.[4]

But the tradition of ballpark organists playing live is waning. Two-thirds of the teams don't even have an organist anymore, and the remaining teams have greatly curtailed their playing time.[5] Organists "are a dying breed, replaced . . . by another DJ blasting canned rock; squeezed out by M&M races, text message quizzes, and other forms of JumboTron techno-blather designed, it seems, to entertain bored teenagers," writes Melissa Isaacson in the *Chicago Tribune*.[6] "Our fans, and our players, have been

At Wrigley Field, recorded music is kept to a bare minimum, in favor of that organ wafting gently on the breeze.

vocal in their requests for a more up-tempo experience," said one Dodger executive in 2004.[7]

Players for many clubs request snippets of their favorite tunes when they come up to bat or take the mound. Al Leiter liked to warm up to Springsteen's "Tenth Avenue Freeze Out," and both Mariano Rivera of the Yankees and Billy Wagner of the Mets like to warm up to Metallica's "Enter Sandman." And they don't want Metallica played on an old-fashioned organ, they want the real thing. So almost gone is the opportunity for organists to individualize the game, such as when the Cubs' Pressy played "At the Hop" when Sammy Sosa was announced, a reference to Sosa's trademark hop coming out of the batter's box after hitting a home run.

The Cubs are the lone holdout in the race to restrict organists to just "Take Me Out to the Ball Game" and accompanying on the national anthem. At Wrigley Field, recorded music is kept to a bare minimum, in favor of that organ wafting gently on the breeze. The Cubs have always marketed an old-time ballpark experience, according to former club president John McDonough, who says that seeing a game at Wrigley Field is "like walking into a time capsule."[8]

Over on the South Side, Nancy Faust, who has missed only five games since 1970, is winding down, as the White Sox join the trend of playing lots of recorded media between innings. Faust is responsible for a bit of baseball's musical history. In 1977, when the White Sox were playing very well, she started the tradition of

playing Steam's "Na-Na-Hey-Hey, Kiss Him Goodbye," which became a rallying cry for fans, who would sing it after every Sox victory. The song is one of the most closely associated songs with any major league team. She was also the house organist when Harry Caray began his tradition of singing "Take Me Out to the Ball Game" live every game. According to Faust, Caray would lean out of the broadcast booth and shout "Come On, Nancy," which is how fans first became aware of her as a ballpark personality.[9] There were some lean years for White Sox fans, of course, prompting owner Bill Veeck to quip, "Last year, Harry and Nancy were the only performers we had." [10]

Where once there was creativity and spontaneity, now there is the same loud music all through the majors. "We're hearing the same music you hear at the shopping malls," says Faust. "There's nothing baseball about it."[11] Jane Jarvis was even more direct: "After I left the New York Mets, there wasn't any more music there."[12]

THE SOUND TRACK
OF SUMMER

IN MANY MODERN ballparks, each time a hitter strolls to the plate or a pitcher warms up, he is accompanied by a personally selected theme song. While many fans have noticed this trend, few have thought of its deeper implications for popular culture. Nothing defines a culture at the popular level better than its music, something which almost everyone enjoys—try to find someone who doesn't like music on at least some level. Another great indicator of a society's cultural values and passions is its sports. So when Roger Clemens grooves to Elton John's "Rocket Man" or Al Leiter gets pumped while warming up to Springsteen's "Tenth Avenue Freeze Out," it is not just a fun moment in the ballpark; it also tells us something about these players and more importantly something about ourselves. This recent development is only the latest of dozens, if not hundreds, of connections between music and baseball.

Surveying the thick file of clippings labeled "music" at the National Baseball Hall of Fame Library, we find many more. References to the giant Margaret and Franklin Steele sheet music collection and to the now nine-disc-strong *Diamond Cuts* baseball music compilations are side by side with other great information. There are so many connections between base-

Al Leiter.

Roger Clemens.

ball and music that it's safe to say there are two national pastimes!

The first two baseball songs, "The Baseball Polka" and "Baseball Days," were written in 1858. The first ballpark organ was installed at Wrigley Field in 1941. Just five years later, the National League felt it necessary to ban the song "Three Blind Mice," after Ebbets Field organist Gladys Goodding made a habit of playing it after close calls that went against the Dodgers. The Brooklyn Sym-Phony was an inspired group of fans who serenaded the Ebbets Field crowd, without the benefit of formal musical training.

The Yankees have even inspired a Broadway musical, *Damn Yankees*, about the team that's so hard to beat one's thoughts turn to desperate measures.

There have been several teams with theme songs–the 1979 Pirates bonded over Sister Sledge's "We Are Family." The Yanks of 1940 liked to "Roll Out the Barrel," and of course the 2004 Red Sox breathed new life into "Tessie," the theme song of the old Royal Rooters as performed by the Dropkick Murphys.

The list of players with musical talent is quite long. Former Padre infielder Tim Flannery has released several country-folk CDs that are quite good. Denny McLain played the organ, both in clubs and on his own records. Jack McDowell's second career is as a rock and roll guitarist with his band Stickfigure. Bernie Williams has recorded a classical guitar album, and Tony Conigliaro released a few singles as a singer. Mudcat Grant has a band, and Bronson Arroyo released an album called *Covering the Bases*. And don't forget Deion Sanders's 1995 CD,

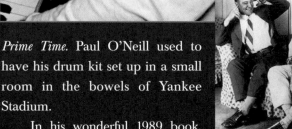

Babe Ruth is not music to Lou Gehrig's ears.

Prime Time. Paul O'Neill used to have his drum kit set up in a small room in the bowels of Yankee Stadium.

In his wonderful 1989 book, *Everything Baseball*, James Mote named an all-time All-Star Team of ballplayer/musicians: Maury Wills on the banjo, Carmen Fanzone on trumpet, Pepper Martin on guitar, Babe Ruth on the sax, Charlie Maxwell on drums, Bob Kennedy on xylophone, Phil Linz on harmonica, Frankie Pytlak on mandolin, and Denny McLain on organ.[1]

"Take Me Out to the Ball Game" has been recorded by big league ballplayers twice, once by a quartet that featured Phil Rizzuto, Ralph Branca, Roy Campanella, and Tommy Henrich, in 1950. Braves pitcher Buzz Capra recorded a version in 1975. The song was also recorded by one umpire, Joe West (1984), and one owner, Bing Crosby, part owner of the Pirates, in 1960.

There are also many players who've been mentioned in popular songs, or who have had entire songs written about them, such as Bill Lee, immortalized in a song called "Bill Lee" by the late Warren Zevon. Richie Allen got a poignant appreciation from folksinger Chuck Brodsky in his song "Letters in the Dirt." Vida Blue has a whole band named after him. Jimmy Buffett and Johnny Ramone are among the many musicians who've been great baseball fans. Emmylou Harris has been quoted as saying: "Let's just say I'm a National League girl, because I don't believe in the designated hitter." Country legend Charley Pride played baseball in the Negro Leagues. Duke Ellington enjoyed the game as a young man. Carly Simon, who does a definitive version of "Take Me Out to the Ball Game" on the sound track to Ken Burns's *Baseball* documentary, grew up in Stamford, Connecticut, where her parents were friends with Jackie and Rachel Robinson. Carly would often ride to Ebbets Field in Jackie's car and would sit in the dugout before games.[2]

The list of American musicians, songwriters, and composers who've written on the game is a Hall of Fame in itself: George M. Cohan, John Philip Sousa, Irving Berlin, Charles Ives, Frank Sinatra, Chuck Berry, Bob Dylan, John Fogerty, Jonathan Richman, Dave Frishberg, Paul Simon, Count Basie, Woody Guthrie, and Bruce Springsteen.

Writers have also gotten into the game, musically speaking. Ring Lardner wrote a bouncy little number called "Gee It's a Wonderful Game," in 1911. Peter Gammons is a well-known devotee of the independent music scene, as well as a songwriter and musician in his own right.

Henry Chadwick, the father of baseball writing, also wrote and published approximately fifty instrumental compositions, according to new research by Cooperstown-based baseball historian Peter Nash, himself the former leader of a rap band called 3rd Bass, whose several baseball songs included one on Ted "Double Duty" Radcliffe, the recently deceased star of the Negro Leagues.

A surprising number of Hall of Famers have been deeply involved in music. According to former HOF historian Ken Smith, Frankie Frisch played the violin, Mickey Cochrane favored the saxophone, Waite Hoyt was a fine singer (and a painter, too) and Bill Terry possessed a "clear-voiced baritone."

Terry Cashman's 1981 hit, "Talkin' Baseball, Willie, Mickey, and the Duke," celebrated the golden era of both baseball in general and center fielders in particular. At a time when fans were enduring the first major baseball strike, they enjoyed a bit of pure nostalgia for simpler times, thanks to Cashman's infectious melody and clear love for the game. Mays was mentioned in Bob Dylan's "I Shall Be Free" and also was the subject of the infectious "Say Hey (The Willie Mays Song)" by the Treniers. Mantle had his own musical tribute, Teresa Brewer's' "I Love Mickey."

"Where have you gone, Joe DiMaggio?" asked

Paul Simon poignantly in the song "Mrs. Robinson," and the great center fielder was also the subject of two songs:

"Joltin' Joe DiMaggio" by Les Brown and His Band of Renown and "Joe DiMaggio Done it Again" by Woody Guthrie.

Irving Berlin's 1926 composition "Along Came Ruth" was one of nearly a dozen songs inspired by the Babe's home run prowess.

Ernie Harwell penned a 1974 tribute to Babe and his successor, Hank Aaron, entitled "Move Over Babe, Here Comes Henry."

Like dozens of other ballplayers, including the Babe, Rube Marquard had a vaudeville routine. He was also the subject of a popular song, "That Marquard Glide." Mike Schmidt, along with teammates Garry Maddox, Dave Cash, Larry Bowa, and Greg Luzinski, recorded "Phillies Fever" in 1976. Bob Dylan wrote an ode to Catfish Hunter in the 1970s, with the prophetic couplet: "Every season twenty wins/Gonna make the Hall of Fame."

There is an alternative rock band called Ty Cobb, whose sound has been described as "hard driven and purely American." Sounds like they picked a good name. Richie Ashburn's 1962 collision with Elia Chacon has resulted in another band name, the veteran New Jersey rockers known as Yo La Tengo, which is Spanish for "I got it," which Chacon yelled and Ashburn didn't understand, resulting in the collision. Songwriter Evan Johns has written "Bill Veeck the Baseball Man" about the great showman. And who can ever forget Stan Musial playing "Take Me Out to the Ball Game" on his harmonica or Gary Carter singing "Oh Canada" at the induction ceremonies, let alone Johnny Bench's hilarious send-up of Harry Caray's singing? Hall of Famers have indeed made their marks in the world of music as well as in the game itself.

From 1858 to 2008, there has been a strong relationship between our great game of baseball and the timeless world of music. For fans of both, there is far more than initially meets the eye or, in this case, the ear.

Johnny Bench imitates Harry Caray at the National Baseball Hall of Fame.

Roger Maris trades his Louisville Slugger for Guy Lombardo's baton.

106

AFTER PEANUTS—
BEFORE CRACKER JACK

I figured there had never been a baseball song written.
—Jack Norworth

CONTRARY TO POPULAR belief, "Take Me Out to the Ball Game" was not the first song about baseball. Not by a long shot. According to the Library of Congress, there were sixty-one songs written about the sport (see the discography for the complete list) prior to 1908! Sixty-one! Jack Norworth apparently wasn't aware of any of them, despite the fact that one of them, "Slide, Kelly, Slide," published in 1889, was a number one hit across America and the first known baseball recording ever made, having been issued on an Edison cylinder in 1893.

The earliest extant song about baseball, "The Base Ball Polka," was written in 1858 by J. R. Blodgett, an amateur ballplayer on the Niagara Baseball Club in Buffalo. The early songs existed purely in sheet music form, as the advent of sound recording didn't happen until 1877. Many of the earlier songs were purely instrumental–sans vocals–and written in the form of quicksteps, marches, and polkas.

As strange as it may sound today, songs about baseball were quite common in 1908. And that makes the success of "Take Me Out to the Ball Game" all the more puzzling. What is clear is that in 1908, the year the song was published, eight other songs about baseball were quickly released, including such non-memorable hits as "Base Ball," "Between You and Me," "Cubs on Parade," "The Glory of the Cubs," "Hoo-oo (Ain't You Coming Out To-Night)," "One-A-Strike," and "Take Your Girl to the Ball Game."

"Take Your Girl to the Ball Game" (the title was no coincidence) was written soon after "Take Me Out to the Ball Game" by legendary Broadway and Tin Pan Alley songster George M. Cohan. He and Norworth were the same age—friends and colleagues as it were—but Cohan was Cohan. He'd already had several hits under

his belt ("Give My Regards to Broadway" and "The Yankee Doodle Boy," to name a few) and was not about to be outdone by the lesser known Norworth. But Cohan's version flopped and Cohan couldn't figure out why. According to Norworth, Cohan believed his version flopped due to its untimely release soon after "Take Me Out to the Ball Game": "I didn't write mine soon enough," Cohan explained, to which Norworth proudly replied, "Or good enough. If it's any news to you. Who ever heard of a baseball song with 'in the stands it's so grand if you're holding her hand at the old ball game.'"

The competition to displace "Take Me Out to the Ball Game" as baseball's greatest hit increased substantially the following year, in 1909. No less than twenty-two new songs about the sport were published that year, including:

First page of sheet music to "Take Your Girl to the Ball Game."

"The Banshee"

"Base Ball Ditties"

"Base Ball Game of Love"

"Baseball Brains"

"Baseball Fans"

"The Baseball Man for Me"

"Come on Play Ball with Me Dearie"

"Follow the Crowd to the Ball Game"

"The Grand Old Game"

"He's a Fan, Fan, Fan!"

"I Want to Go to the Ball Game"

"In Wise King Solly's Days"

"Let's Get the Umpire's Goat"

"The National Game"

"Oh You Tigers: Rag Two-Step"

"Root! Root! Root!"

"Slide, Bill, Slide!"

"The Spectator March and Two-Step"

"Theirs Is a Glory That Lasts But a Day"

"This Sweetheart of Mine"

"Those Grand Old Words 'Play Ball!'"

"The Triumphant March Two-Step"

In the two decades following "Take Me Out to the Ball Game," songs continued to be written about baseball, but they produced no hits. In 1913, Irving Berlin had the distinction of writing, according to the New York *Daily News*, the worst baseball song ever: "Jake! Jake! The Yiddisher Ball-Player."[1] Berlin would avenge himself, however, when his song "Always" became a hit when sung in the film *Pride of the Yankees*.

The first baseball song to give "Take Me Out to the Ball Game" a run for its money came in 1941 with "Joltin' Joe DiMaggio," followed by "Did You See Jackie Robinson Hit That Ball?" in 1947. In 1956, singer Teresa Brewer and Yankee slugger Mickey Mantle recorded the rather self-serving semi-hit "I Love Mickey" with

Brewer swooning, *"I love Mickey,"* to which Mantle replies lackadaisically, *"Mickey who? Mickey me."*

The year 1957 produced several memorable tunes, including the song "Heart" from *Damn Yankees* as well as baseball's one and only protest song, "Let's Keep the Dodgers in Brooklyn." In 1970, Dave Frishberg's "Van Lingle Mungo" was perhaps baseball's most unique song: the lyrics consisted of nothing more than odd and unusual names of ballplayers. In 1981, Terry Cashman's "Willie, Mickey and 'The Duke' (Talkin' Baseball)" was a hit, and John Fogerty's "Centerfield" became a hit, too.

Since the first music written about baseball in 1858, over 1,000 songs have been written about the sport.[2] It can be said with a modicum of certainty that, next to love, more songs have been written about baseball than any other subject. Besides, when was the last time you heard a decent golf song?

WHERE'S THE MUSIC?

THE RICH HISTORY of baseball music is housed in four principal locations: The Margaret and Franklin Steele Sheet Music Collection at the National Baseball Hall of Fame and Museum in Cooperstown, New York; The Lester S. Levy Collection of Sheet Music at Johns Hopkins University in Baltimore, Maryland; The Newberry Library's Driscoll Collection in Chicago, Illinois; and The Library of Congress in Washington, D.C. Together these four research institutions document over 1,000 musical works about baseball.

Play this RECORD on
your PHONOGRAPH
78 rpm speed (manual)

This postcard included a clear-vinyl overlay, which was a working record of "Take Me Out to the Ball Game."

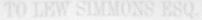

MUSIC OF THE SPHERE

THIS IS A LISTING of all commercially printed music about baseball in the collection of the Library of Congress. Together with hundreds of other songs never commercially published in sheet music form, there exist over 1,000 songs about baseball, stretching back to 1858.

(1858) "The Baseball Polka"
(1860) "The Live Oak Polka"
(1861) "Home Run Quick Step"
(1861) "Tiger Polka"
(1867) "The Base Ball Fever"
(1867) "Base Ball Polka"
(1867) "The Base Ball Quadrille"
(1867) "The Bat and the Ball Song"
(1867) "Home Run Polka"
(1867) "Union Base Ball Club March"
(1868) "Hurrah for Our National Game"
(1869) "Home Run Gallop"
(1869) "Red Stockings Schottisch"
(1870) "The Atlantic Polka"
(1870) "Baseball!"
(1874) "Base Ball Song"
(1874) "Una Schottische"
(1877) "Tally One for Me"

(1878) "The Day I Played Base Ball (Irish Comic Song)"
(1885) "Base Ball Quickstep"
(1885) "Base Ball Waltz"
(1886) "Base Ball"
(1886) "Base Ball March"
(1888) "Angela, or The Umpire's Revenge"
(1888) "Ball Club March"
(1888) "The Baseball Song"
(1888) "Our Champions March"
(1889) "Slide, Kelly, Slide!"
(1889) "Steal! Slide! Anyway!"
(1890) "Clancy Wasn't in It"
(1890) "Finnegan the Umpire"
(1890) "For We Were Boys Together"
(1890) "I'm a Jonah"
(1890) "Silver Ball March"
(1891) "O'Grady at the Game"
(1892) "The Base Ball Fan"

Cover depicts the baseball scene from the 1908 Ziegfeld Follies—celebrating one of the biggest hits of the year.

(1893) "Baseball Days"

(1894) "Our Orioles March"

(1894) "The Temple Cup Two-Step March"

(1895) "At the Game of Ball"

(1895) "The Game the Phillies Play"

(1895) "Games We Used to Play"

(1895) "The Giants' Mascot March"

(1895) "Who Would Doubt That I'm a Man?"

(1896) "'Win Mercer' Caprice"

(1897) "The Ball Player March/Two-Step"

(1897) "Magnates March: Two-Step"

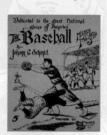

(1897) "Our Ball Team: March and Two-Step"

(1902) "The Base-Ball Fiend"

(1902) "Three Strikes Two-Step"

(1903) "Boston Americans March (Two Step)"

(1904) 'Husky Hans: A Stirring March and Two-Step"

(1905) "Base Ball"

(1905) "Base Ball Cake Walk"

(1905) "The Baseball March and Two-Step"

(1905) "Pals, Good Old Pals"

(1905) "The Umpire Is a Most Unhappy Man"

(1907) "Baseball"

(1907) "Connie's Little Elephant"

(1907) "Cubs on Parade, the Great March–Two-Step"

(1907) "The White Sox March"

(1908) "Base Ball"

(1908) "Between You and Me"

(1908) "Cubs on Parade"

(1908) "The Glory of the Cubs"

(1908) "Hoo-oo (Ain't You Coming Out To-Night)"

(1908) "One-A-Strike"

(1908) "Take Me Out to the Ball Game"

(1908) "Take Your Girl to the Ball Game"

(1909) "The Banshee"

(1909) "Base Ball Ditties"

(1909) "Base Ball Game of Love"

(1909) "Baseball Brains"

(1909) "Baseball Fans"

(1909) "The Baseball Man for Me"

(1909) "Come On Play Ball with Me Dearie"

(1909) "Follow the Crowd to the Ball Game"

(1909) "The Grand Old Game"

(1909) "He's a Fan, Fan, Fan!"

(1909) "I Want to Go to the Ball Game"

(1909) "In Wise King Solly's Days"

(1909) "Let's Get the Umpire's Goat"

(1909) "The National Game"

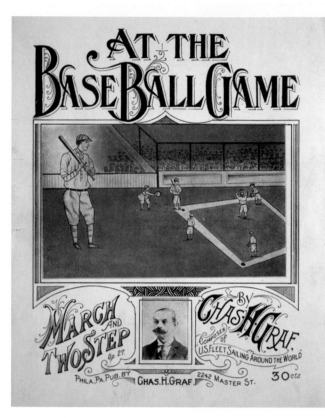

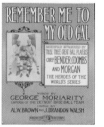

(1909) "Oh You Tigers: Rag Two-Step"

(1909) "Root! Root! Root!"

(1909) "Slide, Bill, Slide!"

(1909) "The Spectator March and Two-Step"

(1909) "Theirs Is a Glory That Lasts But a Day"

(1909) "This Sweetheart of Mine"

(1909) "Those Grand Old Words 'Play Ball!'"

(1909) "The Triumphant March Two-Step"

(1910) "At the Baseball Game: March and Two-Step"

(1910) "Back to the Bleachers for Mine"

(1910) "Base Ball Rag"

(1910) "Baseball on the Brain: A Song for the Fans"

(1910) "I Can't Miss That Ball Game"

(1910) "I'm on the Right Side of the Right Girl at the Right Time and Place"

(1910) "Little Puff of Smoke Good Night"

(1910) "Oh You Reds, Song and Chorus"

(1910) "Put the Ball Over the Pan, McCann"

(1911) "The Base-Ball Bug"

(1911) "The Baseball Boy"

(1911) "The Baseball Glide"

(1911) "The Baseball Team"

(1911) "The Climbers Rag"

(1911) "Come On to the Baseball Game"

(1911) "Dear Old Home of Childhood"

(1911) "Gee! It's a Wonderful Game"

(1911) "Home Run Bill"

(1911) "I've Been Making a Grand Stand Play for You"

(1911) "Manda at the Base Ball Game"

(1911) "Marty O'Toole Base Ball Song"

(1911) "The National Game"

(1911) "National Sports"

(1911) "Remember Me to My Old Gal"

(1911) "Rooters March Two-Step"

(1911) "They're All Good American Names"

(1911) "We're Going to See a Base Ball Game!"

(1911) "World's Champions March"

(1912) "The Base Ball Fever"

(1912) "Baseball vs. Opera, or Want to See Big Mike McGee and Houlihan Play Ball"

(1912) "The Champs of 1912"

(1912) "I Won't Go Home 'til the Last Man's Out"

(1912) "If You Can't Make a Hit in a Ball-game, You Can't Make a Hit with Me"

(1912) "King of Clubs"

(1912) "Oh You Red Sox"

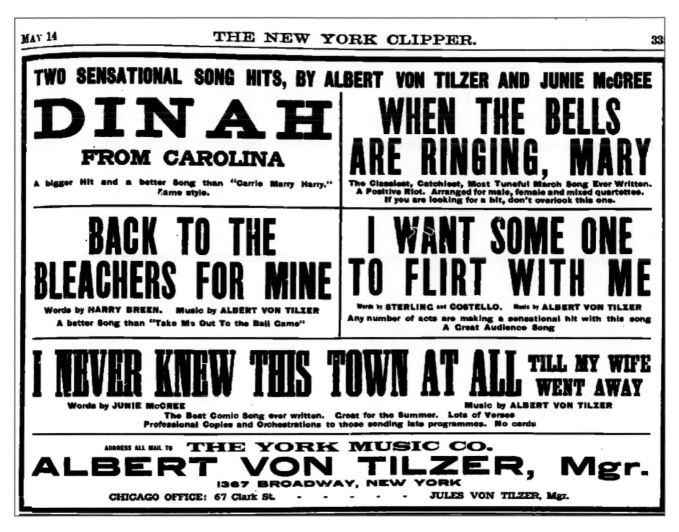

MAY 14   THE NEW YORK CLIPPER.   33

TWO SENSATIONAL SONG HITS, BY ALBERT VON TILZER AND JUNIE McCREE

DINAH
FROM CAROLINA

A bigger Hit and a better Song than "Carrie Marry Harry." Same style.

WHEN THE BELLS ARE RINGING, MARY

The Classiest, Catchiest, Most Tuneful March Song Ever Written. A Positive Riot. Arranged for male, female and mixed quartettes. If you are looking for a hit, don't overlook this one.

BACK TO THE BLEACHERS FOR MINE

Words by HARRY BREEN.   Music by ALBERT VON TILZER

A better Song than "Take Me Out To the Ball Game"

I WANT SOME ONE TO FLIRT WITH ME

Words by STERLING and COSTELLO.   Music by ALBERT VON TILZER

Any number of acts are making a sensational hit with this song
A Great Audience Song

I NEVER KNEW THIS TOWN AT ALL TILL MY WIFE WENT AWAY

Words by JUNIE McCREE   Music by ALBERT VON TILZER

The Best Comic Song ever written. Great for the Summer. Lots of Verses
Professional Copies and Orchestrations to those sending late programmes. No cards

ADDRESS ALL MAIL TO **THE YORK MUSIC CO.**
ALBERT VON TILZER, Mgr.
1367 BROADWAY, NEW YORK

CHICAGO OFFICE: 67 Clark St. - - - - - JULES VON TILZER, Mgr.

An ad in which Albert Von Tilzer proclaims another baseball song he published is "A better song than 'Take Me Out to the Ball Game'!"

(1912) "The Red Sox Speed Boys"

(1912) "Three Cheers–Base-ball Is a Grand Old Game"

(1913) "Base Ball Day"

(1913) "Base-Ball"

(1913) "The Baseball Fan"

(1913) "The Baseball Game"

(1913) "I Want to Go to the Ball Game"

(1913) "Jake! Jake! The Yiddisher Ball-Player"

(1913) "Pennant Rag"

(1913) "Take Me Dearie to That Grand Old Base Ball Game"

(1913) "That Baseball Rag"

(1913) "They All Knew Cobb: Baseball Song and Chorus"

(1914) "Base-Ball"

(1914) "Baseball"

(1914) "The Fed's Are Here To Stay"

(1914) "I'm Baseball Crazy, Too"

(1914) "Those Days of Childhood"

(1915) "Hoop, Hoop Hooper Up for Red-Sox Baseball Song"

(1915) "You're Hitting a Thousand in the Game of Love"

(1917) "Attaboy ('That's the Boy')"

(1918) "Batter Up Uncle Sam Is at the Plate"

(1919) "America" 'Pinch Hit' March: The Hit That Ended the World's Greatest War"

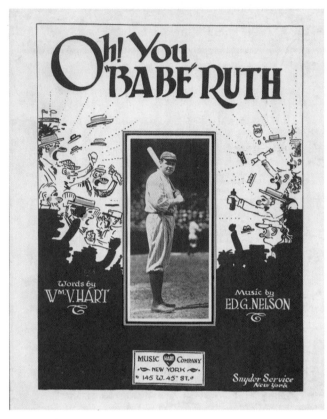

(1919) "The Baseball Rag"
(1920) "Casey at the Bat"
(1921) "Babe Ruth"
(1922) "Babe Ruth"
(1922) "Play Ball! Pray All! There's a Man Named Holy Moses Coming to Our Town"
(1923) "Babe Ruth Blues"
(1923) "Babe Ruth: He Is a Home Run Guy"
(1924) "The Base Ball Blues"

(1924) "Baseball Jim"
(1924) "Our Old Home Team"
(1925) "I Want to Go Out to the Ball Game To-Day"
(1925) "The National Game"
(1926) "Along Came Ruth"
(1927) "'Batterin' Babe'—Look at Him Now"
(1927) "Take Me Out to the Ball Game"
(1933) "I Know a Foul Ball"
(1933) "Let 'Em Eat Cake"
(1933) "Nine Supreme Ball Players"

(1933) "No Better Way to Start a Case"
(1933) "Play Ball!"
(1933) "That's What He Did!"
(1933) "Throttle Throttlebottom"
(1933) "Up and at 'Em, On to Victory"
(1933) "The Whole Truth"
(1935) "I Can't Get to First Base with You"
(1936) "Home-Run on the Keys"
(1936) "You Better Play Ball with Me"
(1937) "Come on You Cubs Play Ball"
(1937) "March of the Cardinals: Official March of the St. Louis National Baseball Club"
(1938) "The 'A's' Are the Craze"
(1938) "Batter Up"
(1938) "Cheer for the Cubs"
(1938) "Cin-c-i-n-n-a-t-i"
(1938) "A Cowboy's Life"
(1938) "Drifting"
(1938) "Here Come the Yanks"
(1938) "The Indian Song"
(1938) "It's Detroit"
(1938) "It's in the Cards"
(1938) "The Pirates Are on Your Trail"
(1938) "Root for the Boston Red Sox"
(1938) "The St. Louis Browns"
(1938) "There's Gold in Them There Phils"
(1938) "Victory for the Bees"
(1938) "Watch the Senators"
(1938) "We're the Boys from Brooklyn"
(1938) "When a Cowboy Goes to Town"
(1938) "The White Sox Are Coming Home"
(1938) "You Can't Go Wrong"
(1939) "BAM! It's Going, Going, Gone"
(1939) "Base Ball the All-American Game"
(1939) "Baseball (America's Favorite Game)"
(1940) "At the Old Ball Game"
(1941) "Joltin' Joe DiMaggio"
(1941) "The March of the Champs"
(1941) "Watch the Cubs Play Ball"
(1943) "Hail to the Senators!"
(1943) "Hurrah! For the Grand Old Game"
(1943) "Leave Us Go Root for the Dodgers, Rodgers"

(1943) "You're Gonna Win That Ball Game–Uncle Sam!"

(1945) "Base Ball Billy"

(1945) "Casey the Pride of Them All"

(1946) "Ball Game"

(1946) "The Brooklyn Dodgers"

(1947) "Albuquerque"

(1947) "Babe"

(1947) "Casey at the Bat"

(1947) "The Dodger Polka"

(1947) "Follow the Dodgers"

(1947) "Jackie Robinson"

(1948) "Casey at the Bat"

(1948) "Come Out to Braves Field"

(1948) "The First Baseball Game"

(1948) "Home-Run"

(1948) "It's the Crack of a Home Run"

(1948) "Our Bambino: Baseball's National Anthem"

(1948) "Rickey"

(1948) "Safe at Home"

(1949) "At the Ball Game"

(1949) "Brooklyn Baseball Cantata"

(1949) "Dem Flatbush Bums"

(1949) "He Was the Greatest of All"

(1949) "It Happens Every Spring"

(1949) "Let's Go Out to the Ballgame"

(1949) "O'Brien to Ryan to Goldberg"

(1950) "The Baseball League"

(1950) "The Baseball Polka"

(1950) "The Fightin' Phils"

(1950) "Grand Old Man of Baseball"

(1950) "I'll See Ya' at the World Series"

(1950) "Wanna Go to the Baseball Game"

(1950) "Whiz Kids"

(1951) "Babe Ruth"

(1951) "Baseball Papa"

(1951) "Flatbush Waltz"

(1951) "Here Comes the Baseballman"

(1951) "Let's Have a Ball at the Ball Game"

(1951) "Play Ball"

(1951) "There's No Place Like First Place"

(1951) "35th Street Chant (Go-Go-Go-Go-Go)"

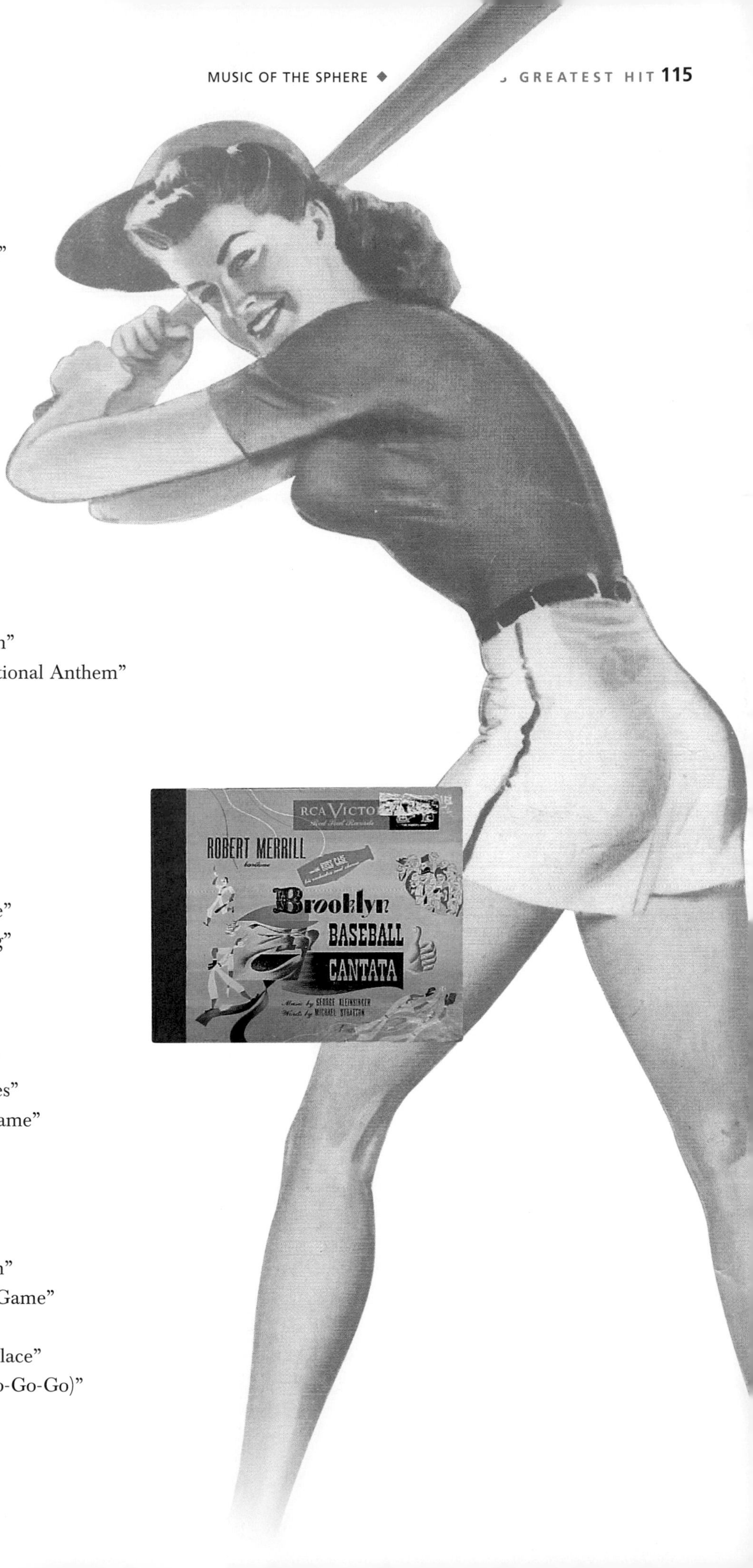

(1952) "Baseball Time in Brooklyn"

(1952) "I'm in Love with the Dodgers"

(1952) "O! Watch Oom Swing That Bat"

(1952) "Play Ball"

(1952) "Play Ball, You All"

(1953) "The Ball Game"

(1953) "I Love an Ol' Ball Game"

(1953) "The Milwaukee Braves Song"

(1953) "Who's Gonna Win the Pennant This Year?"

(1954) "Baseball, Baseball"

(1954) *Baseball in Music and Song; a Series in Facsimile of Scarce Sheet Music*

(1954) "Gay Ballplayers Play"

(1954) "The Mighty Casey"

(1954) "The Mighty Casey: A Baseball Opera in Three Scenes"

(1954) "Our Milwaukee Braves Polka"

(1954) "Sports with Vim Ballplayers Win"

(1954) "Those Cleveland Indians (of Ohio)"

(1955) "The Ball Game Is Over"

(1955) "Batter Up, Batter Up, Play Ball!"

(1955) "Guys with Vim Go Getters Win"

(1955) "Kansas City A's"

(1955) "Let's Play Ball"

(1955) "Let's Play Ball with the A's"

(1955) "Whoops Boom!"

(1956) "Batter Up! Whop!"

(1956) "Grand Slam Home Run"

(1956) "I Love Mickey"

(1956) "Mickey Mantle Mambo"

(1956) "Slam-Bang Home-Run"

(1956) "Winning Home Run"

(1957) "The Baseball Game Is On"

(1957) "Damn Yankees"

(1957) "The Game"

(1957) "Heart"

(1957) "I Like to Go to the Ball Games"

(1957) "Let's Get a Hit (for Ol' L.A.)"

(1957) "Let" Keep the Dodgers in Brooklyn"

(1957) "Little League: Official March of Little League Baseball"

(1957) "Shoeless Joe from Hannibal Mo."
(1957) "Six Months Out of Every Year"
(1957) "Song of the Milwaukee Braves"
(1957) "(Tell de Batter to) Hit de Long Ball"
(1957) "Young and Gay"
(1958) "Baseball Baby"
(1959) "At the Old Ballgame"
(1959) "Baseball Baseball"
(1959) "Charge!"
(1959) "Gimme the Good Ol' American Pastime Baseball"
(1959) "Go, You White Sox! Go, Go, Go!"
(1959) "I Love to Play Baseball"
(1959) "Play Ball, You All, Play Ball!"
(1959) "The Sox Are Home Again Hip, Hooray!"
(1959) "The World Series–The Festival in the Fall"
(1959) "Wow, Wotta Wallop!"
(1960) "The Cardinals Are Charging"
(1960) "Dodgers Charge 1960"
(1960) "Go, Go, Go, Sox 1960"
(1960) "It's a Beautiful Day for a Ball Game"
(1960) "Little Leaguer Base Ball Man"
(1960) "You Ought to See the Dodgers"
(1961) "Bye-Bye Baby (Giants Fight Song)"
(1962) "Let's All Go to the Ball Game"
(1963) "The All-Star Game Is Coming Up Real Soon"
(1963) "Angeltown"
(1963) "Baseball Bounce"
(1963) "Baseball Foxtrot"
(1963) "The Beanball"
(1963) "Beyzbo Mombo"
(1963) "Don'cha Never Bump an Ump!"
(1963) "Don't Kill the Umpire Until the Last Man's Out!"
(1963) "Foul Ball Song"
(1963) "The Game's Never Over Till the Last Man's Out!"
(1963) "The Giants Are Home Again Hip, Hooray!"
(1963) "Going, Going, Gone"
(1963) "Hear the 'Mudville Nine'"
(1963) "I'd Rather Dig the Score of Nine Innings
of a Ballgame Than the Score of Lud Beethoven's
Big Nine"

(1963) "I'm a Fan, Man! Yes I Am!"

(1963) "Let's ALL Play Ball!"

(1963) "Lose It, or Else Get Lost!"

(1963) "Mister Baseball"

(1963) "Our Old Home Team"

(1963) "The Spikes"

(1963) "Stand Up! (Brother Jasper Stretch)"

(1963) "Take a Tip from Diz, Kids!"

(1963) "Take Me Out to the Ball Game"

(1963) "To Be a Good Pitcher"

(1963) "Who's on First?"

(1963) "Yakyu Kyo (That Means 'Baseball Tonight')"

(1963) "You Didn't Bunt Much"

(1964) "Dozens o' Diamond Ditties"

(1964) "Giants Fight Song"

(1964) "Our Washington Senators"

(1965) "The Baseball Game"

(1965) "Casey at the Bat"

(1965) "Little League Polka"

(1966) "California Angels 'A-OK'!"

(1967) "A Ball Player"

(1967) "Cheer the Red Sox"

(1967) "Here Come the Yankees!"

(1967) "I Want to Be at the Ballgame"

(1967) "Stars of Fame"

(1968) "The Ball Game Isn't Over 'til the Last Man Is Out"

(1968) "Batter Up"

(1968) "Shall We Gather at the Ball Park?"

(1968) "Up the Hill with Gil!"

(1969) "Le Baseball Est Ici (They're Playin' Ball Again in Montreal)"

(1969) "Batter Up"

(1969) "The Chicago Cubs Song–Hey Hey! Holy Mackerel!"

(1969) "Go! Go! Go! Chicago Cubs!"

(1969) "Meet the Mets"

(1970) "Home of the Braves"

(1970) "Van Lingle Mungo"

(1971) "The Baseball Song"

(1971) "The First Time"

(1971) "It's a Girls Game Too"

(1971) "The Johnny Bench Song Book"

(1971) "The Most Welcome Sound"

(1971) "Pizza Party"

(1971) "Rainy Saturday"

(1971) "The Rookie"

(1971) "South Paw"

(1971) "Teamwork"

(1971) "Victory Song"

(1972) "The Superbuc Song"

(1973) "Base Ball"

BASEBALL

Words and Music by RICHARD WOLFE

THE MAJOR LEAGUE BASEBALL SONG

BAYBERRY MUSIC INC. and
HASTINGS MUSIC CORPORATION
NEW YORK, N.Y.

$1.00

Distributed by
big3

(1973) "Baseball" 1973 "Song of Roberto"

(1973) "There Used to Be a Ballpark"

(1974) "There Goes the Old Ball Game"

(1974) "You Make a Hit with My Heart"

(1976) "(He's) Daddy's Little Leaguer"

(1977) "Baseball Boogie"

(1977) "Batting Slump"

(1977) "The Kansas City Royals Are on the Go"

(1979, 1986) "Baseball"

(1979) "Baseball Girl"

(1981) "The First"

(1981) "Willie, Mickey and 'The Duke' (Talkin' Baseball)"

(1982) "Superstar"

(1986) "The Boys of Summer"

(1986) "Chaser"

(1986) "Diamonds"

(1986) "Diamonds Are Forever"

(1986) "Escorte Moi"

(1986) "Favorite Sons"

(1986) "He Threw Out the Ball"

(1986) "Hundreds of Hats"

(1986) "In the Cards"

(1986) "Ka-Razy"

(1986) "Ka-Si Atta Bat"

(1986) "Let's Play Ball"

(1986) "1919"

(1986) "Song for a Hunter College Graduate"

(1986) "Song for a Pinch Hitter"

(1986) "Stay in Your Own Back Yard"

(1986) "Vendors"

(1986) "What You'd Call a Dream"

(1986) "Winter in New York"

(1990) "The Artful Dodgers"

(1990) "The Danville Dodgers Rap"

(1990) "I'm Goin' to a Baseball Game"

(1990) "I've Got Confidence in Me"

(1990) "Teamwork"

(1990) "Tomorrow Is Another Day"

(1990) "Triple Play!"

(1990) "We Are the Winners"

(1991) "Take Me Out to the Ballgame: A Celebration of Baseball in Song"

Edison wax cylinders of "Take Me Out to the Ball Game."

ANDY PLAYS POST
OFFICE

IN 1999, THE AMERICAN public was asked by the United States Postal Service to cast their ballots and select those subjects, events, and/or personalities of each decade of the twentieth century that should be celebrated on stamps. Once again I found myself rooting for baseball player Roger Maris, as I did when he joined the Yankees in 1960. I was twelve years old when Maris joined the Yankees and he instantly became my childhood hero.

A stamp was issued in 1999 to commemorate Maris breaking Babe Ruth's single-season home run mark. It was one of nineteen different stamps selected by the American public to represent the 1960s, and I had the good fortune to attend the First Day Issue ceremony in Green Bay, Wisconsin.

During the ceremony proceedings, I met a number of United States Postal Service (USPS) employees who had helped stage the event. While there, I developed a friendship with Leslie Corban of the USPS, who remarked to me that when you meet people, the relationship takes on one of the following characteristics: a season, a reason, or a lifetime. I had never heard that adage before, but it resonated with me. Since then whenever I meet someone for the first time, I imagine which of the three categories our friendship will become.

It appears that another USPS employee, Greg Allen, has fallen into the "for a reason" category, but I'm thinking there's a good chance that it will change to "a lifetime." It was Greg who would play a very important role a few years later, when I decided to propose a stamp to commemorate the one hundredth anniversary of the song "Take Me Out to the Ball Game."

Greg provided me with the support and guidance for my proposal. There's little magic in the process of submitting a proposal to the Citizen Stamp Advisory Committee for its consideration. I'll never forget Greg's

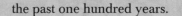

reaction to my concept, "the group receives as many as fifty thousand proposals, but only thirty to forty-five subjects are selected." Ouch.

My proposal for the consideration of a "Take Me Out to the Ball Game" stamp would be brief, entertaining, and informative. My rationale in celebrating the song is that, unlike other recent baseball-themed stamps, this one would be celebrated not only by fans of the Cleveland Indians, Seattle Mariners, or Roberto Clemente but by all baseball fans around the world regardless of team loyalty or favorite player. I included a CD that demonstrated the diverse music genres the song has been recorded in, publicity photos from the movie of the same name that was produced in 1949 starring Frank Sinatra, examples of the popularity of the song since 1908, and what I felt was a significant baseball treasure. It was a letter explaining the desire to have the song celebrated with a stamp, signed by fifteen Baseball Hall of Famers. That's what is known in baseball as a closer.

According to sources inside the USPS, once the proposal was up for consideration in their meeting, the group spontaneously broke into singing the baseball classic. The USPS will print millions of "Take Me Out to the Ball Game" stamps, and I'm looking at that as the number of baseball fans who have sung the song over the past one hundred years.

After the stamp had been selected, I was on the phone with a number of people involved in the promotion of the stamp when Greg referred to me as "the father of the stamp." Not a bad legacy for a guy who never was good at playing post office.

GOT 'IM, GOT 'IM, NEED 'IM, GOT 'IM

FOR MILLIONS OF FANS, one of the highlights of attending a baseball game is the souvenir experience. For me, that experience has always meant a lot of looking and maybe buying.

I remember staring at all the stuff Manny's Baseball Land had for sale across the street from Yankee Stadium in the 1950s and 1960s. I would stand and gaze at yearbooks, caps, magazines, picture packs, buttons, plastic statues, pennants, pencils, etc. The souvenirs were arranged outside the store as if the wind was holding them up on a fence.

Before every Yankees game I budgeted enough time so that I could stand in front of the store looking for that one item that I had to have. Unfortunately my budget rarely was equal to the total cost of my desires. I sometimes fantasized about Manny's home. I figured that he had every room filled with great baseball items.

Immediately after the game I would return to Manny's Baseball Land and stand in almost the exact same spot and gaze over the hundreds of baseball-related products that I had stared at just a few hours earlier in the day. It was as if I was looking for something that I hadn't seen earlier that day or for that matter earlier that week. This was the eye candy of my youth.

Interestingly Manny's didn't carry items relating to the song "Take Me Out to the Ball Game." My guess is that it was

"Take Me Out to the Ball Game" collectibles owned by Andy Strasberg, including Spanish and French movie posters.

not a big seller and the profit margin wasn't as dramatic as perhaps a pencil with Mickey Mantle's facsimile autograph or the offset printing of an 8 x 10 inch Don Mossi picture.

Originally there were only a couple of ways that the song was merchandised. It was either sheet music or a recording. Imagine walking into a music store and selecting a few pieces of sheet music and then handing it over to a person sitting at a piano, who would then play the sheet music for you so that if you liked the tune, you would purchase it.

Jack Norworth was curiously smart and a marketer back in those days. He decided to incorporate dozens of different performer's images on the sheet music of "Take Me Out to the Ball Game." In part it was to acknowledge those entertainers who were singing his

song, but it also raised the desire that if you wanted the "set," you had to buy them all. An example of that today is when *Sports Illustrated* prints different covers of the same issue that will sell better in certain parts of the country. Oh, those smart marketers.

The first recording of the song was by the Haydn Quartet and released around September 1908. This recording was on a disc and not a cylinder.

The song's popularity rose slowly and so did those products embracing the name. Postcards were the earliest products that capitalized on the name recognition of the popular song. It wasn't until the 1950s that "Take

Me Out to the Ball Game" felt the merchandising embrace of a diverse group of products. Marketers realized that the name was synonymous with baseball and that there was little risk involved. The name appeared on a variety of items.

With the acceptance of the purchasing public, the Internet has become a place to shop and, to a great degree, eliminated the lifelong yearning search for new items. The products available are as diverse as the musical styles in which the song has been recorded. In addition to the different recordings of the timeless classic, type the name in a search engine and the variety of products that use the name come pouring out. There are "Take Me Out to the Ball Game" rubber stamps, signs, trading cards, plates, tote bags, figurines, candles, cake decor, clothing, music boxes, doorbells, walking

sticks, piano rolls, video games, plush toys, Pez dispensers, mobiles, scrap-booking supplies, wallpaper, and more. Many times, people who are selling tickets to baseball games use the song title in their description.

But my favorite story about the marketing of the song was how Jack Norworth himself worked it. Jack would occasionally handwrite the lyrics of the song and give it to a friend or admirer as a gift. As I researched Jack and his songwriting, it became very clear that among Jack's talents was a high-level ability to promote himself. I can just imagine Jack sending someone a copy of his song "Ball Game," as he always referred to it, as a gift. After all, it was a simple piece of paper with his lyrics on it.

Lucky for us baseball fans that Manny and Jack knew how to sell baseball.

THE CRACKER JACK CONNECTION

ONE OF LIFE'S MYSTERIES is: How did the stuff we like to eat come to be? Can you imagine the day before bread was invented—how did people eat their peanut butter and jelly sandwiches? Was there a time when mankind didn't know what to do with eggs or the animals that laid them? And if you really want to comprehend the incomprehensible, imagine what the world was like when Jell-O, Baby Ruth candy bars, and Kool-Aid didn't exist. Someone had to invent all the stuff we like to eat, like Cracker Jack.

The beginnings of the product actually came about as a result of the Great Chicago Fire of 1871. A young German immigrant, Frederick Rueckheim, began selling popcorn to the workers who were rebuilding the city. The earliest form of the modern product made its debut at the World's Columbian Exposition held in Chicago in 1893.[1] It was popcorn mixed in tubs with peanuts and molasses, sold in paper bags. It took three years for the concoction to earn a name—Cracker Jack is slang for something that's very good.[2]

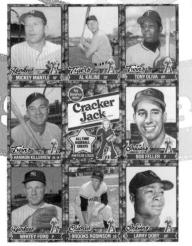

Cracker Jack first appeared in a major league ballpark in 1907, and a year later, Jack Norworth forever linked the confection to the game.

In 1899 Cracker Jack joined the industrial revolution. It became a boxed product that could be mass-produced and sold days later. There was, however, still one element missing, but it should not be a surprise to anyone who has had that Cracker Jack experience. In 1912, the "added value" element of a prize was incorporated in each box.[3] The early prizes didn't have a baseball theme until 1914 when Cracker Jack inserted a baseball card in each box. Cracker Jack first appeared in a major league ballpark in 1907.[4]

Marty Appel, a baseball promoter, was on the advisory committee of the Cracker Jack Old Timers Day Games from 1984 through 1990. The games brought back notable retired players, who played before local fans and a nationally televised audience. While most of us are used to eating Cracker Jack out of a box, Appel recalls a time when Cracker Jack, as part of the old timers games, was once cooked on site for players and officials.

"The scent of hot Cracker Jack was almost indescribably wonderful. I'll always associate Cracker Jack with baseball, and the smell of hot Cracker Jack with

the fun of those old timers games."

So how did Cracker Jack become part of the song's lyrics? Jack Norworth wrote songs because he enjoyed it and he got paid for his efforts. Did Norworth work any backroom deals with Cracker Jack so as to include them in the song? We don't know. We do know that Cracker Jack rhymes with "never get back," and for songwriters, it's all about what rhymes.

Baseball and music are part of the entertainment business—with the emphasis on business. Those who work in either are trying to make a living. They may enjoy what they do, but make no mistake: at the end of the day, they want to get paid.

Businesses are always looking for an edge to make their product more successful. Norworth must have realized this on some level. By using a popular product in a newly minted song, he must have hoped to make "Take Me Out to the Ball Game" instantly recognizable and accessible. And his plan, if it was one, worked. We'd all agree that Cracker Jack and "Take Me Out to the Ball Game" enjoy a symbiotic relationship.

Readers may wonder if Norworth's use of Cracker Jack was an early example of product placement. However, the practice didn't begin in earnest until post–World War II. For example, there's a scene in the 1951 movie *The African Queen* where Katharine Hepburn's character dumps Gordon's Gin overboard. Legend has it that Gordon's Gin paid the producers to use their prod-

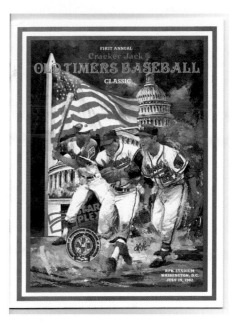

uct, and as a result, Gordon's Gin received enormous exposure. It is not by chance that you see a specific soft drink in a movie scene or a certain car driven by a leading actor. The popularity of a movie and its actors often cause the products they are seen using to become popular as well. In 1966, when cult hero Steve McQueen got behind the wheel of a Dodge Charger in the movie *Bullitt*, every red-blooded American male wanted to be McQueen or at least drive the same car. And in 1985 Reese's Pieces' sales soared after a certain adorable extra-terrestrial took a liking to the candy.

While product placement has become a cottage industry in the movie and TV business, there doesn't appear to be financial rewards for product mentions in music, at least not yet. But maybe that was what Meat Loaf was after when he wrote "Two Out of Three Ain't Bad," which once again included Cracker Jack!

We doubt Meat Loaf received free Cracker Jack for using it in his song, but if you see him drive by in a Cadillac Coupe de Ville eating Cracker Jack, you'll know why.

So here, unsolicited, is our Cracker Jack Marketing Top Ten List:

Each season insert prizes that will let fans fly to see games in ballparks (either major league or minor league) around the country.

Invite fans to submit photographs of folks eating Cracker Jack at ball games for possible inclusion in advertisements.

Host a traveling "Take Me Out to the Ball Game" muse-

The First Lady takes John F. Kennedy, Jr., out to the ball game and buys him Cracker Jack, April 14, 1967.

um containing artifacts of the song and Cracker Jack to appear at different baseball parks throughout the season.

Stage a contest around the country, with the finals taking place at "Coney Isle," to determine which fans can whistle "Take Me Out to the Ball Game" the fastest after consuming a package of Cracker Jack.

When the score is 2–2, have fans text-message "CJ" to Cracker Jack and possibly win a prize.

Have fans write, in 250 words or less, who they believe to be the greatest woman baseball fan each year. The recipient will receive the prestigious "Katie Casey Cracker Jack" diamond pendant.

Hire "Cracker Jack" jugglers to juggle boxes of Cracker Jack and tour ballparks during the season.

Produce a commemorative coin (a sou) to celebrate the song and its relationship with Cracker Jack.

Sell T-shirts made to resemble old-time baseball jerseys. The graphics would integrate the song and Cracker Jack.

E-mail Cracker Jack a new version of the lyrics for the year 2108 and win a prize.

THE PERFECT PITCH

THE LEAD BASEBALL STORY of July 29, 2007, was not about a dramatic ending to a ball game or a franchise player being traded. Rather the story was the astronomical number of baseball fans that attended the Baseball Hall of Fame induction ceremony in Cooperstown, New York. The previous largest crowd to attend the annual summer induction was set in 1999 when approximately 50,000 fans descended upon the village of Cooperstown, whose daily population is about 2,500. A reported estimate of 75,000 fans attended the induction ceremony for Tony Gwynn of the San Diego Padres and Cal Ripken, Jr., of the Baltimore Orioles. This crowd saw history and made history at the same time.

The new inductees each spent his entire baseball career with one team—Ripken for twenty-one years, Gwynn twenty. The length of these careers is only one remarkable aspect of these players' Hall of Fame credentials. What really makes Ripken and Gwynn so special is their loyalty to their respective teams, especially considering the opportunity of free agency that hundreds of players took advantage of during this period. Both players could have taken that option many times, and, like the others, earned more loot. Instead, they chose to stay where they began their Major League Baseball careers. In fact, each player has deep roots in his team's city: Tony went to college in San Diego, and Cal grew up in the Baltimore area. This degree of loyalty is amazing and refreshing, a fact apparently not lost on their legions of fans.

With the induction ceremonies over, Cooperstown slowly began to empty out. But not everyone was leaving this day. A special photo session was about to take place, and the subjects—a group of baseball immortals—

An estimated 75,000 fans attended the 2007 Baseball Hall of Fame induction ceremonies for Tony Gwynn and Cal Ripken, Jr.

For the first time ever, a recording would be made of over fifty living Hall of Famers singing "Take Me Out to the Ball Game."

slowly wended their way to a secured location. This annual rite captures on film all of the returning Hall of Famers attending Induction Weekend. The year 2007 hosted fifty-five of these living legends. The setting–a gorgeous backdrop of lush green Catskill Mountains connecting a light blue twilight sky with dark blue Otsego Lake–perfectly complemented the baseball talent assembled. Each was colorful, breathtaking, majestic, and legendary. Benches had been set up for players to sit on and stand behind, posing in what appears to be a baseball team photo. Except in this picture, the "team" is dressed in chic and dapper civilian clothes.

The assembled baseball talent was overwhelming. The list begins with Gaylord Perry, Robin Roberts, Frank Robinson, Monte Irvin, Billy Williams, and baseball executive Lee McPhail. Some Hall of Famers are recognizable to fans by just their last names: Bench, Schmidt, Lasorda, Kell, Gwynn, Morgan, Doerr, Aparicio, Brett, Bunning, Palmer, Sutton, Brock, Seaver, Carew, Kaline, Kiner, Sutter, and Yount. Other players need just one name: Sandy, Whitey, Yogi, Lefty, Cal, Sparky, Cha-Cha, Rollie, Fergie, Maz, Knucksie, Doggie, Brooksie, Pudge, Winny, Boggsie, Eck, Gibby, Molly, Ryno, and Stretch.

And then there's a group of players whose nicknames are used affectionately no matter how old they are: The Say Hey Kid, The Duke of Flatbush, The Kid, Rapid Robert, Mr. October, The Wizard, The Dominican Dandy, The Killer, and The Earl of Baltimore. Baseball Commissioner Bud Selig and Hall of Fame President Dale Petroskey are also part of the "team photo."

In preparation for this momentous assemblage, we met a few weeks earlier with the executives of the National Baseball Hall of Fame. In addition to the photo, we proposed, let's have the attending Hall of Famers sing baseball's anthem. The reaction to this idea was overwhelmingly positive. For the first time ever, a recording would be made of over fifty living Hall of Famers singing "Take Me Out to the Ball Game."

At the photo session, Dale Petroskey stepped in front of the ultimate elite gathering of baseball players. He explained that to celebrate the one hundredth anniversary of the song "Take Me Out to the Ball Game," the group would sing and record the song. And then, with a spot-on impression of Harry Caray, Johnny Bench stood up and counted out the song.

And that's how it happened. It was as if all the living members of the Rock and Roll Hall of Fame got together at Woodstock and sang "It's Only Rock and Roll." Well kinda' like that.

The song was over in less than thirty seconds. Friends and families of the Hall of Famers on the porch of the Otesaga Resort Hotel burst into applause at its conclusion. Most realized that they had just witnessed a song fest of historical baseball proportions.

PARODIES

NEARLY EVERY AMERICAN knows the refrain to "Take Me Out to the Ball Game," and for that reason, the song is easy to adapt and parody. Here are some of the best parodies we've found.

When television loomed on the horizon for baseball in the 1940s, there was a good amount of fear that if games were televised, no one would ever come out to the ball game but would sit and watch it at home—for free. Parodies were a staple of the annual New York Baseball Writers' Association dinner, and, in 1949, this one was sung:

Take us home to the ball game.
Take us home to the wife.
Get us our slippers; they're just the style,
Plug in the gadget and spin the old dial.
Then we'll root for plenty of action.
If a tube blows out, it's a shame.
But no matter what happens, we'll never go out
To the old ball game."[1]

Jack Norworth was a lover of tongue twisters, jokes, and wordplay in general, so we hope he saw this item in the *Los Angeles Times* back in 1956. While we listened to many hundreds of recorded versions of "Take Me Out to the Ball Game" in selecting the tracks for the accompanying CD, we guarantee that this is the strangest adaptation of the song you'll ever see:

Tag meow Tudor Paul came
Tag meow tooter kraut.
Pie meerschaum paynotes

And craggy checks,
Iodine caravan after compact.
Lad mere root, trued, rude
Farther him dame,
Phaeton windage ash aim;
Ferrets wand, who, tree stricture rout
Eddie all bald came.[2]

Now, tee-ball is a wonderful thing, but in some places, it differs from baseball in that every child gets a hit, scores a run, and both teams win. This was parodied in a 2007 newspaper column by the syndicated columnist Lenore Skenazy:

"Take Me Out to the New Non-Competitive Ball Game"
Take me out to the ball game
For cooperative fun!
Buy me some sunscreen so I won't burn
I just hope that we all get a turn!
For it's root, root, root for the two teams
Whoever wins it's the same—all the same
'Cause we don't! Keep! Score! Anymore
At the new ball game.[3]

The best parody I've ever heard was sung to me by ten ladies who played in the All-American Girls' Professional Baseball League (AAGPBL), during a 1995 visit to the Baseball Hall of Fame. I recently called the song's writer and copyright holder, Lavonne "Pepper" Paire Davis, a ten-year veteran catcher in the league. I remembered the first line, "Take me out of the ball game," but could not remember any more, except for the spirit of gently poking fun at the oft-injured, highly paid players of today. Here's Pepper's effort:

Take me out of the ball game
I don't think I can play
I've got a headache and a hangnail too,
What's more I think I'm coming down with the flu.
So please,
Take me out of the ball game,
If we don't win it's a shame

But I'll still get my
One, two, three million or more
At the old ball game.[4]

Pepper, who as soon as she heard about this book, broke into a lovely rendition of Jack Norworth's "Shine On Harvest Moon," is quick to point out that not all of today's players are described by her parody, but notes that her song is directed at those who fit the bill. She notes that old players like Duke Snider and Ernie Banks, and others of their era love her take, and that Ernie always asks her to sing it when their paths cross, as they often do at card shows and charity events.

Davis is also credited with writing the official song of the AAGPBL, the one from the movie *A League of Their Own* that goes: "We are the members of the All-American League / We come from cities, near and far . . ." She's written songs and poems since she was a young girl.

Our final parody comes from Cherie Cirlin, a cousin of author Andy Strasberg, who heard this one year at Passover Seder:

Take me out to the Seder
Take me out with the crowd
Feed me some matzah and chicken legs
I don't care for the hard-boiled eggs.
And it's root, root, root for Elijah
That he will soon reappear
And let's hope, hope, hope that we'll meet
Once again next year.

Take me out to the Seder
Take me out with the crowd.
Read the Haggadah
And don't skip a word.
Please hold your talking,
We want to be heard.
And lets, root, root, root for the leader
That he will finish his spiel
So we can nosh, nosh, nosh and by-gosh
Let's eat the meal!!!

A family Seder,
circa the 1950s.

THE NATIONAL ANTHEM

THE TRADITION OF singing the national anthem before every home game began in 1942, at a time of fervent patriotism and great challenge to this nation. World War II had only just begun, and the outcome was by no means certain. The anthem had made a brief appearance during the 1918 World Series between the Red Sox and the Cubs, only to recede as that war came quickly to a close. But after the Second World War, the anthem continued unabated, and once again baseball led the way for other sports to follow.

Although this list is by no means complete, we know of four players who have performed the national anthem prior to a game: Lamar Johnson of the White Sox, Nelson Briles at the 1973 World Series, and former Cubs Carmen Fanzone and Dwight Smith before Cubs games.

Profile Of the Blauers

The Miniature Peddler's Shop®

LITTLE BIG MAN

Born in San Francisco, Decem-
r 31, 1926, John M. Blauer ha
en a collector and creato of
niatures since his early
ildhood. At the age of 14, he
nt to work for a theatrical cos-
ne house that supplied
Grand Opera, stag
tion pictures. He
rking during summe
d weekends while h
n Francisco State Col
earned the Alpha C
tor Award in 1951, a
work full-time after
lege.

the widow of the famous songwriter
Jack Norworth whose "Shine on
Harvest Moon" and "Take Me Out
to the Ball Game" are now
American song classics. There
were over 10,000 individual pieces

Through correspondence and
phone conversations, a great en
husiasm developed between the
two. Ellen, who had created some
miniatures for her own collection
started to create commercially for
ture Mart. The secret o
was a painstaking at
etail, countless hours of
eweler-like craftsman-
natural artistic talent,
made her one of the
leading miniature
n. There are many
credit in the world of

> "Wanted. At All Times, anything tiny and curious, small books, model engines, guns, etc. Everything must be small. Send nothing on approval. Will also buy ship models up to 2 ft. overall. Must be well made.—Jack Norworth, 8872 Sunset Blvd., West Hollywood 46, California."
>
> —Jack Norworth (an ad he placed in *Hobbies* magazine, July 1944)

JACK NORWORTH WAS a man of many talents, chief among them what would later be called "living large." He was described by the *Los Angeles Times* as "the eternal playboy."[1] He liked the best in everything and spent money just as fast as he could make it, or faster, on cars, fine lodgings, horse races, marriages, travel, and most of all, on the lifelong hobby he shared with his father—collecting miniatures—extremely tiny things. According to the 1943 book *Miniaturia: The World of Tiny Things*, Jack Norworth was the dean of miniature collectors in America— and indeed throughout the world. His collection numbered 25,000–30,000 little objects.

The book says that Norworth's father, Theodore, picked up the hobby in the 1870s, and later kept adding items while traveling as the treasurer with Buffalo Bill's Wild West Show. As a youth, Jack Norworth had been consigned to sea by his father and visited ports of call all around the globe. Each time he arrived back in the States, he would stretch out the suspense by not showing the new miniatures to his father

Miniature piano, five inches across, containing Jack Norworth's tiny sheet music to "Shine On Harvest Moon," along with gumball-size skull given to Norworth by John Barrymore (who played Hamlet), and miniature liquor bottles filled with real liquor, a gift from W. C. Fields. Also, Norworth's miniature checkbook.

until after dinner. Then he would bring out Buddhas carved from a single grain of rice, camels small enough to pass through a needle's eye, and similar treasures.[2]

When Norworth lived in England from 1913 to 1917, he was intrigued by models of ships that were being made by sailors as they whiled away long hours on calm seas. It was in England that Norworth opened his first small shop, an unobtrusive place with a sign in front saying "Ship Models Bought and Sold." Any attempts to buy the models on display were met with outrageously high prices, but when someone brought in a model to sell, it was accepted "on consignment" and then would become part of the Norworth collection.[3]

His prize ship was a four-and-a-half-inch model of Lord Nelson's *Victory*, which Norworth had to pursue for years before its owner would sell. When the ship

was finally sent to the States, it was damaged in transit, making it necessary to repair the ship's rigging, made of human hair. The highest rigging was actually made from split hairs, to keep scale accurate.

In addition to ships, Norworth had many miniature books, musical instruments, shoes, kitchen and household utensils, and on and on. He exhibited his collection in 1940 in Manhattan, and in 1941 at Coney Island, before moving in the mid-1940s to Hollywood, where he opened a shop called It's a Small World on the Sunset Strip. The *Chicago Tribune* called this shop "more of a rallying place for his old Broadway cronies than a place of business."[4] Norworth rarely would sell anything from his collection and once even turned down $5,000 from Errol Flynn for a model ship.

After three years, he moved the shop to his new home of Laguna Beach, but still was unlikely to part with anything, preferring to show off his treasures. He

July, 1944   HOBBIES—

tion of the ingenuity our ancestors employed to make their homes comfortable. Such remarks as 'that is so old-fashioned' have changed to those of respect for our forefathers' ideals, ingenuity, and determination to make their homes places of comfort and beauty, which involved a sacrifice greater than many are now willing to make.

"It is gratifying to hear our young folks express a real pride in those important early steps that our ancestors took to make possible the America that we have known. It is encouraging for me to note, too, that some old Welsh dressers, what-nots,

MINIATURIA

WANTED

WANTED, AT ALL TIMES, anything tiny and curious, small books, model engines, guns, etc. Everything must be small. Send nothing on approval. Will also buy ship models up to 2 ft. overall. Ship models in bottles. Must be well made.—Jack Norworth, 8872 Sunset Blvd., West Hollywood 46, California.   n122901

SOLDIERS: Collector wants to buy lead soldiers. Particularly Mignot, Heyde and Britains. Standard size. Give details and price.—Frank L. Hnida, 37-50 78th Street, Jackson Heights, N. Y.   jly6844

WANTED: Miniature books or miniature objects of book form, only.—Thomas Kneeland, c/o Schrafft's, Boston, 29, Mass.   ap12844

FOR SALE

FOR SALE: Blystone's "Lord's Prayer in pen and ink on a human hair." Exhibited at three world's fairs. Described in Ripley's new book. First $1200 takes it. Can be exhibited for profit.—Jack Norworth, 8872 Sunset Blvd., West Hollywood 46, Calif.   au2294

FOR SALE: Now selling all duplicates from my vast collection of miniatures. Send for list.—Jack Norworth, 8872 Sunset Boulevard, West Hollywood 46, Calif.   mh128001

THE FAMOUS Miniature Bible now only 5c.—George Irwin, 3415 Drexel, Dallas 5, Texas.   n120501

had a cannon less than an inch long that fired, a camera of a similar size that took actual pictures, and a tiny phonograph that played tiny records—of Jack Norworth songs. He had a bust of himself small enough to fit into a willi-willi seed, a tiny crystal radio that could pick up stations up to fifteen miles distant, an oil painting of George Washington painted with a single human hair on the head of a pin, two hundred carved ivory elephants that fit inside a single carved seed from India, and a teapot made from a copper penny.

A visitor to the Norworth home in Laguna Beach wrote an appreciative catalog of the place shortly after Jack's death. Noting that the miniatures room was "a museum," our correspondent went on to say: "Never to be left without a gag, he had the hugest toothbrush in the bathroom and after a tour of the miniatures, this sight was always good for a laugh."[5]

Norworth's widow sold his collection to noted miniaturist John M. Blauer upon his death in 1959. The pieces have since been dispersed to individual collectors. We located one such collector, Judith Armitstead, who was kind enough to share the photos that accompany this essay. My personal favorite is a miniature piano, measuring just five inches across. It comes complete with Jack's little sheet music for "Shine On Harvest Moon." There is also a miniature liquor set—containing real booze—a gift to Norworth from W. C. Fields, and a miniature skull given to Norworth by John Barrymore, who himself was given the tiny skull when he played Hamlet.[6]

OUR TOP TEN
BASEBALL SONGS

ANDY

"It's a Beautiful Day for a Ball Game" by Ruth Roberts, William Katz, Gene Piller, and Harry Simeone–Next to "Take Me Out to the Ball Game," this stimulates my baseball game-experience senses. You gotta go.

"Baseball Blues" by Claire Hamil–Love the blues. Love baseball. This marries them. Oh, what a union!

"Baseball, Baseball" by Jane Morgan–Great singing voice. The only thing better than baseball is "Baseball, Baseball."

Damn Yankees' "Six Months Out of Every Year"–My life is broken up into the baseball season and the off-season of baseball. This song captures the baseball season part of the year.

"The Baseball Song" by Tim Flannery–"Flan" was a player, is a coach, and knows baseball and music. On top of that, he is sensitive, caring, has a great sense of humor, and is passionate about life. He'd make a great big league manager.

"There Used to Be a Ballpark" by Frank Sinatra–Sentimental song about my childhood ballparks that are either gone or disappearing. Frank is singing about our ballpark.

"Take Me Out to the Ball Game" by the Ink Spots–Soulful rendition of the timeless classic. Someone make sure this is played at my funeral, please.

"Take Me Out to the Ball Game" by Harpo Marx–I love it. Very ethereal.

"Roger Maris" by Steve Vaus – My heart will always wear number 9.

Open and closing theme from HBO's *When It Was a Game* by Brian Keane–Genius music that stimulates baseball memories and feelings. Add the poignant script and the voice-over to the music and it's the most powerful baseball sound track ever produced.

BOB

"Forever Spring" by composer Fred Sturm–This nine-movement jaw-dropping tour de force for orchestra and narrator celebrates the essence of the game. It's the world Series of baseball music. Just ask Tony Kubek, Dave Winfield, or voice of the Cubs announcer Wayne Messmer, all of whom have narrated it.

"Did You See Jackie Robinson Hit That Ball?"–It's a great tune. Period. But the recording with the Basie Band is a classic.

"Joltin' Joe DiMaggio"–Les Brown and His Band of Renown deliver big-time.

"The Baseball Polka"–Written in 1858, by an amateur ballplayer no less, this tune is the first song written about the sport, and it's rather catchy (pun intended).

"Slide, Kelly, Slide"–This number one hit in America in 1889 is a comical tribute to the great Michael King Kelly.

Music from the film *The Natural*–There's a place in the universe where music, cinema, and baseball intersect and composer Randy Newman is standing in the center of it. I've conducted music from *The Natural* with many an orchestra, and I still get goose bumps–even at rehearsals.

"Let's Keep the Dodgers in Brooklyn"–Baseball's one and only protest song sung by Phil Foster. Move over, Bob Dylan.

"Say Hey (The Willie Mays Song)"–The Treniers do an outstanding job of paying tribute to one of the greats.

"Knock It Out the Park" by Sam and Dave with the Dixie Flyers.–It's got groove.

"Take Me Out to the Ball Game"–Version sung by my children while sitting in the backseat of the car. Granted, they take some liberties with the lyrics (*Buy me some Kleenex and Mac Attacks*), but their version reminds me that baseball is, at its best, the domain of children.

TIM

"Take Me Out to the Ball Game"–as interpreted by Dr. John–You just can't beat that swamp boogie.

"Did You See Jackie Robinson Hit That Ball?" by Count Basie–Infectious swing, tightly written, impeccably performed, and bursting with ethnic pride and joy.

"Matty" by Dave Frishberg–Frishberg's "Matty" captures the elegance that was Mathewson in a lovely composition, both musically and lyrically.

"Van Lingle Mungo"–Fun for its sheer improbability–this was Frishberg's third set of lyrics to the tune, composed after purchasing the first edition of *The Baseball Encyclopedia* in 1969. A beautiful reference book became a beautiful, wistful song, a story to melt the heart of a librarian like myself.

"Heart" by Richard Adler and Jerry Ross, from the musical *Damn Yankees*–This song brilliantly captures the innocent optimism of Washington Senators fans, and by extension, fans of the Cubs, Phillies, Brooklyn Dodgers, and similar teams. Only one team wins the World Series each year, and the rest of us gotta have heart. And once you start singing it, it sticks in your head.

"The Dying Cub Fan's Last Request"–Do they still play the blues in Chicago when baseball season rolls around? Indeed they do, and for anyone who grew up with the Cubs, Steve Goodman nails Wrigley Field in all it's sublime glory: frosty malts, the "El" tracks, crushed beer cups, the organ, Ernie Banks, Jack Brickhouse, the wind, the bleacher bums, p.a. announcer Pat Pieper's "have your pencils and scorecards ready," sunny day games, and Waveland Avenue. It's a poem set to music, really, by Goodman, who wrote the song in 1983, and sadly, died at age thirty-six on September 20, 1984, four days before his beloved Cubs clinched the NL East title, their first championship in thirty-nine years. As in the song, some of his ashes were scattered at Wrigley Field.

Mickey Cochrane on the saxophone.

"Gee It's a Wonderful Game"—Fascinating for the way it invokes dead ball–era baseball from within, this 1911 gem was a collaboration between two amazingly talented baseball men: writer Ring Lardner and Guy Harris "Doc" White, a big league pitcher, dentist, composer, singer, and writer. Any song that so jauntily mentions Frank Chance, John McGraw, Napoleon Lajoie, and Christy Mathewson is worth a listen.

"Joltin Joe DiMaggio"—Those Horns! They "glorify the horsehide sphere." The Les Brown Orchestra swings with the same proficiency and headlong rush of Joe DiMaggio and his stellar fifty-six-game hitting streak in 1941, which inspired the song.

"Take Me Out to the Ballgame" by Carly Simon—It's time for female baseball fans—the Katie Caseys of the world—to reclaim the song as their own. It's a women's song. Carly Simon does the definitive version by a female singer.

"Gone to Heaven" by Chuck Brodsky—"Max Patkin made the children laugh, and for that he's gone to heaven." One of the greatest figures in baseball music is singer-songwriter Chuck Brodsky, who has done an entire album of baseball ballads based on baseball figures. "Gone to Heaven" melodically tells the story of the last "Clown Prince of Baseball," Max Patkin, who performed his great shtick throughout the minor leagues from the 1940s to the late 1990s. Brodsky's song is evocative, and both the melody and the lyrics are beautiful.

RECORD COLLECTORS

WE ARE A SOCIETY of collectors. You might have started off collecting dolls, trading cards, stamps, records, teddy bears, or comics, but after a while your collection appeared. You might not have realized why you kept stuff in the closet, attic, basement, or garage, but you did and over the years you have amassed a lot of stuff with a theme.

One of us is guilty of being a baseball collector. Maybe guilty is not strong enough. Very guilty. Okay, one of us is obsessed with collecting, so much so that his doorbell plays "Take Me Out to the Ball Game" and his kitchen cabinets are filled with Cracker Jack. But this isn't about Andy's collection of baseball artifacts that includes anything pertaining to "Take Me Out to the Ball Game." It's about his brethren. He understands them. He gets it. Even if we don't.

Andy reached out to other collectors who had a specialty and interest in the song "Take Me Out to the Ball Game" and asked them a series of questions. Here are their responses.

45 RPM

TAKE ME OUT
TO THE BALL GAME

Producer — ELLIOT FIELDS
Engineer — STEVE MITCHELL
Writer — Jack Norworth and
Albert Von Tilzer
Publisher — Vogel Music
Trumpet Solo —
Lee Montgomery
Arranged by: Roy Phillippe

ASCAP

Copyright 1982
CHEESE & OLIVE RECORDS
8950 Beverly Blvd.
Los Angeles, CA 90048
(213) 273-8817

Duplication Unlawful

Ollie Mitchell's
SUNDAY BAND

Time: 2.9 minutes
ALL RIGHTS RESERVED

MARK ATNIP— KNOXVILLE, TN

What do you like most about the song?

On a personal level, I like the song because it embodies the spirit of the game itself. "Take Me Out to the Ball Game" was originally written as a waltz. A nice, slow early recording of the song makes a wonderful waltz. Waltzes imply leisure and class. The relaxing meter of the song hearkens back to the golden age of the game, when games were played in early afternoon, in parks under sunlight. Ladies wore dresses, men wore hats, and there was a touch of class about going to a game. Almost elegance. Not only about what was taking place on the field, but about the fans and the way they understood and respected the game they enjoyed.

Why do you collect recordings of "Take Me Out to the Ball Game?"

I was loitering in a record shop with a friend of mine. He was digging through stacks of records looking for rare blues records while I passed the time chatting with the proprietor of the shop. He asked me where my collecting interests were, and upon being informed that the dead-ball era of baseball history was what filled my time, he produced a copy of "Take Me Out to the Ball Game" performed by Harvey Hindermeyer. I not only purchased it but spent a couple of days searching through his store looking for other variations and recordings. I purchased seven different recordings that week and quickly discovered that not only had I found a relatively inexpensive hobby, but that it was one that was fairly uncommon in the memorabilia world. I still know of only a handful of people that collect baseball-related recordings.

How many recordings do you have?

My main focus of interest is on 78-rpm and cylinder recordings. My collection currently consists of eighty-nine different recordings of "Take Me Out to the Ball Game"; however, that list includes several identical recordings that appeared on multiple labels and label variations. Over the years I have picked up several 33-rpm and 45-rpm copies; however, I haven't cataloged them.

Do you have a favorite recorded version of the song?

There is something very "dead ball" about the early releases of "Take Me Out to the Ball Game" that contain the verses. Many baseball fans are unaware that the song that is sung during the seventh-inning stretch is the chorus of the song. I would like to see the perplexed faces in the crowd if the seventh-inning-stretch performance began with the first verse of the song as opposed to the chorus.

The early Haydn Quartet, Fred Lambert, and Harvey Hindermeyer versions are three of my favorites. The Lambert and Hindermyer versions sound as if they were recorded off of vaudeville.

As for the more modern recordings . . .

Ken Griffin's organ solo sounds like what you would hear if you were attending a game before the era of Herculean sound systems. I suppose it just sounds like a 1940s baseball game should sound.

Four New York–area players, Tommy Henrich, Ralph Branca, Phil Rizzuto, and Roy Campanella; recorded a fabulous version in 1950 that was issued on several labels, and even given away as a paper record on the back of Wheaties boxes in the mid/late '50s (The singers were not credited on the Wheaties box version).

Pete Daily's Chicagoans released a relatively obscure and scarce version in 1951 that is one of the best as well. As with many of the later (post-1930) recordings, Dailey converted the meter to 4/4 as opposed to the original Waltz. The elimination of the verses allowed groups to easily convert the meter from 3/4 to 4/4, and therefore most versions that don't feature verses are found in 4/4 time. One other very popular 4/4 version was the

Hoosier Hotshots' 1936 recording that was released on at least five different labels.

Having listened to over one hundred different versions of "Take Me Out to the Ball Game," I must admit, however, that my favorite recordings, and the ones that I most value in my collection, were homemade recordings that were sent to soldiers overseas during WWII. Over the years, I have come across several acetate discs that were recorded by families sitting around a home disc recorder. In the process of recording messages from as many family members as possible (Hey, Billy! It's Uncle Joe! Ethel is doing well. We hope to see you at Christmas this year, etc.), there were families that felt the best way to make their soldier feel most at home was to sing a song. For many of those soldiers, the song they heard was "Take Me Out to the Ball Game."

Without exception, the recipients of these recordings have remained anonymous other than their first name. The labels generally bear a simple handwritten message consisting of something to the effect of "For Billy, we miss you . . . Mom and Dad." The fact that Mom and Dad would sing "Take Me Out to the Ball Game" says more about what the song meant to America and Americans than anything else I can imagine. They knew what their boy wanted to hear and they knew what made him happy. The recordings consist of all types. A cappella, duets, piano solos, and one disc

that contains nothing but someone whistling. No greetings, no messages from home. Just a song. These homemade recordings: faint, off-key, a cappella recitations show that the game and its anthem were, at least at one time, far more that a sport.

Is there an artist you'd like to hear record "Take Me Out to the Ball Game?"
It would be a bit on the silly side, but I would have loved to see what the Muppets could do with this song. They took so many vaudeville tunes and turned them into modern fun.

I would have liked to have heard a recording by the Mills Brothers.

On a more modern note, Karen Carpenter would have done a fabulous version.

Will "Take Me Out to the Ball Game" still be popular one hundred years from now?
Alas I have to say no. The song will still be the anthem of the game; however, I feel that the game has damaged itself too deeply for it to remain "the national pastime" for another hundred years. It will still be played during the stretch and will still be loved by baseball fans, but I don't know if it will enjoy the public recognition that it has in the past. I hope I'm wrong on this one.

What is the worst recording you've heard?
I really don't have a least favorite version of the song. I have heard versions performed by modern rock/pop bands that were borderline unlistenable; however, I have no idea which bands they were.

I once had a very astute nine-year-old look at my collection and explain to me that I was renting everything. "No," I explained to him, "I own it." He then explained to me that in reality I was just renting the items because eventually my collection would be sold or passed along to someone else.

The kid was right.

MIKE BROWN— EAST BRUNSWICK, NJ

What do you like most about "Take Me Out to the Ball Game"?
First, this is truly the anthem of baseball. If you are a fan of baseball, you can't help but identify with the lyrics– the food, the crowd, the cheers, and for me, "I don't care if I never get back" is the same as Yogi said some forty-five years later "It ain't over till it's over," that is, to stay the course and not leave just because you're team is behind (*or way ahead*).

Second, as a collector of baseball recordings and memorabilia, my family is very attuned to the sport and my love of it. Each of my children taught the song to each of my grandkids, who in turn sing it to me . . . over the phone, when visiting, or just to cheer me up.

Why do you collect "Take Me Out to the Ball Game" memorabilia?
I don't actually collect "Take Me Out to the Ball Game" . . . I collect baseball *music.* It all began with a couple of 78-rpm Wurlitzer jukeboxes that I owned. Needing records to fill them, I remembered a couple of tunes from my childhood–"Joltin' Joe DiMaggio" and "I Love Mickey." As both of these were issued on vinyl 78-rpm, I knew they could be played in my jukeboxes, so I began scouring record stores, baseball shows, and *Goldmine* magazine for the dozen or so baseball recordings that I thought existed. Much to my amazement, I discovered that there were not a dozen 78-rpms, but well over a hundred and even more on 45 and 33 1/3 rpm, plus a smattering on cylinder, and I don't even want to think about what's on CD.

As my baseball music collection grew, so did [the versions of] "Take Me Out to the Ball Game." As the anthem of baseball, I gathered over one hundred vinyl records (from pop, jazz, country, rock, sing-along) and about twenty-five pieces of sheet music issued from 1908 through the current times. How many different pieces exist may never be answered, but based on conversations with the writers of this book and other collectors, there are at least 300 versions by artists from every musical genre.

What is your favorite rendition of "Take Me Out to the Ball Game"?
To my mind, there are two incredible renderings: Bruce Springstone (Cold Cuts, 45 rpm, CC902) and Ella Logan, (Columbia, 78 rpm, 36257).

The Springstone is the artist's rendering of how "The Boss" would have sung the song if he made it. And the orchestration will knock you off your feet.

The Ella Logan rocks . . . and this was when rock meant a large stone or something you did to a baby in a cradle. And the intro is unique, having nothing to do with Nellie Kelly or Katie Casey, but words from a forgotten song.

What artists would you like to hear record "Take Me Out to the Ball Game"?
I have given this question a fair amount of thought as I do not keep up with the entertainers of the '80s to today. My ear for music is the '40s to the '70s from Glenn Miller to Creedence, from big band to '50s R&B to '60s and '70s rock.

I want an entertainer that loves the sport and has the creative ability to be original when it comes to presenting their version of 'Take Me Out to the Ball Game."

Here's my want list:

James Earl Jones—Imagine his presentation, a cappella or with music behind him. His voice would resonate well beyond the cheap seats.

Billy Crystal—The antithesis to Mr. Jones's resonant sound, presented with humor, love, and a word or two about Mickey.

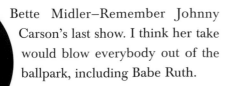

Bette Midler—Remember Johnny Carson's last show. I think her take would blow everybody out of the ballpark, including Babe Ruth.

Penny Marshall—I saw her present her baseball memorabilia collection on TV and expound on her love of the Dodgers. Most important to me, however, is her prized baseball sheet music collection, a collection that she insisted be shown to the viewers before closing out the program. (A woman I would love to meet because her collection is comparable to or better than mine and I own over 500 sheets.)

Will the song still be popular one hundred years from now?
We got past the Black Sox, expansion, strikes, and eventually drugs and steroids.

As long as there are dads and kids, there will be baseball. As long as there is baseball, there will be "Take Me Out to the Ball Game."

How many different recordings do you own of the song?
At last count, I can account for 115 versions, two on cylinder, forty-eight on 78 rpm, twenty-eight on 45 rpm, and thirty-eight on LP. Some of the LP versions are reissues of the original 78- or 45-rpm recordings. Also included are multiple versions recorded by the same artist.

What's your favorite recording?
Any version as sung at ballparks all over the world, particularly that voiced by the "mellifluous" Harry Caray and equally "honey voiced" fans at Wrigley for years. (Caray recorded "Take Me Out to the Ball Game" on Churchill [CR 7714] in 1978.)

What is the worst recording you've heard?
There is no such thing as a bad version of "Take Me Out" unless you consider the rendition of yours truly, who can't carry a tune to save himself and who in the sixth grade was told by his music teacher to "mouth the words" to the songs sung at auditorium.

Jack Norworth as "The College Boy," a stage persona he developed early in his career.

ADDENDUM

PROFESSOR HEADLAM'S FORMAL MUSICAL THEORETICAL
ANALYSIS OF "TAKE ME OUT TO THE BALL GAME" (WARNING:
THIS IS ONLY FOR THOSE OF YOU WHO CAN KEEP SCORE!)

"TAKE ME OUT to the Ball Game" is in a verse-chorus, two-part form characteristic of American popular songs in the Tin Pan Alley tradition. (Typically people remember the chorus and forget the verse in these songs.) Both the verse and chorus are in two parts, labeled A A' and B B', with the second part a varied repetition of the first part in each case. Within each part, the four lines are organized musically into a three-part structure, with a first line, then a close variant or repetition of that line in the second line, then the last two lines joined together and set with different musical material. This "aab bar" form is typical of popular songs and of blues forms. In the first A of the verse, after the first line "a" (Katie Casey) the second line is a sequence on the first, sung a step higher. The third and fourth lines form a "sentence" structure of xxy, divided by the "/"s in the example. Notice that this little sentence, xxy, is a smaller version of aab. Such similar patterns on different levels add to the interest of this song. In the varied repeat within the verse of part A as A', the third musical part ("To see a show . . . can do") is varied into a two-part statement, preparing us for the chorus.

EXAMPLE

Verse

A	a		Katie Casey was baseball mad
	a	sequence	Had the fever and had it bad
	b	xxy	Just to root for the / home town crew,
			Ev'ry / sou Katie blew

A'	a		On a Saturday, her young beau
	a	sequence	Called to see if she'd like to go
	c	xy	To see a show, but Miss Kate said,
			"No, I'll tell you what you can do"

Chorus

B	d		Take me out to the ball game
	d	slightly varied	Take me out with the crowd
	e	xy	Buy me some peanuts and Cracker Jack,
			I don't care if I never get back

B'	d		(Let me) root, root, root for the home team,
	f		If they don't win it's a shame
	g		For it's one, two, three strikes, you're out
			At the old ball game

The chorus B part is also in a three-part form, of dd'e, like the verse parts. After the famous initial statement of "Take me out to the ball game," the musical setting repeats, slightly varied. The third musical part is E xy, a two-part contrast. The most interesting part, however, is the final B' of the chorus. Here, for the first time, each musical line is different, as dfg. After the "(Let me) root, root, root for the home team" line, which is the same as in the B chorus, the "If they don't win it's a shame" line is now different, preparing for the famous last two lines "For it's one, two, three strikes you're out / At the old ball game." Here the singer metaphorically "hits" the three notes/strikes to end the song. The combination of repetition and contrast in the aab, aac, dd'e, dfg structure of the musical setting of the text allows for memorability, but yet we are intrigued enough to come back to the song again and again.

More details on the musical setting are given with the musical example that follows.

The bottom three staves show the melody with a piano accompaniment in two parts (two hands of the piano). To read the added details, think of a scale as a set of numbers: "Twinkle, twinkle, little star" is 1-1-5-5-6-6-5-4-4-3-3-2-2-1, or "Happy Birthday" is 5-5-6-5-1-7-()-5-5-6-5-2-1. These numbers indicating notes of the scale are shown between the staves: they also have added #'s and b's, which indicate that the notes are raised or lowered out of the scale for an effect. The patterns shown, such as 6-b6-5, create "chromatic" ("color") notes and patterns out of the scale and are very characteristic of barbershop quartet singing, which was a popular activity in the early 1900s, when this song was written. An interesting effect occurs when a note is respelled: the Bb b6 in m. 2, where Bb acts as a passing tone between B and A, returns as A# in a neighbor role to B ("Buy me some . . .").

The top staff is a "reduction," showing the larger succession of notes A-B-C#-D. These longer-range patterns reveal the "skeleton" holding the melody together–try to sing the melody while playing the reduction on the piano, or get another person to sing the melody and reduction together. A solid underlying line like the one shown here is the hallmark of a good and memorable piece as well. The counterpart to such an underlying line is contrapuntal interest, from little counter-melodies to the main melody. Throughout the song, little melodies emerge in the accompaniment: for instance, in the chromatic ascent from A to D, which bridges the verse and the chorus, and the counter-melody under "ball game" in line Bd.

The harmony is written below the staff in roman numerals with little numbers indicating the bass note of the chords. The chords correspond to the notes of the scale in the same way: 1 = I, 2 = II, etc. The key of D major (the home key–think of home plate) is never in

doubt in the piece, but there is harmonic interest in the opening phrase, which starts off tonic and only ends securely, and in chromatic inflections of the note and harmony based on the note B. The opening phrase is actually the ending phrase, which also acts as an introduction in a setting very characteristic of the style. The first few harmonies are ambiguous; it is really the chromatic voice-leading that governs the motion and leads into the cadence ("old . . . ball . . . game"). The second chord is an "augmented sixth" chord, a somewhat exotic chord for the style. There is actually another augmented sixth chord, in the chorus leading to "Buy me some . . . ," but this chord there leads to V/II, a B-major chord. This chord, with its chromatic note D#, is part of the "story" of the note B in this song. The note B is scale-degree 6; it is the first bass note, and it is a prominent note in its melodic role as a neighbor to A (scale-degree 5, which along with the note D defines the key) and in its harmonic role as V of II (the dominant of E). A charming moment in the song is the V-chord accom-

paniment to a melodic B in line Ab ("knew . . . ev'ry"). But it is the embellishing role of B that keeps us coming back to this song: in the verse B as V/II is hinted at in the second line (Aa), B returns in a stronger role in lines Aa and Ac, and is on full display in the chorus line Be, where the progression V/II-II–V/V–V changes the E-minor-II chord to an E-major V/V (V/A) chord in a very characteristic change.

Although there is plenty of chromatic motion, and the tonic is even undermined momentarily by a move to IV in line Bf, throughout the chromatic notes and harmonies are paired with clear voice-leading for a effective balance. All in all, the song achieves a balance between repetition and contrast, notes within the key and chromatic notes, unfettered upper melody and inner counterpointing voices, clear form and expression of the text. These all contribute to our affection for this song, whether we're hearing and singing it for the first or the hundredth time.

DISCOGRAPHY

IF YOU WERE BORN after Joe Charboneau made his 1980 debut with the Cleveland Indians, you are probably not familiar with the concept of how music on vinyl records was enjoyed by millions. In the early 1980s, the commercial compact disc was a few years away from being introduced and accepted by the general market, and downloading music was still years away from becoming a reality, changing the face, or in this case, the ear of music.

"Take Me Out to the Ball Game" has spanned the evolution of how music was and is enjoyed by the public. This is certainly another testimony to its popularity and staying power. Therefore this discography of the song will be different from those that you have seen in the past. This is the most comprehensive discography of recordings for "Take Me Out to the Ball Game" ever published. However, it is by no means complete. Old recordings are being rediscovered and new recordings are produced frequently.

To begin with, I have included many of the different media formats in which the song has appeared. It's not just records, but cylinders, piano rolls, post cards, toys with sound chips, music boxes—all of which play a rendition of the song.

But first a clarification and explanation of each medium, for those of you born after "Super Joe" stepped into the batter's box of Cleveland's Municipal Stadium.

CYLINDERS

The earliest recordings were made in the 1880s on metal cylinders and were known as "records." Cylinders evolved into different forms (wax) and identifications (length of time—two or four minutes).

RECORDS

Flat records (discs) were introduced in the 1890s and were made of celluloid and rubber-based compounds.

These discs were made of shellac and could easily break but sounded better than the first generation of discs. The records were played by rotating at 78 revolutions per minute (rpm) and placing a needle in the grooves to transmit the recorded sound. The first records were ten inches across and then became seven inches and also twelve inches. Although not commercially produced, there were sixteen-inch records, which were used primarily at radio stations.

The first recording of "Take Me Out to the Ball Game" was a ten-inch record by the Haydn Quartet on the Victor label. The record was released around September 1908.

The rotational speed of records changed from 78 rpm (in the 1930s) to 45 rpm (in the late 1940s) and 33 1/3 rpm (in the 1950s). Grooves on a 78-rpm record are much more coarse than the 33-rpm and 45-rpm ones. There are many combinations of record size and rpm, but the most common were seven-inch, 45-rpm and twelve-inch, 33 1/3-rpm records.

Recordings of "Take Me Out to the Ball Game" can be heard on ten-inch, one-sided records that played at 78 rpm. There were also two-sided records that played at 78 rpm, 45 rpm, and 33 rpm.

A vinyl phonograph record introduced in the early 1950s consists of a disc of polyvinyl chloride plastic, engraved on both sides with a single concentric spiral groove in which a sapphire or diamond needle—stylus—is intended to run from the outside edge toward the center.

While a 78-rpm record is brittle and relatively easy to break, both the microgroove 33 1/3-rpm record and the 45-rpm records are made from vinyl plastic that is flexible and relatively sturdy.

COMMON FORMATS

12" (30 cm), 331/3-rpm, long-playing (LP) format
7" (17.5 cm), 45-rpm (single) format

LESS COMMON FORMATS

12" (30 cm), 45-rpm, extended-playing single, maxi single, and EP format

10" (25 cm) 33 1/3-rpm, long-playing (LP) format

10" (25 cm) 45-rpm, extended-playing (EP) format

7" (17.5 cm) 331/3-rpm, extended-playing (EP) format

16 2/3-rpm format for voice recording

12" (30 cm), 10" (25 cm), and 7" (17.5 cm) picture discs and shaped discs

Specialty sizes: 5" (12 cm), 6" (15 cm), 8" (20 cm), 9" (23 cm), 11" (28 cm), 13" (33 cm)

Flexidiscs, often square, 7"s (17.5 cm)

Vinyl recording standards for the United States follow the guidelines of the Record Industry Association of America. The inch dimensions are not actual record diameters but a trade name. The actual dimension of a twelve-inch record is 302 mm (11.89 in), for a ten-inch record, it is 250 mm (9.84 in), and for a seven-inch record, it is 175 mm (6.89 in).

PIANO ROLLS

Piano rolls operate similarly to a music box. The notes played on a piano come about as a result of perforations on a piece of paper that corresponds to the movement of a key on a piano. A piano roll could be inserted into a player piano that is set up to "read" the perforated sheet and play the desired song. The "master original sheet" is created by a musician playing the desired song on the piano and perforating the sheet.

TOYS

This catchall category includes novelty products that produce the instrumental music of the song. It could be watches, doorbell chimes, games, signs, phone ring tones, plush toys, clocks, etc. Many of these products have a musical chip inside that plays "Take Me Out to the Ball Game" when activated. In other words, these are toys.

TAPE

Magnetic-tape recording, which originated in laboratories in the 1920s, began as a "reel to reel" in the late 1940s. Utilizing the essential component of magnetic tape, the format changed in the 1960s to 8-track and cassette.

MUSIC BOXES

Music boxes now are often anything but boxes. They appear in many forms such as ceramic figurines and tin canisters. They play "Take Me Out to the Ball Game" through the music box inside, which dates back to the eighteenth century.

SOUND SHEETS

In the 1950s records could be produced on flexible sound sheets and played like records. The earliest known sound sheets were the ones that were produced on packages of cereal in the 1950s. These were inexpensive to produce and became premium items. Sound sheets were produced as a stand-alone product or as part of an item that could be played. One of the more unique sound sheets was applied to postcards that could be played. There are three postcards that when the hole is punched out can be placed on a turntable to play "Take Me Out to the Ball Game." The pictures on the postcards are a ballpark (Milwaukee County Stadium), the National Baseball Hall of Fame in Cooperstown, New York, and a cartoon of a batter swinging.

FILM

Movies shown in theaters were produced on film with a sound strip. These were called "talkies." Films came in 35 mm, 16mm, 8 mm and Super-8.

LASER DISC

These discs looked like large silver records but contained video.

VIDEO

VHS and Beta tapes were the next step in the video evolutionary process. In the 1970s, movies and TV shows were the primary subjects of these tapes. Eventually this was developed into DVDs.

CD

Compact discs (CDs) are starting to lose favor with the new generation of listeners as music can be downloaded from the Internet to computers and MP3 players.

SPECIAL NOTE: In 1994, Ken Burns produced a 690-minute documentary on the history of baseball and utilized "Take Me Out to the Ball Game" throughout the film. Many of the segments had the song as a musical background over which the narrator talked. At other times, the song was the center of interest. The finished project provided a multitude of versions including country and western, jazz, violin, Delta blues, and swing. Many of the people who were interviewed for the documentary also sang the song. Some of the singers included Bob Costas, Doris Kearns Goodwin, Stephen Jay Gould, Roger Angell, Daniel Okrent and Curt Flood. As a result, there's a conglomerate-of-voices segment edited so that pieces of different lyrics and singers create a unique multi-personality version of the song. The highlight of singers include Billy Crystal singing it like Mickey Mantle would have and Buck O'Neil singing it like a man who enjoyed life and loved baseball.

DOWN NOTE: There have been many unrecorded renditions of "Take Me Out to the Ball Game" by notable music talents. According to baseball music historian Warner Fusselle, Eddie Duchin performed a classic version on the piano, Melba Moore performed it for the National Baseball Hall of Fame, the Five Blind Boys of Alabama gave it a gospel feel, and Meat Loaf crooned it at a MLB All-Star Game. Joel Brandon, the national and international champion "Master Whistler" whistled it for Johnny Carson on *The Tonight Show*; and in Austria, Phil Rizzuto, Yogi Berra, Whitey Ford, and Enos Slaughter (among others) sang it with the Vienna Boys Choir.[1]

LAST NOTE: "Take Me Out to the Ball Game" is used constantly in connection with commercials. Advertisers recognize that the music triggers a general positive correlation with baseball. They are right. The renditions are as varied as the products featured. Recent examples of products and services using the music ranges from Ensurance to Baby Ruth candy bars. The song works!

ARTIST	TITLE ALBUM (S = SIDE/ D= DISC/ T = TRACK)	LABEL
52 Key French Gasparini Carousel	*The World's Most Famous French Casparini Carousel* (T1)	Gold 20
The 1,000 Strings	*More Golden American Waltzes* (T5)	Crownstar Records
Abbott and Costello	*Abbott and Costello in the Movies*	
Abbott and Costello	Who's on First	Castle
Rich Acocella	*Disc Jockey*, Vol. 5 (T8)	Rock'nmania
Albatross	*The Albatross Is Your Boyfriend Now* (S1/T5)	Pennsylvania Six 5000
Alf	"Take Me Alf to the Ball Game"	Alien Productions
Ted Alvetta	*Pianola Pete and His Honky Tonk Rag Pickers*	Treasure
Andrews Sisters/ Dan Dailey	"Take Me Out to the Ball Game"	American Movie Classics
Andrews Sisters/Dan Dailey	"Take Me Out to the Ball Game"	Decca
Andrews Sisters/Dan Dailey	"Take Me Out to the Ball Game"	MCA
Anonymous	Gerbert	Les Music
Anthony Brown's Orchestra	*Rhapsodies* (T/10)	Water Babies
Armed Forces Radio Service	"Take Me Out to the Ball Game"	Basic Musical Library
Ted Auletta	*Honky Tonk Rag Pickers* (S1/T7)	MVM
Roy Ayers	*Roy Ayers Fever* (S1/T3)	Polydor
Ben Baker	*A Salute to Ken Griffin* (SA/T2)	Hudson
Duck Baker	*There's Something for Everyone in America* (S2/T1)	Kicking Mule
Lowery Ballew	*Music for Sporting Events* (T5)	Music for All Occasions
Banjo Barons	*36 Golden Banjo Favorites* (S2/T3)	CBS
Banjo Barons	*55 Golden Banjo Favorites* (S1)	Good Music
Banjo Barons	*Banjo Back in Town* (S2/T4)	Columbia
Banjo Barons	*Jockey Short Cuts* (S1/T3)	Columbia
Banjo Barons	*Music at the Turn of the Century* (S1/T4)	Heritage
Banjo Kings	*The Banjo Kings, Nostalgia Revisited in Hi-Fi* (S1/T3)	Good Time Jazz Records
Banks/Carey	*Big League Rocks* (T14)	EMI
Ernie Banks	*Big League Rocks* (T7)	EMI
H. B. Barnum	"Take Me Out to the Ball Game"	RCA Victor
Emma Barrett	*Sweet Emma Barrett* (T8)	JHB
K. and G. Barrymore	*Million Dollar Vaudeville Show*	Lion
Lionel Barrymore	"Casey at the Bat"	MGM
Benders	*Oldies and Goodies Sing Along with the Benders*	Modern
Lou Bennett	"Take Me Out to the Ball Game"	Columbia
Ben Yost Singers	*Let's All Sing* (S1/T4)	Varsity
Ben Yost Singers	*Let's All Sing* (S2/T4)	Varsity
Ben Yost Singers	*Old Timers Series E*	Sonora
Ben Yost Singers	"Take Me Out to the Ball Game"	Royale
Ben Yost Singers	"Take Me Out to the Ball Game"	Varsity
Leon Berry	*Merry Go-Round and Circus Calliope Music* (S1/T1)	Audio Fidelity
Leon Berry	*The Best of Theatre Organ*	Audio Fidelity
Leon Berry	*The Best of Theatre Organ* (S1/T3)	Audio Fidelity
Big League Quartet	"Casey at the Bat (Lionel Barrymore)"	MGM
Jimmy Blaine	"Take Me Out to the Ball Game"	Caravan
Steve Blane	"Take Me Out to the Ball Game"	Scholastic
Bob and Larry's Backyard Party	*Veggie Tales Sing-Alongs* (T1)	Big Idea
Boilermaker Jazz Band	*Jazz Baby* (T4)	Phono-Lithic
Pascal Bonniere	*Wood Wind and Steel* (T11)	Pascal Bonniere
Boston Pops	*American Bicentennial Salute* (SC/T4)	RCA

	CATALOG NUMBER	FORMAT (INCHES/RPM)	TIME (MINUTES)	YEAR	NOTES
		CD	3:06	2006	
		CD	2:06	2006	
		VHS			
		10"/78			
	RMCD-5	CD	1:24		
	PA 65000	12"/33			
		5 1/2"/33			Paper picture disc, parody
		12"/33			
		7"/45		1992	American Movie Classics promo
	24605A	10"/78		1949	
	MCA-65016	7"/45		1949	two different label designs
		CD	2:19	1989	
		CD	0:44	2005	
		16"/33			
	MVM 131	12"/33			
	PD1 6204	12"/33	4:12		
	263	12/33			
	KM 124	12"/33	2:18		
	25028	CD	4:49		
	P19940	12"/33			
	GMC 80034	Cassette			
	CL 1581	12"/33			two different label designs
	XLP 56383	12"/33			Not for sale
	P 12718	12"/33		1975	
	L-12029	12"/33			
	72435-22858-22	CD		2000	
	72435-22858-2-2	CD	4:00	2000	
	47-8155	7"/45	2:29		
	BCD-141	CD		1994	
		12"/33			
	S35	10"/78		1954	
		12"/33			
	DB 7296	7"/45			
	6911	10"/33			
	6911	10"/33			
	MS 1084	10"/78			Four-record set
	525	10"/78			
		10"/78			
	AFLP 1903	12"/33	1:27		
	6139	12"/33		1965	
	AFSD6139	12"/33	1:50	1965	
	535	10"/78			
	C25	10"/78			Red vinyl
	0439187168	Cassette		1993	
		CD			
		CD	2:37	2004	
		CD	1:54	2007	
	R223611	12"/33			

ARTIST	TITLE ALBUM (S = SIDE/ D= DISC/ T = TRACK)	LABEL
Boston Pops	*Arthur Fiedler Our Man in Boston* (S2/T1)	RCA Victor
Boston Pops	*Concert in the Park* (S2/T6)	RCA Victor
Boston Pops	*Song Fest* (S1/T4)	RCA Victor, Red Seal
Boston Pops Orchestra	*Song Fest*	RCA Victor
Leo Bradley	*One Bounce and You're Out*	Hurdy Gurdy
Brave Combo	*Let's Kiss* (T4)	Rounder Records
Brave Combo	*Let's Kiss* (T12)	Rounder Records
Teresa Brewer	"I Love Mickey"	Coral
Chuck Brodsky	*The Baseball Ballads* (T7)	ChuckBrodsky.com
Lori Brooks	*The Original Baseball Sing-Along*	Brentwood Music
Brother Bones	"Take Me Out to the Ball Game"	Theme
Jason Brown	"Take Me Out to the Ball Game"	DreamMakers
Joe E. Brown	"How to Play Baseball"	RCA
Jimmy Buffett	*Live at Fenway Park* (Disc 2/T6)	Mailboat Records
Bugs	*The Ballgame II*	RSP
Bunker Hillbillies	"Take Me Out to the Ball Game"	Seville
Roy Burns	*Skin Burns* (SB/T3)	Roulette
Sam Bush	*Diamond Cuts* (T18)	Hungry for Music
Sam Bush	*Howlin' at the Moon* (T14)	Sugar Hill
Sam Bush and George Winston	*Nolan Ryan, a Musical Tribute* (T18)	Hungry for Music
General Caine	"Baseball"	Tabu
The Californians	"Take Me Out to the Ball Game"	Featha
Mike Campbell and Tom Garvin	*Blackberry Winter*	ITI Records
Freddy Cannon	*Palisades Park* (S1/T6)	Swan
Buzz Capra and Atlanta Braves	"Take Me Out to the Ball Game"	Atlantis
Captain Jack	*Dancemania Speed 9* (T20)	Toshiba
Dutchie Caray	*Harry Caray Tribute* (T13)	WGN
Harry Caray	*Chicago Cubs Greatest Hits* (T10)	Sony
Harry Caray	*A Commemorative Tribute, Harry Caray* (T12)	
Harry Caray	*Harry Caray Tribute* (T1)	WGN
Harry Caray	"Take Me Out to the Ball Game"	Churchill
Harry Caray	*White Sox '76 Fan Appreciation*	7Up/Evatone
Wynona Carr	"The Ball Game"	Fidelity
Jeannie Carson	*Hey, Jeannie* (TV Show)	
Terry Cashman	"Talkin' Baseball (Willie, Mickey and The Duke)"	Lifesong
Pete Cavano	*Out of the Blue* (T10)	Westgate Music
Chicago Cubs (1969)	*A Day at the Ballgame* (S1/T2)	Quill
Children	*Children's Pop* (SB/T1)	Parade
Children	*Our America*	Medalist
Cincinnati Pops	*Casey at the Bat* (S1/T1)	MMA
Cincinnati Pops	*Play Ball* (T9)	Telarc
Jim Collier	*30 Trumpet Favorites* (S2/T8)	Wyncote
Computer	"Take Me Out to the Ball Game"	N/A
Dave Conner	*Sesame Street Sing-A-Long* (S2/T3)	Sesame Street
J. Lawrence Cook	"Take Me Out to the Ball Game"	QRS
Billy Corgan	"Take Me Out to the Ball Game"	
Countdown Kids	*Children's Sing A-long Favorites* (D2/T7)	Madacy
Countdown Kids	*Mommy and Me*	Madacy

CATALOG NUMBER	FORMAT (INCHES/RPM)	TIME (MINUTES)	YEAR	NOTES
LM 2599	12"/33			
LSC-2677	12"/33			
ERA 58	7"/45			two different picture sleeves
118453	12"/33			
	CD			
	CD	2:09	2005	
	CD	2:53	2005	
61700	10"/78		1956	
	CD	0:33		
C5177N	Cassette			
UR 165014	10"/78	3:00		
	CD			Private recording, two versions
H351				
	CD	1:44	2005	
4488	7"/45	3:10		
106	7"/45			
R52095	12"/33			
	CD	4:17	1997	
SHCD-3876	CD			
HFM-008	CD	4:17	1999	
Z5502947	7"/45	3:48	1982	First two lines
FJ4/3003	7"/45			
9	12"/33			
LP 507	12"/33			
3245	7"/45	1:30	1975	
64177	CD		2002	Japanese
	CD		1998	
	CD		1999	
	CD		2006	
	CD		1998	
CR 7714	7"/45			
	7"/33			Largest band
855	10"/78		1953	
	VHS		1956	
	7"/45	3:10		Opens with "Ball Game," many team versions
	CD			
800Q-1001	12"/33	1:07		
SP 341	12"/33			
	CD			
MMG 1127	12"/33			
	CD			
SW-9122	12"/33		1964	Stereo and mono; three different labels
	Floppy disc			Computer generated
CTW 22098	12"/78			Jim Henson as Ernie
8720	Piano Roll			
	CD			Private
	CD		1999	
	CD			

ARTIST	TITLE ALBUM (S = SIDE/ D= DISC/ T = TRACK)	LABEL
Countdown Kids	*Rock-A-Bye Baby* (T13)	Madacy
Crazy Otto	"Take Me Out to the Ball Game"	Camden
Bing Crosby	*Armed Forces Radio and TV Service* (T1)	Armed Forces
Bing Crosby	*Join Bing and Sing Along, 33 Great Songs* (S1/T1)	RCA Victor
Bing Crosby	*Join Bing and Sing Along, 33 Great Songs* (S1/T1)	Warner Bros.
Bing Crosby	"Take Me Out to the Ball Game"	E P Pro
Da Brat	*Hardball* (T10)	Sony
Dan Dailey	*Diamonds on the Silver Screen*	American Movie Classics
Pete Dailey	*Dixie by Daily* (S1/T6)	Capital
Pete Dailey	"Take Me Out to the Ball Game"	Capital
Dan Hornsby Quartet	"Take Me Out to the Ball Game"	Columbia
David and the High Spirit	*The Complete Jewish Kids Party, Vol. V* (T28)	
Helen Dell	"Take Me Out to the Ball Game"	Malar
Déjà vu	*Pastiche* (T-1)	LMP
Frank DeVol	*The Old Sweet Songs with Frank DeVol* (S1/T2)	Columbia
Frank DeVol	*The Old Sweet Songs with Frank DeVol*	Columbia
Dixie	"Take Me Out to the Ball Game"	Wheaties Red, Our Favorite Album
Donald Duck	*Mickey Sports Songs* (S1)	Walt Disney
Donald Duck	*Disney's Star Show Singles*	Disney
Don Doane	*Ready to Swing* (S1/T3)	Outer Green Records
Doogleberry Family	*Golden Car Songs Songfest USA*	Gallimaufry Music
Ken Double	*Ken Double Live Plus* (T7)	
Dr. John	*Baseball, a Film by Ken Burns* (T27)	Elektra
Fred Duprez and Bob Roberts	*Blitz and Blatz at the Ball Game*	Columbia
Bob Dylan	*XM's Theme Time Radio Hour*	
Paul Eakins	*Gypsy Queen, Vol. 2* (SB/T4)	Gold 20
Paul Eakins	*A Musical Tribute to St. Louis* (T1)	
Eddie Burleton's Band	*Unexpurgated Jazz* (SB/T3)	Audiophile
Ed Sullivan's Gang	*Ed Sullivan's Let's All Sing* (S1/T4)	Little and Ives
Electronic Music Player	"Take Me Out to the Ball Game"	Radio Shack
Don Elliott	"Take Me Out to the Ball Game"	Savoy
Don Elliott	"Take Me Out to the Ball Game"	Savoy
Don Elliott	*The Versatile Don Elliott*	Quality
Don Elliott	*The Versatile Don Elliott*	Savoy
Don Elliott and Cal Tjader	*Vibrations*	Savoy
Vern Elliott	"Take Me Out to the Ball Game"	Aeolian
El Paso Wind Symphony	*Classics with a Twist* (T/7)	Summit Records
Emeril	"Take Me Out to the Ball Game"	
Emily	"Take Me Out to the Ball Game"	
Buddy Emmons	*One for the Road* (T5)	Buddy Emmons Music
Lee Erwin	*50 Years of Theatre Pipe Organ* (S6/T2)	Somerset
Lee Erwin	*Oldies for Pipe Organ* (S2/T2)	Somerset
Andy Farber and Andrew Williams	*Double "A"* (T9)	After 9
Father and Daughter	*Diamond Cuts* (T17)	Hungry for Music
Nancy Faust	*Crowd Pleasing Favorites* (S1/T3)	Faust Presents
Ferko String Band	*Ferko String Band* (SB/T1)	Regent
Ferko String Band	"Take Me Out to the Ball Game"	Palda 113-B
Ferko String Band	"Take Me Out to the Ball Game"	Palda 115-B

CATALOG NUMBER	FORMAT (INCHES/RPM)	TIME (MINUTES)	YEAR	NOTES
	CD	2:05		
CAE 3000	7"/45			
SSL-12708	16"/33			
LPM 2276	12"/33			
WS 1363	12"/33			
126	7"/33	3:01		
	CD			Rewrite
	7"/45			
T385	12"/33			
1588	10"/78		1951	
15440D	10"/78			
	CD	1:06		
MAS 2024	7"/45			
	CD	2:24		
CS 8209	12"/33			
	Reel Tape			
	7"/78			
	Cassette			
	CD			Mini CD in Donald Duck cutout
	12"/33		1986	
	Cassette		1994	
	CD			
	CD and cassette	2:52	1994	
1137	Two-minute cylinder		1910	Parody
82876891942	CD			Promo, not for sale
AFSD 5212	12"/33			
	CD	2:53		
AP-43	12"/33			
ESS 1008	12"/33			
	microchip			
1103	7"/78			Free sample
S1103	10"/78			
9033	10"/33			
V-37	10"/33			
MG 12054	12"/33			
1034	Piano Roll			
	CD	0:43	2003	
	VHS			Recorded from TV show
	DVD			Friend of Duane's
	CD			
SFG52-3B	12"/33			Box set
SF-12600	12"/33			Blue label + gray label + blue with red
	CD	5:12		
	CD	0:27	1997	
	12"/33		1983	Autographed
MG 6007	12"/33			
	10"/78			
	10"/78			

ARTIST	TITLE ALBUM (S = SIDE/ D= DISC/ T = TRACK)	LABEL
Arthur Fiedler	*50 Years 50 hits* (Program 4/T5)	RCA Victor
Arthur Fiedler	*Boston Pops*	RCA Victor
Arthur Fiedler	*Our Man in Boston*	RCA Victor
Arthur Fiedler	*The Songs of North America* (S1/T13)	RCA Victor
Arthur Fiedler	*Those Were the Days* (S2)	RCA
Irving Fields	*Year Round Party Fun* (S2/T2)	Oceanic
Fireside Gang	*Everybody Sing* (SA/T2)	Golden Tune
Fireside Gang	*Let's All Sing* (SA/T2)	Mayfair
Fireside Gang	*Let's All Sing*	Tops
Firstcom Productions	"Take Me Out to the Ball Game"	
Glen Fisher	"Take Me Out to the Ball Game"	
Tim Flannery	"The Baseball Song"	PSB Records
Marc Fortier	*Les Expos de Montreal* (SA/T3)	GSI
D'Anna Fortunato	*Hurrah for Our National Game* (T22)	Newport
Four of a Kind– The Trombone Quartet	*Four of a Kind 2* (T22)	Summit Records
Four Roses Society	*Sing with the Four Roses Society* (S1/T4)	RCA Victor
Fourth of July	*Fourth of July* (T/11)	Disc Eyes
Phil Foster	*A Brooklyn Baseball Fan*	Coral
Fred Frank	*Ken Griffin Styled Organ* (SA-T1)	Evon
Madeline Franks	*Music for Baseball* (S1/T2)	
Curtis Gadsen	"Take Me Out (to the Ball Game)"	Go 4 It
Sam Gainer	*The Rinky Dink Piano of Sam Gainer at the Barn* (S2/T8)	Austin Custom Records
Gale Force V	*Diamond Cuts–Top of the Sixth* (T7)	Hungry for Music
Saul Galperin	*The Sidewalks of New York, Tin Pan Alley* (T7)	Winter and Winter
Kelly Garrett	"Take Me Out to the Ball Game"	MGM
Grady Garters	*The Longest Piano in Town*	Columbia
Grady Garters	"Take Me Out to the Ball Game" (S2/T3)	
Danny Gatton	*Danny Gatton Rarities* (T14)	
Terry Gibbs	*Swing's the Thing*	Savoy
Gigi and Mike	*Crunchy Party Mix* (T/3)	Maremel Music
Goo Goo Dolls	"Take Me Out to the Ball Game"	WB
Vince Gomez	"Take Me Out to the Ballpark" (T1)	
Steve Goodman	"Take Me Out to the Ball Game"	Red Pajama Records
Bee and Ray Goman	*Gay 90's in San Francisco* (S1/T3)	San Francisco Records
Grasshoppers	*Happy Crickets* (SA/T2)	Happy Time
Grasshoppers	*Sing Along with the Grasshoppers* (S1/T2)	Diplomat
Grasshoppers	*Sing Along with the Grasshoppers*	Happy Time
Grasshoppers	*Sing Along with the Grasshoppers*	Pirouette
Great Lakes Chorus	*2001 International Barbershop Quartet - Final Round, Vol. 2 Live* (T2)	Naked Voice Records
Greater Stringhands Overbrook String Band	*Best of the Mummers* (SC/T2)	Sure
Bobby Gregg	"Take Me Out to the Ball Game"	Epic
Ken Griffin	*Ken Griffin, the Wizard of the Organ* (SB/T3)	Rondo
Ken Griffin	*My Blue Haven* (S2/T5)	Allegro
Ken Griffin	"Take Me Out to the Ball Game"	Rondo
Ken Griffin	"Take Me Out to the Ball Game"	Rondo
Ken Griffin	"Take Me Out to the Ball Game"	Esquire
Johnny Guarnieri	"Crazy Otto Medley"	Camden
Johnny Guarnieri	*Hey, Mr. Banjo Rag* (S1/T2A)	Camden

CATALOG NUMBER	FORMAT (INCHES/RPM)	TIME (MINUTES)	YEAR	NOTES
DVS2-0420	8-track		1973	
	7"/45			
	12"/33			
PRM-259	12"/33			
LSC-3261	12"/33			
OCP-501	10"/33			
14044-A	12"/33			
96515	12"/33			
12-608-1A	7"/45			Picture sleeve
	Cassette			Studio production, not for sale
	CD			Private
	CD			Padres Crowd Opens
GSI 7001	12"/33			
LC 8554	CD	2:47	1994	
	CD	2:15	2003	
K8OP-6582	12"/33			two different cover images
	CD	1:41	2006	
61200	10"/78			three different labels
315	12"/33			Red and black label
	Cassette			
GFI 1985	7"/45	2:53	1985	Picture sleeve
WAM-33-6528	12"/33			
	CD			
	CD			Yiddish version
	12"/78			
C58794	12"/33			
	Cassette			
AV 389	CD			Promo only
Mg-12062	12"/33			
	CD	1:47	2005	
	CD	0:58, 1:00		Promo, two versions
	CD			Indie
RP 1001	7"/45	2:58		
M33011	12"/33			
HT-1006-A	12"/33			Happy Time = Red
2215-A	12"/33			
	12"/33			
FM56	12"/33			
	CD	3:21	2006	
57-2	12"/33		1976	
5-9601	7"/45			Radio station copy
RLP-27-B	10"/33			Red vinyl
1728	12"/33			
R-197-B	10"/78			
45197-B	7"/45			
5-082	10"/78			
	7"/45			
CAE 300	7"/45			Picture sleeve

ARTIST	TITLE ALBUM (S = SIDE/ D= DISC/ T = TRACK)	LABEL
Johnny Guarnieri	*Superstride* (S2/T3)	Taz-Jaz
Lalo Gurrero	"Take Me Out to the Bull Fight"	Real
Tardo Hammer	*Something Special* (T5)	Sharp Nine
Pappy Hanahan	*Honky Tonk in Percussion* (SA/T3)	Grand Prix
Happy Harts	*Banjos and Minstrels in Stereo* (S1/T2)	Kapp
Happy Harts	*Play Mr. Banjo* (S1/T2)	Kapp
Lisa Harris	*Magic Wand* (T28)	Tenacious
Hayden Causey Trio	*Hayden Causey Trio Takes a Trip* (S1/T3)	Total
Hayden Quartet	"Take Me Out to the Ball Game"	Victor
Ernie Hays	*Organ for All Seasons* (S2/T1)	Entertainment Extraordinaire
Porter Heaps	*The Good Old Songs* (S2/T3)	Columbia
Horace Heidt	"Casey at the Bat"	Magnolia Records
Wayne Henderson	*Made and Played* (T5)	Wayne Henderson
Hey Mabel	"Take Me Out to the Ball Game"	Pavis
Bill Heyer	"Take Me Out to the Ball Game"	Epic
John Higgins	*New Horizons for Jazz Ensemble* (SA/T3)	Jenson
Murray Hill	"Take Me Out to the Ball Game"	Victor
Harvey Hindermeyer	*Baseball, a Film by Ken Burns* (T5)	Elektra
Harvey Hindermeyer	*Eljer 7th Anniversary Album*	RCA Victor
Harvey Hindermeyer	"Take Me Out to the Ball Game"	Harmony
Harvey Hindermeyer	"Take Me Out to the Ball Game"	Lakeside
Harvey Hindermeyer	"Take Me Out to the Ball Game"	D and R
Harvey Hindermeyer	"Take Me Out to the Ball Game"	Vocallion
Harvey Hindermeyer	"Take Me Out to the Ball Game"	Standard Disc
Harvey Hindermeyer	"Take Me out to the Ball Game"	Columbia
Harvey Hindermeyer	"Take Me Out to the Ball Game"	Standard Disc
Harvey Hindermeyer	"Take Me Out to the Ball Game"	Columbia
Harvey Hindermeyer	"Take Me Out to the Ball Game"	Standard Talking Machine
Harvey Hindermeyer	"Take Me Out to the Ball Game"	United Record
Henstooth Discs	"Take Me Out to the Ball Game"	
The Hit Crew	*Drew's Famous 57 Greatest Kids Songs* (T31)	Turn Up the Music
Gary Hoey	"Take Me Out to the Ball Game"	Surf Dog Records
Kathleen Holeman	*Don't You Wonder?* (T11)	Kathleen Holeman
Leroy Holmes	"Take Me Out to the Ball Game"	MGM
Leroy Holmes	"Take Me Out to the Ball Game"	MGM
Honky Tonks	*Sing Along* (S1/T2)	Somerset
Honky Tonks	*Sing Along with the Honky Tonks* (SA/T2)	Somerset
Hoosier Hot Shots	*Are You Ready, Hezzie? It's the Hoosier Hot Shots* (S2/T5)	Sunbeam Records
Hoosier Hot Shots	*Are You Ready, Hezzie?* (S2/T5)	Sandy Hook
Hoosier Hot Shots	*Going, Going, Gone* (T1)	Sony
Hoosier Hot Shots	"Take Me Out to the Ball Game"	Melotone
Hoosier Hot Shots	"Take Me Out to the Ball Game"	Columbia
Hoosier Hot Shots	"Take Me Out to the Ball Game"	Columbia
Hoosier Hot Shots	"Take Me Out to the Ball Game"	Vocallion
Hoosier Hot Shots	"Take Me Out to the Ball Game"	Melotone
Dan Hornsby	"Take Me out to the Ball Game"	Columbia
Hot Buttered Elvis	*Occupado!* (T/6)	Hot Buttered Elvis
Hot Frittatas with Sam Page	"Take Me Out to the Ball Game"	

CATALOG NUMBER	FORMAT (INCHES/RPM)	TIME (MINUTES)	YEAR	NOTES
TJZ-1001	12"/33	2:57		
	10"/78		1955	
	CD	4:57		
K161	12"/33			
KS-3012	12"/33		1959	Blue label + red label
KL 1115	12"/ 33			
	CD	2:19	2007	
TLP1-331	12"/33			
5570	10"/78			one-sided
DF 108	12"/33			
45 11023	12"/33			
45-1001	7"/45	2:45		Open
	CD	2:49	2006	
PD 102	10"/78	2:40		
9050	10"/78	1:52		Not for sale
JP 3008	12"/33		1978	Not for sale
16954	10"/78			
	CD and Cassette	2:04	1994	
DPL1-0375	12"/33			
A586	10"/78		1908	
70812	10"/78			
3596	10"/78			
3736	10"/78			
A586	10"/78			
3917	10"/78		1908	one-sided
3917	10"/78			
3392	Two-minute cylinder			
	10"/78			Large hole
A586	10"/78			Extra-large hole
AD30-H321	Thorens/Reuge 4.5" disc			
	CD	0:43	2007	
	CD			Private recording
	CD	3:13	2003	
11016	10"/78		1951	
K11016-B	7"/45		1951	
SF 305-2A	12"/33			Box set
Mill 300	12"/33			
MFC-10	12"/33			
SH2086	12"/33	1:27	1984	
A 24540	CD	2:41	1994	
61051	10"/78			
20432	10"/78			
	12"/78			
3736	10"/78		1936	
C1401	10"/78			
15444-D	10"/78		1929	
CD		0:54	2006	
	CD			Private recording

ARTIST	TITLE ALBUM (S = SIDE/ D= DISC/ T = TRACK)	LABEL
Armand Hug	*Armand Hug, His Piano in New Orleans* (S1/T3)	Southland
Hula Monsters	*Diamond Cuts—Bottom of the Fifth* (T7)	Hungry for Music
William Hung	*Miracles: Hung for the Summer* (T16)	KOCH
Hurdy Gurdy	*Volume 7: Sound Effects*	
Hurst, Trevor	*Due South, Vol. II* (T9)	Unforeseen
Ink Spots	*The Ink Spots in the Spotlight* (Vol. 3/T5)	Mayfair
Ink Spots	*The Ink Spots in the Spotlight* (Vol. 3/T5)	Mayfair
Ink Spots	*The Ink Spots in the Spotlight* (Vol. 3/T5)	Tops
Don Ippolito	*Latin Dance Party* (S1/T2)	Audio Cab
Don Ippolito	"Take Me Out to the Ball Game"	Deluxe
Don Ippolito	"Take Me out to the Ball Game"	Deluxe
I.R.M. Crew	*Baseball*	Cahill
Robert Irving	*The Frogs of Summer* (T8)	Macola
Ishikawa	*Ishikawa Million Stars* (T4)	BCL
Shot Jackson	*Rural Rhythm Presents Beautiful Waltz Melodies* (SA/T9)	Rural Rhythm
Jacksonville BB Club	"Take Me Out to the Ball Game"	
James	*TMOTTBG (Take Me Home from the Ball Game)*	CMG
Bernell James	*Take Me Out to the Ball Game* (T2)	CMH
Dave Jasen	*26 Happy Honky Tonk Memories* (T8)	Special Music
Hattie Jessup	*A Night at the Red Dog Saloon*	Royal
Jesters	*Safe at Home Babe Ruth Tribute* (S2)	20th Century
Jesters	"Take Me Out to the Ball Game"	20th Century Records
Joe Doyle Duo	*Ragtime Favorites* (S1/T9)	Barre
Joe Reichman's Chorus	"Take Me Out to the Ball Game"	National Hollywood
Billy Joel	"Take Me Out to the Ball Game"	
Buddy Johnson	"Did You See Jackie Robinson Hit That Ball?"	Decca
Samuel Johnson	*Honky Tonkin''* (S1/T7)	Tiffany
Victor Johnson	*Kid at Heart* (T12)	P-POP
The Jukebox Puppet Band	*A Day in the Life*	Kid Vision
Jutoupi	*Jutoupi Funny Rap 2: Happy New Year* (T6)	Rock Records
Michael Kamen	*Frequency* (T7)	
Karaoke	*Karaoke—Specialty Songs—Vol. 1* (T1)	Sound Choice Karaoke
Gene Kelly	*Gene Kelly Songs* (T6)	Suisa
Gene Kelly and Betty Garrett	*Million Dollar Vaudeville Show* (S1/T4)	Lion
Gene Kelly and Betty Garrett	"Take Me Out to the Ball Game"	MGM
Gene Kelly and Betty Garrett	"Take Me Out to the Ball Game"	MGM
Kerry Kearny Band	*Kerry Kearny* (T13)	Palmetto
Key Artizan Organ	*River Bank Razzmatazz* S2/T1)	Melody Music
Keyboard Kingston	*Honky Tonk Hits* (SA)	Waldorf
Kidzup Production, Inc.	*Kindergarten Songs* (T22)	Kidzup Production
J. Kiley and R. Petrocelli	*Red Sox Organ Music* (S1/T1)	Ace
John Kiley	*Great Organ Favorites* (T4)	Spin O Rama
Kim Loo Sisters	*Kim Loo Sisters*	
King Curtis	*Baseball, a Film by Ken Burns* (T23)	Elektra
King Curtis	*Home Cookin'* (SA/T5)	Trip
Kings Men/Mitchell Boys Choir	*The Babe Ruth Story* (SB/T1 and T7)	RCA Victor
Kryczko/Torent	"Take Me Out to the Ball Game"	Walt Disney
L.A. Air Force	*The Ball Game*	

CATALOG NUMBER	FORMAT (INCHES/RPM)	TIME (MINUTES)	YEAR	NOTES
LP 244	12"/33			
	CD	2:35	2002	
	CD	1:42	2005	
	12"/33			
	CD			
96855-A	12"/33			Blue label
9685-S	12"/33			Yellow vinyl
L 1685	12"/33			Black label
AL 1535	12"/33			
45-GR15294	7"/33	2:00		Not for sale, DJ special
2035	7"/45	2:00		DJ copy
NU 6820	12"/45		1987	Opens with the song
			1997	Frogs croaking
73247	CD		2007	Japanese
RRBW 203-A	12"/33			
	12"/78			Private, genuine steam calliope
	CD			
	CD			
SCD-4529	CD	2:17		
RR-112	7"/45		1959	EP, picture sleeve
1631	10"/78			
1631	10"/78			Flip side: Babe Ruth tribute
BRA6-464A	12"/33			
	12"/78		1942	From Joe Reichman Show
	CD			
24675	10"/78		1949	
1021-A	12"/33		1960	
	CD	1:48	2005	
	VHS			
	CD	3:54	1995	
	CD			
	CD	1:52	2005	
DVGH 708-2	CD			Italy
L70089	12"/33			
30193	10"/78			
5012	10"/78			Australian issue
	CD	0:55	1999	
8267	12"/33			
	10"/78			
	CD	1:45	2005	
MG 7201862	12"/33			
S-135-A	12"/33			Box set
	16-mm soundies			
	CD and Cassette	2:07	1994	
TLX-9508	12"/33			
	16"/33	1:02, 4:45		
	Cassette			
	Cassette	0:30		instrumental sloppy version

ARTIST	TITLE ALBUM (S = SIDE/ D= DISC/ T = TRACK)	LABEL
Fred Lambert	"Take Me Out to the Ball Game"	Oxford Disc Record
Fred Lambert	"Take Me Out to the Ball Game"	Zon-O-Phonerecord
Fred Lambert	"Take Me Out to the Ball Game"	Zon-O-Phonerecord
Fernand Lapierre	*Fernand Lapierre a L'orque au Parc Jarry* (T10)	Trans Canada
Late Night Band	"Take Me Out to the Ball Game"	Letterman Show
Christine Lavin	*Beau Woes*	
Eddie Lawrence	*German Baseball*	Coral
Eddie Lawrence	*German Baseball*	Coral
Eddie Layton	*Eddie Layton's "Ya Gotta Have Heart"* (S1/T1)	Silva
John Lee	*"Kids Stuff"–Tunes to Grow On* (T6)	John Lee
Bernie Leighton	*Dizzy Fingers*	Cameo
Eddy J. Lemberger	*Eddy J's Fun Songs for Kids!* (T/3)	
Eddy J. Lemberger	*Eddy J's Fun Songs for Kids!* (T/13)	
J. L. Lewis and Neil Sedaka	*Shindig Presents Jerry Lee Lewis*	Rhino
Liberace	*The Golden Age of Television, Vol. 5* (T8)	The Liberace Foundation
Liberace	*Liberace, Vol. 2*	MPI
Liberty Baptist College Singers	*Look Up America (Billy Sunday)* (S2/T6)	Impact
Life Action Singers	*America, You're Too Young to Die* (S1/T3)	Life Action Music
Enoch Light	*Pops for Tots* (SB-T/4)	Waldorf Music Hall
Little Tino	"Crazy 'Bout Those Tigers"	Teenage
Living Voices	*Song Fest Fun at Home* (S2/T1b)	RCA Camden
LL Cool J	*Major League Beat* (T11)	PolyGram
LL Cool J, Aretha Franklin, et al	*What a Game* (T2)	
Ella Logan	"Take Me Out to the Ball Game"	Columbia
Lonestar	*Everyone''s Hero* (T9)	Columbia
Los Straitjackets	*Diamond Cuts–Triple Play* (T1)	Hungry for Music
Loumel Morgan Trio	"Take Me Out to the Ball Game"	V-Disc
Loumel Morgan Trio	"Take Me Out to the Ball Game"	V-Disc
Loumel Morgan Trio	"Take Me Out to the Ball Game"	No label
Loumel Morgan Trio	"Take Me Out to the Ball Game" (S1/T5)	V-Disc
Frank Luther	"Take Me Out to the Ball Game"	Decca
Frank Luther	"Take Me Out to the Ball Game"	Decca
Cherie Lynn	*Shades of Cherie* (T-8)	Norva
Liz Magnes and Sandra Bender	*Two White Mothers* (T13)	JazzD Recordings
Chuck Mahaffay	"Take Me Out to the Ball Game"	Jerden Music
Frank Malone	*Hail, Hail, the Gangs All Here* (SB/T4)	Somerset
Gap Mangione	*Take Me Out to the Ball Game* (T1 and T2)	Josh
Mark-ettes	"Take Me Out to the Ball Game"	Big 20
Freddy Martin	*27 Great Waltzes, Vol. 1* (S1/T3)	Kapp
Freddy Martin	*Freddy Martin and His Orchestra–53 All-Time Waltzes*	Kapp
Freddy Martin	*Freddy Martin and His Orchestra–54 Great Waltzes* (S1/T3-C)	MCA
Freddy Martin	*Great Waltzes of the World* (S1/T3)	Kapp
Tony Martin	"Take Me Out to the Ball Game"	RCA Victor
Tony Martin	"Take Me Out to the Ball Game"	RCA Victor
Harpo Marx	*I Love Lucy "L.A. at Last"*	CBS Fox
Frankie Masters	*Spotlight on Frankie Masters* (S1/T1)	Joyce
Frankie Masters	"Take Me Out to the Ball Game"	Vocalion
Chet Mauthe	"Take Me Out to the Ball Game"	Ken Kay

CATALOG NUMBER	FORMAT (INCHES/RPM)	TIME (MINUTES)	YEAR	NOTES
1185	10"/78		1908	single sided
1185	10"/78		1908	single sided
5371	10"/78		1909	
	CD			
	VHS		September 1, 2003	Recorded from TV show
9-61799	7"/45			Opens with the song
61799	10"/78		May 2005	Opens with the song
SSC 1073	Cassette			
	CD	2:24	2005	
1005	12"/33			
	CD	2:24		With vocals
	CD	2:24		Instrumental
	VHS		1992	
	CD	1:36	2004	
	VHS		1991	
R3979	12"/33		1983	Opens with the song
LRR 402	12"/33			
MH 33166B	10"/33			
711 LML	7"/45			Opens with the song
CAS-714	12"/33			
	VHS			
	CD		1996	four versions
36257	10"/78			
	CD			
	CD		1999	
258B	12"/78			
478B	12"/78			
478	12"/78			One-sided
Warner	CD		1992	
3212B	10"/78			
3210A	10"/78			
NOCD5631	CD			
	CD	2:15	2005	
PAN 1067	8"/45			Audio disc
MI 900	12"/33			Blue and yellow label + three album covers
JM-4029	CD	2:08	1997	
869A	7"/45	2:15		
KS 3261	12"/33			
KT 41115	Reel to reel			
MCA2-4021	12"/33		1973	Label with and without clouds
KS-3261	12"/33			
204216-A	10"/78			Not for sale
47-4216-A	7"/45			Two blue labels
2303	VHS		1989	Appearance on I Love Lucy
LP 4008	12"/33			
4915	10"/78			Fox-trot
113	10"/78			

ARTIST	TITLE ALBUM (S = SIDE/ D= DISC/ T = TRACK)	LABEL
Terri McCallister	*Wordy Birdy*	Wordy Birdy
Stuart McCay	*Reap the Wild Winds*	RCA Victor
Stuart McCay	*Reap the Wild Winds* (S1/T3)	RCA Victor
Stuart McCay	"Take Me Out to the Ball Game"	RCA Victor
Stuart McCay	"Take Me Out to the Ball Game"	RCA Victor
Gordon McCrae	*Songs for an Evening at Home* (S1/T6)	Capital
Bob McGrath	*If You're Happy and You Know It Sing Along with Bob, Vol. 1* (S2/T10)	Kids Records
Tom McHenry	*Rock Creek Yonder Come Day* (T12)	
Edward Meeker	"Take Me Out to the Ball Game"	Borri Record
Edward Meeker	"Take Me Out to the Ball Game"	Edison
Melody Makers	*Music Album Songs to Remember*	Castle Films
Tom Memoli	"Take Me Out to the Ball Game"	Windsor
Jack Mercer	*Popeye the Sailorman* (SB/T9)	Golden
Jack Mercer	*Popeye the Sailorman and His Friends* (SB/T9)	Merry
Jack Mercer	*Popeye the Sailorman and His Friends*	Wonderland
Wayne Mew	"Take Me Out to the Ball Game"	
Mitch Miller	*Songs for Children* (SA/T3)	Golden
Million Dollar Violins	*Melody of Love* (S1/T3)	Baccarola
Frank Mills	*Gather Around the Piano with Frank Mills* (T2)	Capital
Billy Mitchell	*Base Ball Papa*	Blue
Bob Mitchell	*Baseball's Best* (S2/T2)	NAN
Dr. Bill Moffitt	"Take Me Out to the Ball Game"	Bellaire
Max Morath	*Max Morath*	Epic
Max Morath	*Presenting Max Morath* (S2/T1)	Epic
Max Morath	*Who Is Max Morath?*	Epic
Jane Morgan	*Jane Morgan at the Coconut Grove* (S2)	Kapp
Peter Moses	*90 Nifty Songs* (T3)	Peter Moses
Jack Mudurian	*Downloading the Repertoire*	
(T 72)	*Duplex Planet*	AA-057
Billy Mure	*Strickly Cha Cha*	Everest
Clark Murray	*Swing Out America* (T/9)	Orchard
Stan Musial	*Diamond Cuts–Turning Two* (T15)	Hungry for Music
Stan Musial	*Stan the Man's Hit Record* (S1)	RCA Victor
Stan Musial	*Take Me Out to the Ball Game*	Melbay
Music Box	"Take Me Out to the Ball Game"	N/A
Natalie Music	*ESPN's Hustle Movie Sound Track*	
N/A	*Finger Jantz*	Hasbro
N/A	*Giant Pez*	Pez
Nashville Fiddles	*Nashville Fiddles Play for America* (T5)	King
Nashville Mandolins	*Nashville Mandolins, 30 Mandolins Classics* (T28)	King
National Geographic Society	*In the Good Old Summertime* (S1/T4)	National Geographic Society
National Pastime Orchestra	*The Sporting News: A Century of Baseball in Song* (T1)	CC Entertainment
Pamela Neal	*Charlie Hustle*	Free Flight
W. Nelson and A. Amado	*Play Ball! Diablos El Paso* (T1 and T10)	Subway/Network
Ronnie Neuman	*K-Tel Presents: Take Me Out to the Ball Game* (T/10)	K-Tel
New York Mets	*The Amazin' Mets* (SA/T2)	Buddah
New York Military Band	"Waltz Medley"	Edison Amberol
Al Nichols	"Take Me Out to the Ball Game"	RCA

CATALOG NUMBER	FORMAT (INCHES/RPM)	TIME (MINUTES)	YEAR	NOTES
	CD		1997	
EJC 1021	7"/45			Picture sleeve
LJM-1021	12"/33			Label nipper in color and no color
47-6168	7"/45			Not for sale
20-6198	10"/78			
T-1251	12"/33			
KRL 1009	12"/33		1984	
	CD			
03-25-04-11	Wax cylinder		2004	Two-minute reissue
9926	Two-minute cylinder			
	16 mm			
R-604-B	10"/78			
LP 56B	12"/33			
MR 602B	12"/33			
LP 56B	12/ 33			
	CD			Private recording
LP 72	12"/33			Red and yellow label
C80121A	12"/33			Made in Germany
S2 80012	CD			
126	10"/78		1951	
SN 4020	12"/33			
5022-A	7"/45			
	12"/33			
BN 26066	12"/33			
2LP 75702	7"/33			
KS-3268	12"/33			
	CD	0:38	2005	
CD		1996		
SD-1120	12"/33			
	CD	2:54	2000	
	CD		1998	
PNRM 3988	12"/33			Opens with the song
MB 95288C	Cassette		1994	Two versions
	Hand-crank music box			
	CD			Theme, not for sale
	Toy			
	Toy			
PKCD-10535	Cassette			
	CD			
07818	12"/33		1979	
	CD	1:07	1989	
JM 11555	12"/33		1979	Opens with the song, picture disc
FAV-1	CD			Custom promotional CDs, two versions
	CD	0:39	2005	
METS 1969	12", 33			
45	Four-minute cylinder		1908	Ends with the song
755004	7"/45			

ARTIST	TITLE ALBUM (S = SIDE/ D= DISC/ T = TRACK)	LABEL
Nicotine	*Take Me Out to the Ball Game* (T1)	Sky Records
Johnny Nielson	*Magnificent Waltzes* (S2A/T5)	Vogue
Larry Norred	"Take Me Out to the Ball Game"	FJH Music Co.
N Sync	"Take Me Out to the Ball Game"	
Nuclear Whales Saxophone Orchestra	*Thar They Blow* (T14)	
King Quartet Odom	*Amazin' Willie Mays*	Perspective
Ace O'Donnell	*Honky Tonk Piano* (SB/T3)	Tops
Shamus O'Gould	*At the Golden Nugget* (SB/T2)	Design
Happy O'Hallihan	*Percussive Honky Tonk* (SA/T3)	International Award
The Old Timers Orchestra and Jimmy Ray	"Take Me Out to the Ball Game"	Blue Bird
The Old Timers Orchestra and Jimmy Ray	"Take Me Out to the Ball Game"	Blue Bird
Joe Knuckles O'Leary	*Honky Tonk Piano* (SB/T3)	Craftsman/Gold
Ollie Mitchell's Sunday Band	"Take Me Out to the Ball Game"	Cheese and Olives Records
Omega Studios	*Tillie and Hermann's Favorite Songs* (T22)	Iron
Orchestra Ensemble Kanazawa	*Hikari No Michi* (T5 and T6)	Victor
Original Cast	*Take Me Out to the Ball Game* (Movie Sound Track)	Curtain Calls
Joe Fingers O'Shay	*Honky Tonk Piano* (SB/T2)	Golden Tone
Lisa Otey	*Lisa Otey Trio* (T8)	Owl's Nest productions
Knuckles O'Toole	*26 Ragtime Honky Tonk Hits*	Waldorf
Knuckles O'Toole	*Baseball Special*	Grand Award
Knuckles O'Toole	*Baseball Special*	Grand Award
Knuckles O'Toole	*Honky Tonk*	Waldorf
Knuckles O'Toole	*Honky Tonk Piano* (SB/T3)	FDR Dynamic
Knuckles O'Toole	*Knuckles O'Toole Plays Honky Tonk Piano* (S2/T1)	Grand Award
Knuckles O'Toole	*Ragtime Piano Honky Tonk*	FDR
Knuckles O'Toole	"Take Me Out to the Ball Game"	Top Hits
Jamie Palumbo	*Distant Star* (T/12)	jaDapa
Mandy Patinkin	*Mamaloshen* (T14)	Nonesuch
Les Paul	"Take Me Out to the Ball Game"	
Pearl Jam	*Pearl Jam, Live #2*	
Pete Daily's Chicagoans	"Take Me Out to the Ball Game"	Capital
Peter Pan Kids	*Sing-A-Long*	Parade
Peter Pan Orchestra	"Take Me Out to the Ball Game"	Peter Pan
Mark Pearman	"Take Me Out to the Ball Game"	
Stacy Phillips	*Fiddle Tunes for Beginning Cello*	Melbay
Pianola Pete	*Pianola Pete and His Honky Tonk Rag Pickers, Vol. 2* (SA)	Fortuna
Pianola Pete	*Pianola Pete and His Honky Tonk Rag Pickers, Vol. 2* (SA/T7)	Treasure
Pilot Quartet	*The Gay 90's* (SA/T1)	Waldorf Music Hall
Pixies	*The Chipmunk Song* (S1/T3)	Diplomat
Player Piano	*Original Player Piano Roll Gems* (S2/T1)	Crackerbarrel
David Polansky	*32 Familiar (Mostly) Kids Songs* (T15)	Perfect Score
Steve Poltz	*Live at the Basement*	
Poolesvile Youth	*Children's Songs* (T9)	AmeriMusic
Porter Music Box	*Music Box—Past and Present* (T6)	Porter
Porter Twin Disc Music Box	*Music Box—Past and Present* (S1/T6)	Porter
Sandy Posey	*American Country Bluegrass* (T21)	King
Poway High School Band	"Take Me Out to the Ball Game"	
Andre Previn and Russ Freeman	*Double Play!* (S1/T1)	Contemporary Records

CATALOG NUMBER	FORMAT (INCHES/RPM)	TIME (MINUTES)	YEAR	NOTES
	CD		2003	Japanese
VS103-2A	12"/33			Box set
	CD			
	Cassette			Singing at Cubs game—bootleg
	CD			
5001	10"/78		1954	
L1509	12"/33			
DLP 42	12"/33			Stereo and Spectra
AK 161	12"/33			
B-7457-B	10"/78			With Bird Only
B-7457-B	10"/78			With Nipper
C 8009	12"/33			Yellow vinyl, red vinyl + black vinyl
	7"/45	2:00	1982	Picture disc
	CD			
	CD		2007	Japanese
	12"/33			
C 4009	12"/33			
	CD	4:29	2005	
S-2-A	10"/33			
1004A	7"/45			
GA78-1004A	10"/78			
MH 45-163	7"/45			
MH 33-139	10"/33			
GA 33-324	12"33			
	7"/45			
H-401	10"/78			
CD		0:56	2005	
	CD			Yiddish
	CD			
	CD			Bootleg
F1588	7"/45			
	VHS (video)			
471	7"/78		1957	
	CD	1:56	2007	Private recording
	CD			
905	12"/33			
805A	12"/33			
MHK33-1203A	12"/33			
SX1723A	12"/33			
9XMLI	12"/33			
	CD	0:36	2005	
	DVD			
	CD	0:34	2006	
	CD			
44477	12"/33			
KG 0356-2	CD and cassette			
	Cassette		1992	All-Star Pre-Game
C3537	12"/33			

ARTIST	TITLE ALBUM (S = SIDE/ D= DISC/ T = TRACK)	LABEL
George Rabbai	*Baseball, a Film by Ken Burns* (T25)	Elektra
Raffi	*One Light One Sun* (S1/T3)	Shoreline MCA
Raggs Kids Club Band	*Red, White and Raggs* (T5)	RAGGS Kids Club Music
Ray Brown Trio	*3 Dimensional* (T8)	Concord
Michael Reed	"Take Me Out to the Ball Game"	Peter Pan Records
Michael Reed	"Take Me Out to the Ball Game"	Peter Pan Records
Michael Reed	"Take Me Out to the Ball Game"	Peter Pan Records
Michael Reed with Peter Pan Orchestra and Chorus	"Take Me Out to the Ball Game"	Peter Pan Records
Dave Remington	*Dixie on the Rocks* (S1/T3)	Vee Jay
Rosemary Rice	*The Wonderful World of Children's Songs* (S1/T4)	RCA Victor
Rosemary Rice	*The Wonderful World of Children's Songs* (S1/T4)	Camden
Paul Richardson	*Paul Richardson Plays Organ for the Phillies*	
Rip Chord	*Honky Tonk* (SB/T3)	Audition
Rizzuto, Branca, Campanella, Henrich	"Take Me Out to the Ball Game"	Golden Records
Rizzuto, Branca, Campanella, Henrich	"Take Me Out to the Ball Game"	Golden Records
Robert DeCormier Singers	*Oh, You Beautiful Doll*	AR
Robert DeCormier Singers	*Oh, You Beautiful Doll* (T13)	Arabesque
C. Barney Robertson	*Kid's Praise! 8* (S1/T1)	Marantha
Dick Robertson	"Take Me Out to the Ball Game"	Victor
Dick Robertson	"Take Me out to the Ball Game"	Decca
Frank Rosolino	*Swing . . . Not Spring* (SB/T5)	Savoy
Frank Rosolino	*The Trombone Album* (T7)	Denon
Murray Ross	*Many Sounds of Murray Ross* (T3)	Murger Music
The Rumors	"Take Me Out to the Ball Game"	Stix, Baer and Fuller
Sadie Mae's All-American Birthday	*Classic Birthday and Event Music* (T12)	Gold 20
Maritz Sales	*Chevrolet Song Parodies*	Premier
Arturo Sandoval	*61* Original Movie Sound Track* (T11)	HBO
Sandpiper Chorus	*Miller's Golden Hits Children*	Golden Records
Sandpiper Chorus	*Songs for Children*	Golden Records
Santiago and His Silver Strings	*American Beauty Waltzes* (S1/T5)	Coronet
Henry Sapoznik	*Diamond Cuts–Bottom of the Fifth* (T14)	Hungry for Music
Henry Sapoznik	*The Life and Times from H. Greenberg*	
The School for Creative and Performing Arts Chorale	*Play Ball* (T29)	TELARC
Jacqueline Schwab	*Baseball, a Film by Ken Burns* (T2)	Elektra
Mabel Scott	*Baseball Boogie*	King
Selvin's Orchestra	*Old Time Waltzes* (Part 7)	Vocalion
SFX Broadcasting	"Take Me Out to the Ball Game"	
Marc Shaiman	*61*, The Sound Track* (T18)	Jelly Bean
Rita Mitzrahi Shamie	*Grandma Rita's Songbook Three* (T7)	Rita's Digest
Spike Shannon	*Ol' Abner Doubleday Has Done It Again*	Funny Bones
W. Sharples	"Take Me Out to the Ball Game"	
Ann Sheridan	*Shine On Harvest Moon*	
Eric Show	"Take Me Out to the Ball Game" (two versions)	
Carly Simon	*Baseball, a Film by Ken Burns* (T29)	Elektra
Frank Sinatra	*MGM Sing-A-Longs*	MGM
Frank Sinatra with Doris Day	*The Radio Duets* (T8)	Digital Dejavu
Frank Sinatra and Gene Kelly, etc.	*Take Me Out to the Ball Game*	Curtain Calls
Sinatra Yankee Announcers	*N.Y. Memories, May 1, 2002*	Yankees

CATALOG NUMBER	FORMAT (INCHES/RPM)	TIME (MINUTES)	YEAR	NOTES
	CD and cassette	1:07	1994	Trumpet solo
MCA-10040	12"/33	2:03		
	CD	2:10	2005	
CCD-4520	CD	4:48	1992	
471	7"/78			
	5"/78			
45-471 A	7"/45			Picture sleeve
45-520	7"/45			Picture sleeve
LP 3009	12"/33			
R220286-1-A	12"/33			
CAL-1079	12"/33			
AZ99961	12"/33		1972	
33-5918	12"/33			
S107A	7"/78			Picture sleeve, black and yellow vinyl
BR 25A	10"/78			Picture sleeve, yellow vinyl
	CD			
Z 6675	CD	2:43		
710-025582-1	12"/33			
4746	10"/78			
1735	10"/78		1938	
MG-12062	12"/33			
SV-0276	CD	2:44		
MMCD-101	CD			
KMOX-2128	7"/45			
	CD	1:05	2007	
	12"/33			
JBR-50472	CD			
	12"/33			
	12"/33			
CX 145	12"/33			Stereo and mono
	CD	1:09		
	Cassette		1999	Yiddish
CD 80468	CD		1998	
	CD and Cassette	1:34	1994	Piano solo
4368	10"/78			
A14563	10"/78			
	Cassette			Studio production, not for sale
	CD			
	CD	2:43	2005	
	7"/45			
	Tape			
	VHS			two versions
	VHS			TV broadcast
	CD and cassette	2:52	1994	
	VHS			
5-131-2	CD	2:12		
	12"/33			Movie sound track
	CD			

ARTIST	TITLE ALBUM (S = SIDE/ D= DISC/ T = TRACK)	LABEL
The Six Fat Dutchmen	*Old Time Waltzes* (S1/T5)	Dot
Skater's Band	"Take Me Out to the Ball Game"	His Majesty's Voice
Skeletons	*The Skeletons in the Flesh* (S2/T6)	The Next Big Thing
Skeletons	*The Skeletons in the Flesh* (T11)	ESD
Willie Smith	*Willie the Lion Smith Live at Blues Alley* (S1/T7)	Halcyon
Wilbur Snapp	"Take Me Out to the Ball Game"	
Bruce Springsteen	*Take Me Out to the Ball Game* (S1/T2)	
Bruce Springstone	*Live at Bedrock* (S1)	Clean Cuts
Bruce Springstone	"Take Me Out to the Ball Game"	Clean Cuts
Bruce Springstone	"Take Me Out to the Ball Game"	Quality
Standard Program Library Themes 2	"Take Me Out to the Ball Game"	Standard Program Library
Standard Sound Effect 404B	"Take Me Out to the Ball Game"	Standard Sound Effect
Cal Stanley	"Take Me Out to the Ball Game"	Victor
Cal Stanley	"Take Me Out to the Ball Game"	Zonophone
F. Stanley	"Take Me Out to the Ball Game"	Oxford
Stay-Up Lates	*Sing Along with the Stay-Up Lates* (SB/T2)	Valiant
Don Sternberg	*About Time* (T/7)	Blue Night Records
Bob Stevens	"Take Me Out to the Ball Game"	Erro
Curtis Stigers	*I Think It's Going to Rain Today* (T12)	Concord
Noel Paul Stookey	*Something New and Fresh* (SB/T5)	M7
Noel Paul Stookey	*Something New and Fresh* (T4)	Sparrow
Jere Stormer	*Lingo* (T1)	
Stubby and His Buccaneers	*Bogle to Boogle to Boone*	Decca
Sweet Toothers	*Those Were the Days* (S1/T3)	Diplomat
Talking Machine	*The Naughty 90's*	Bee and R Goman
Tenor Solo	"Take Me Out to the Ball Game"	Columbia
Tenor Solo	"Take Me Out to the Ball Game"	Standard Disc
Tenor Solo	"Take Me Out to the Ball Game"	Standard Disc Record
Tenor Solo	"Take Me Out to the Ball Game"	Standard Disc
Tenor Solo	"Take Me Out to the Ball Game"	Star
Stradivari Strings	*3 Waltzes: Music in Three-Quarter Time* (S1/T5)	Spinorama
Tiger Stadium Organist		
Tiny Tim	*I Love Me* (T8)	Lumberjack/Mordam Music
Cal Tjader and Don Elliott	*Cal Tjader and Don Elliot*	Savoy
Toadstruck Symphony	*Toadstruck Symphony* (T6)	Toadstruck Symphony
Toadstruck Symphony	*Toadstruck Symphony* (T7)	Toadstruck Symphony
Danny Topaz	*What Are We Waiting For*	Zapot
Shay Torrent	*Angels*	Walt Disney
Shay Torrent	*Centerfield Serenade* (SA/T4)	Do Re Mi
Shay Torrent	*Organ Fantasies in HiFi* (SB/T6)	Mercury
Shay Torrent,	"Take Me Out to the Ball Game"	Vista
Helen Traubel	"Take Me Out to the Ball Game"	RCA Victor
Treehouse Trolls	*The Treehouse Trolls–The Forest of Fun and Wonder*	Good Times Video
Bobby Troup	*Stars of Jazz* (S2/T1)	Bobby Troup
Bobby Troup	*The Navy Swings, #37*	Programs, Inc.
Twin Sisters	*Addition* (T1)	Twin Sisters Production
Twisters	*Doin' the Twist* (SA/T6)	Treasure
United We Sing Chorus	"Take Me Out to the Ball Game"	National

CATALOG NUMBER	FORMAT (INCHES/RPM)	TIME (MINUTES)	YEAR	NOTES
DPL 3599	12"/33	1:50		
S213	12"/78			British
NBT 3302	12"/33			
	CD		1991	
HAL 104	12"/33			
	Cassette			Private recording
	CD			Bootleg (September 6, 2003), Fenway Concert
CC 1202	12"/45	2:40	1982	Also appears on Baseballs Greatest Hit LP
CC 902	7"/45		1982	Picture sleeve
Q2425	7"/45	2:40	1982	Picture sleeve
	16"/33			
97408	10"/78			Four versions
16288	10"/78			
5848	10"/78			
1185	10"/78			
V-4906	12"/33			Blue label and purple label
	CD	4:22	2000	
J90W3159	7"/45	2:08		
	CD	4:03		
MLF-133	12"/33		1976	
NWS 090376	12"/33		1978	
	CD	0:45		
46315	10"/78			
DS-2463	12"/33			
	12"/33			
33292	Cylinder			Two minutes
3917	10"/78			Large hole
3917	10"/78			Large hole, green label/black label/one side
A536	5"/78			Large hole
12	10"/78			
M85A	12"/33			
	VHS		1999	Fan's recording
	CD		1995	
	12"/33		1956	
	CD	1:21	2004	
	CD	2:05	2004	
Z101A	7"/45			Integrated into song
603920	Cassette	1:09	1998	Recorded May 9, 1966
33232-5	12"/33	1:15		
MG 20135	12"/33			Australia
F-451	7"/45	1:08		
49-3790	10"/78			
6326	VHS			
LP 1959	12"/33			
	16"/33			
TW143CD	CD		2001	
TLP 890	12"/33			
	10"/78		1942	

ARTIST	TITLE ALBUM (S = SIDE/ D= DISC/ T = TRACK)	LABEL
Unknown	*25 Organ Favorites* (T25)	TDP
Unknown	*30 Fun Hits*	Alshire Int.
Unknown	*30 Fun Hits to Get the Party Started*	Somerset
Unknown	*50 All-Time Kiddie Records*	Playhour
Unknown	*97 Giants* (2 diff.) (Japanese)	
Unknown	*101 Favorite Children's Songs* (S3/T16)	Special Music
Unknown	*150 All-Time Sing Along Favorites* (Tape 2/SB/T6)	Reader's Digest
Unknown	*1939 Baseball Hoff Games and Introduction*	NBHF
Unknown	*Adventures in Music* (T9)	
Unknown	*All-Time Children's Hits* (S2/T3)	Peter Pan
Unknown	*All-Time Children's Hits, 10 Happy Sing-Along Songs for Boys and Girls*	Peter Pan
Unknown	*All Time Favorites, Vol. 1, Sing Along*	Peter Pan
Unknown	*American Idol TV Commercial*	
Unknown	*Baby Genius—Favorite Children's Songs*	Muze Inc.
Unknown	*Baseball Centennial*	
Unknown	*Beer Drinkin' Sing Alongs* (S1/T2)	Oscar
Unknown	*Best of Sing-A-Long* (T4)	Direct Source
Unknown	*Birthday Songs* (T4)	St. Clair
Unknown	*A Century of Baseball Songs* (T1)	CC Entertainment
Unknown	*A Century of Baseball Songs* (T15)	CC Entertainment
Unknown	*Children's Favorite Songs, Vol. 1* (T12)	Walt Disney Records
Unknown	*Coors Light Commercial*	
Unknown	*Diamond Jubilee, 75 Years of Great American Music* (SB/T1)	Hifidelity
Unknown	*Disney's Children's Favorites, Vol. 1* (S1/T12)	Walt Disney Records
Unknown	*Disney Children's Favorites, Vol. 1* (S1)	Walt Disney Productions
Unknown	*Disney Sing-A-Long Songs, 101 Dalmatians*	Disney Home Video
Unknown	*Disney Take a Song Along* (T7)	Walt Disney Records
Unknown	*Down Memory Lane* (Program 3)	Reader's Digest
Unknown	*Down Memory Lane* (S2/T3)	Reader's Digest
Unknown	*ESPN's Hustle" Sound Track*	Natalie Music
Unknown	*Gay 90's* (SA/T2)	Waldorf
Unknown	*Give My Regards to Broadway*	TDP
Unknown	*The Glory of Their Times*	Sonic
Unknown	*Great American Music* (S2/T3)	Spin-O-Rama
Unknown	*Happy Honky Tonk!* (S2/T3)	Pickwick
Unknown	*Jell-O No Bake Cookies and Cream*	
Unknown	*Kiddie Pop Parade*	Happy Time
Unknown	*Kidsongs* (S1/T8)	TAP
Unknown	*Kidsongs "A Day at MacDonald's Farm"*	Warner Bros.
Unknown	*Kids Silly Song Sing A Long*	Wonder Workshop
Unknown	*Kid Toons Sing Along Songs*	Good Times Home Video
Unknown	*Laser Karaoke Video Sing Along,* Vol. 14	Pioneer
Unknown	*The Leo Lassan Story*	Baseball Record Company
Unknown	*Max Fleisher's Cartoon Capers,* Vol. 2, *Somewhere in Dreamland*	Buena Vista
Unknown	*Mets Greatest Hits* (T21)	
Unknown	*MGM Sing-A-Longs*	MGM
Unknown	*Mickey Sports Songs*	Disney
Unknown	*Mini Victrola Record*	

CATALOG NUMBER	FORMAT (INCHES/RPM)	TIME (MINUTES)	YEAR	NOTES
2516	CD			
	12"/33			
SF 35-2A	12"/33			
TB-47B	7"/45			Box set
	Cassette			
	CD and cassette			
	Tape			
	CD			
	CD	3:34		
8138	12"/33			
	12"/33			
	Cassette			
	CD			TV commercial sound track
	DVD		2007	
DiDX043695	CD		1996	Band, 1939 inductions
OS-130	12"/33			
	CD	1:13		
	CD		2004	
4031-27	CD	1:07	1989	
4031-27	CD	3:36	1989	Instrumental
	CD			
	CD	0:32	August 31, 2004	Parody, two versions
SRM-75	12"/33			
2505	12"/33			
2505	Cassette			
	VHS			
	CD		2004	
RD5 0401/1	8-track			
	12"/33			
	CD			
MHK33-1203	12"/33			
	CD			
K-441	12"/33		1966	Three versions
	12"/33			
SPC-3371	12"/33	2:45		
	VHS			TV commercial, not for sale
HT-1014	12"/33			
6-38235	Laser disc			
	VHS			
WW 41273	Cassette			Canadian
	VHS			
WKST 014A	Laser Disc			
	12"/33		1976	Spoken word, background intro
	VHS			
	CD			Background to '62 opening-day lineup
	VHS			
	Tape			
	2"			

ARTIST	TITLE ALBUM (S = SIDE/ D= DISC/ T = TRACK)	LABEL
Unknown	*Music for Special Occasions* (T6)	MCR Productions
Unknown	*Music from Mary Poppins and Other Children's Film Favorites* (SB/T1)	Twinkle
Unknown	*Music from Walt Disney's Mary Poppins and Others* (S2/T1)	Twinkle
Unknown	*A Musical Portrait of America the Beautiful*	Reader's Digest
Unknown	*Name That Tune* (S2)	Milton Bradley
Unknown	*Nashville Fiddles*	King
Unknown	*Nelvana Presents Animated Ink, Vol. 2*	
Unknown	*Nike TV Commercial*	
Unknown	*Organ Favorites* (SB/T13)	TDP
Unknown	*Play Ball* (T1)	Network
Unknown	*Play Ball* (T9)	Network
Unknown	*Preschool Sign Language*	Cerfor Media
Unknown	*Raggedy Ann and Andy* (D3 T4)	
Unknown	*The Red Skelton Radio Show*	
Unknown	*River Bank Razzmatazz*	Melody Music
Unknown	*Sights and Sounds of Ohio* (S1/T5)	
Unknown	*Silly Songs*	Madacy
Unknown	*Simply the Best Kids Songs* (D2/T4)	Direct Source
Unknown	*Sing Along Fun for the Entire Family*	Parade
Unknown	*Sing Along with the Blenders* (S2/T5C)	Modern
Unknown	*Sing Along with the Gang at McGoo's* (SA/T2)	Tops
Unknown	*Sing Along with the Grasshoppers*	Diplomat
Unknown	*Sing-A-Long with Lil' Lulu*	Dan Dalton Productions
Unknown	*Sing Along with Lil' Lulu*	Simitar
Unknown	*Sing with Tenneco* (S1/T5C)	RCA Victor
Unknown	*Soft Karaoke Lite*	Eatsleepmusic.com
Unknown	*Song Parodies*	Chevrolet
Unknown	*Songs for Children*	Golden Records
Unknown	*Songs 4 Kids on the Go*	
Unknown	*Songs to Remember*	Castle Films
Unknown	*The Songs that Went to War, V-Disc*	Warner
Unknown	"Take Me Out to the Ball Game" (S9/T1)	Children's Treasury of Record Favorites
Unknown	"Take Me Out to the Ball Game"	LL Cook Co.
Unknown	"Take Me Out to the Ball Game"	Skatin' Tunes
Unknown	"Take Me Out to the Ball Game"	Musical Postcard Company
Unknown	"Take Me Out to the Ball Game"	Natalie Music
Unknown	"Take Me Out to the Ball Game"	Puff the Magic Dragon
Unknown	"Take Me Out to the Ball Game"	Shann
Unknown	"Take Me Out to the Ball Game"	Wemp
Unknown	"Take Me Out to the Ball Game"	
Unknown	"Take Me Out to the Ball Game"	
Unknown	"Take Me Out to the Ball Game"	
Unknown	"Take Me Out to the Ball Game"	
Unknown	"Take Me Out to the Ball Game"	Valor
Unknown	"Take Me Out to the Ball Game"	Russell
Unknown	"Take Me Out to the Ball Game"	Valor
Unknown	*Themes 2* (T5)	Standard
Unknown	*Those Were the Days*	Diplomat

CATALOG NUMBER	FORMAT (INCHES/RPM)	TIME (MINUTES)	YEAR	NOTES
	CD	1:23	1990	
TW-31	12"/33			
TW-31	12"/33			
RK5B-004-GW1	VHS			
33				Record in tabletop game
	CD			
961922	VHS		1980	Cartoon background music, three versions
	VHS			Recorded from TV
TDP-11	12"/33		1978	
FAV-1	CD		1997	Additional lyrics by W. Nelson
FAV-1	CD		1997	
	VHS			
	CD			
	cassette		June 3, 1951	Program title and opening
	12"/ 33			
	12"/33			Ballpark recording
	Cassette			
	CD		2001	
	VHS			
M7016	12"/33			Stereo and mono
1729	12"/33			
	12"/33			
	VHS		1991	
	VHS			
M70P-4428	12"/33			
	CD			
	10"/33			Parody
	12"/33			
	CD			
	16 mm			
	CD			
66618-5	7"/45			
JM 132	Postcard (7" x 9")			Milwaukee County Stadium
3061	10"/78			
408	Postcard (6" x 9")			Cartoon player hitting
	CD			
S554B	7"/45			
813-A	7"/45	1:40, 1:17		Two versions
	10"/78			Private label
	CD			Private, Hawaiian style
	CD			Cingular commercial
	2", mini Victrola			
	Postcard (5 3/8"x 3 3/8")			Baseball Hall of Fame
1500	10"/78			
162-A	10"/33	1:43, 0:50		Two versions; Watzclog
1500-A	10"/78			
SRR-2319	16"/33	0:46		
	12"/33			

ARTIST	TITLE ALBUM (S = SIDE/ D= DISC/ T = TRACK)	LABEL
Unknown	*Toddler Sing Alongs* (D3/T8)	St. Clair
Unknown	*Tonka Playtime Tunes* (S2/T14)	
Unknown	*Tonka Play Time Tunes* (D2/T29)	Hasbro
Unknown	*Top TV Themes* (SB/T2)	Vicking
Unknown	*Video Sing Along*, Vol. 2, *Children's*	Pioneer
Unknown	*Yellow Submarine* (SA/T6)	Happy Time
Unknown	*Your Most Requested Songs* (SA/T2)	Aim
Unknown	*Walk to the Beat*	Jamb Productions
Valentine's Day Mob	*Golden 20's*	Power Apple Honey Series
Valentino Production Music	*Specialty*, Vol. 10 (T21)	Valentino Production
Valentino Production Music	*Specialty*, Vol. 10 (T22)	Valentino Production
Eddie Vedder	"Take Me Out to the Ball Game" and Cubs Fans	
Vernon Alley Quartet	*Freedom's Front Door* (T9)	2006 Soundies
Larry Vincent	"Take Me Out to the Ball Game"	Pearl
Larry Vincent	"Take Me Out to the Ball Game"	Pearl
Albert Von Tilzer	*Cavalcade of American Music* (S1/T3)	Ariel
Albert Von Tilzer	*New Medley*	
Donald Voorhees	*Armed Forces Radio Service*	War and Navy
Steve Vozzolo	*I Love Baseball* (T13)	Vozzman
Suzyn Waldman	"Take Me Out to the Ball Game"	
Suzyn Waldman	Take Me Out to Old Fenway	Fenway Productions
Walt Disney Productions	*A Musical Souvenir of "America on Parade"* (S2/T5)	Disney
Art Walunus	"Take Me Out to the Ball Game"	AW
Washington Senators	*Legend to Legend, Bob Wolf Interviews*	National Baseball Hall of Fame
Doc Watson	*Doc and Merle Watson's Guitar Album* (S2/T6)	Aural Tradition
Doc and Merle Watson	*Doc and Merle Watson's Guitar Album* (T11)	Flying Fish
David Weiss	"Take Me Out to the Ball Game	
We Kids Rock	*Everybody Clap Your Hands* (T18)	We Kids Rock
Wellstood, Dick	*Ragtime Piano Favorites* (T15)	Special Music
Joe West	*Blue Cowboy* (S1/T5)	Colonial
Joe West	*Blue Cowboy* (T4)	
Wheaties	"Take Me Out to the Ball Game	Wheaties
Wheaties	"Take Me Out to the Ball Game"	Wheaties
Kenny White	*Sounds of Nashville Baseball Souvenir* (S1/T1)	Hilltop House
Wiggleworms	*Wiggleworms Love You* (T19)	Old Town School Recordings
Kathy Williams	*Crocodiles and Rainbows* (T8)	Kassandra Music Co.
George Winston	*Diamond Cuts–Turning Two* (T6)	Hungry for Music
Wittnauer Choraliers	*An Album of Memories*, Vol. 3	Longines
Floyd Woodhull	*Floyd Woodhull's Favorite Squares* (SB/T2)	Folk Kraft
O. Woodhull	"Take Me Out to the Ball Game"	RCA Victor
Woodhull's Old Tyme Masters	Vol. 2 Woodhull's Old Tyme Masters Plays Square Dances	RCA Victor
George Wright	*Encores*, Vol. 2 (S1/T6)	HiFi
George Wright	*Sherwood Presents the Sound and the City* (S2/T6)	Mark 56
George Wright	"Take Me Out to the Ball Game"	King
Ben Yost	*Let's All Sing Along*	Varsity
Young American All-Stars	*Our America* (T11)	Medalist
Frank Zappa	*You Can't Do That On Stage Anymore*, Vol. 4 (T14)	Ryko

CATALOG NUMBER	FORMAT (INCHES/RPM)	TIME (MINUTES)	YEAR	NOTES
	CD		2005	
	CD			
	CD			
VK 625-B	12",/3			
	VHS			Two versions, with words and without
HT-1044	12"/33			
01024C	12"/33			
SM 4254	Cassette		1987	
DS 414	12"/33			
	CD	0:36	1987	
	CD	0:38	1987	
	VHS			Recorded at Cubs game
	CD	2:31	2006	
1235	7"/45			
1235	10"/78			
CAM 11	12"/33		1982	
	CD			
SSL-1034	16"/33	2:17		
	CD		1994	
	Tape			
	Cassette		1987	Parody
	12"/33		1975	Picture disc
AW 452B	7"/45	2:12		
	DVD		2006	Traditional and rewrite versions
ATR105	12"/33	2:13		Also appears on Baseball's Greatest Hits LP
FF 70301	CD	2:13	1983	
				Private recording
	CD	1:26	2007	
SCD-4528	CD	1:58	1987	
SCLP 1177	12"/33	2:54		
MLUMP	CD	2:54		
	5"/78			Paper cutout from box
GM 68	7"/78			Red and green vinyl
CP 5550	12"/33			
	CD	1:14	2005	
	CD	1:49	2005	
	CD	5:22	1998	
P41806	10"/78			Box set
LP-7B	12"/33			Square dance
28-0439	10"/78			
480156	7"/45			Square dance box set
R 711	12"/33			
561-B	12"/33			
15039-AA	10"/78	2:30		
	10"/33			
60045-2	CD			
RCD 10088	CD	3:02	1991	

NOTES

UNSUNG HEROES

1. Sharon Fay Koch, "Composers' Musical Legacies," *Los Angeles Times*, June 8, 1971.

2. Clyde Snyder, "Lagunan Still Thrills to Baseball Anthem," *Los Angeles Times*, April 13, 1958, OC1.

3. *National Cyclopedia of American Biography*, "Jack Norworth (John Godfrey Knauff)," 391–92.

4. "Jack Norworth, Song Writer, Dies," *The New York Times*, September 2, 1959, 29.

5. Georgene O'Donnell, *Miniaturia: The World of Tiny Things*, (Chicago: Lightner Publishing Company, 1943).

6. "Jack Norworth, Song Writer, Dies."

7. Allen G. Debus, "Celebrity Corner: The Records of Jack Norworth," *Hobbies–The Magazine for Collectors* (September 1957).

8. Mid-Week Theatre Notes, *Brooklyn Daily Eagle*, April 13, 1899, 11.

9. "Albert Von Tilzer Is Dead at 78; Wrote 'Take Me Out to the Ball Game.'" *The New York Times*, October 2, 1956, 35.

10. Ibid.

11. "Harry Von Tilzer," entry on www.parlorsongs.com.

12. "ASCAP Issue of Variety Music 7-31-1940," Harry Von Tilzer file, NYPL for the Performing Arts

13. Allen G. Debus, liner notes to *Nora Bayes and Jack Norworth: Together…and Alone*, Archaophone Records 5007, 2004.

14. "Jack Norworth, Song Writer, Dies."

15. "Nora Bayes Gets Divorce Decree," *Chicago Daily Tribune*, February 23, 1913, 1.

16. Allen G. Debus, liner notes to *Nora Bayes and Jack Norworth: Together . . . and Alone*, citing *Washington Post* of September 6, 1910.

17. Ibid.

18. Ibid.

19. Small notice in scrapbook copied by Bob Thompson at NYPL.

20. "An Afternoon with Nora and Jack Norworth," *Chicago Daily Tribune*, October 2, 1910, B4.

21. "Nora Bayes' Death Ends Great Stage, Marriage Career," *The Washington Post*, March 20, 1928, 3.

22. Debus, liner notes.

23. *National Cyclopedia of American Biography*, 391–92.

24. Debus, liner notes.

25. "Tongue Twisters Found in Odd Sources Snare Unwary," *The Washington Post*, August 29, 1915, A8.

26. www.musicals101.com/bwaypast3b.htm.

27. "Norworth to Be Honored," unsourced clipping, Jack Norworth file, National Baseball Hall of Fame and Museum, June 20, 1940.

28. Oscar Ruhl, From the Ruhl Book, *The Sporting News*, August 15, 1951, 12.

29. "Stars and Suds Open Baseball Race Today," *Los Angeles Times*, April 8, 1944. A6.

30. "Jam Session Thrills 6000" *Los Angeles Times*, January 31, 1944.

31. Photo provided by Gene Felder of Laguna Beach.

32. Snyder, "Lagunan Still Thrills to Baseball Anthem."

33. "Jack Norworth, Song Writer, Dies."

34. "Take Me Out to the Ball Game Day and 2 Awards for Composer Norworth," *The Sporting News*, July 16, 1958, 41.

35. "Jack Norworth Services Set for Tomorrow," *South Coast News*, September 4, 1959; John Weld, Our Town, *Laguna Beach Post*, September 3, 1959.

HIT OR MYTH?

1. John P Carmichael, The Barber Shop, *The Sporting News*, September 9, 1959, 35.

2. *Smithsonian* 35, no. (April 2004): 47–48.

3. *The Sporting News*, September 9, 1959, 35.

4. Ibid.

5. Bob Addie, *The Washington Post*, April 17, 1960.

6. Ibid.

LONG-DISTANCE DEDICATION

1. "Elks Benefit a Success," *Chicago Daily Tribune*, March 25, 1907, 17.

2. "Notes of the White Sox Game," *Chicago Daily Tribune*, May 9, 1907, 6.

3. "New Incorporations," *Chicago Daily Tribune*, May 12, 1907, 11.

4. "Ald. Badenoch, Pedestrian," *Chicago Daily Tribune*, December 4, 1907, 1.

5. "New Incorporations," *Chicago Daily Tribune*, May 26, 1911, pg. 17

A MAGIC LANTERN RIDE

1. "1909 in Music," Wikipedia, http://en.wikipedia.org/wiki/1909_in_music.

CHART TOPPERS

1. Joel Whitburn, *Joel Whitburn's Pop Memories, 1890–1954: The History of American Popular Music: Compiled from America's Popular Music Charts, 1890–1954* (Menomonee Falls, WI: Record Research, 1986).

2. It was later corrected in the Victor catalog that Billy Murray was never on this recording!

BASEBALL IN 1908

1. From a 1925 interview in the *New York Sun*, used as an epigram in *Deadball Stars of the National League*," ed. Tom Simon, (Dulles, VA: Brassey's Inc., 2004).

2. Paul Dickson, *Baseball's Greatest Quotations*, (New York: Edward Burlingame Books/Harper Collins, 1991), 378.

3. Cait Murphy, *Crazy '08*, (New York: Smithsonian Books/Harper Collins, 2007), 182.

4. John Snyder, ed., *Cubs Journal*, (Cincinnati: Emmis Books, 2005), 146.

5. Ibid., 147.

6. Trey Strecker, "Fred Merkle," in *Deadball Stars of the National League*, 61.

7. Snyder, *Cubs Journal*, 147.

TINKERING WITH MUSIC

1. "Evers-Tinker," *The Sporting Life*, November 7, 1908.

A BIT OF A STRETCH

1. "Wolter's Home Run Wins for Yankees," *The New York Times*, April 17, 1910, S1.

2. Dennis D'Agostino, "100 years Old and Stretching," The Associated Press, June 18, 1982.

3. *The Sporting Life*, July 22, 1883, 7.

4. Greg Rhodes and John Erardi, *The First Boys of Summer*, (Cincinnati: Road West Publishing Company, 1994),70.

5. Ibid.

6. Bruce Anderson, "A Pause That Refreshes," *Sports Illustrated*, April 16, 1990.

THE MOVIE WE NEVER SAW

1. Remarks by Dr. Kathryn Fuller-Seeley at New York State Historical Association, September 9, 2007.

2. H. Kent Webster, "Little Stories of Great Films," *The Nickelodeon*, August 1, 1910, 61–62.

3. David Kiehn, *Broncho Billy and the Essanay Film Company*,(Berkeley, CA: Farwell Books, 2003).

DAME YANKEES

1. Jean Hastings Ardell, *Breaking into Baseball: Women and the National Pastime*, (Carbondale, IL: Southern Illinois University Press, 2005), 35.

2. Ibid., 20.

3. Carol DeMare, "President Sought Escape at Ballpark," undated clipping, *Albany (NY) Times Union*, Women in Baseball–Women's Suffrage file, National

Baseball Hall of Fame Library, Cooperstown, NY.

4. Undated letter to Giants' President Horace Stoneham, from Bob Ahearn of the Sports Research Institute. Women in Baseball–Women's Suffrage" file, National Baseball Hall of Fame Library.

5. "Suffragette Day," unsourced newspaper clipping, June 26, 1915, Women in Baseball–Women's Suffrage file, National Baseball Hall of Fame Library.

6. Henry Chadwick, "Ladies at Base Ball Matches," editorial,, *The American Chronicle of Sports and Pastimes*, New York, May 28, 1868, 172.

7. Jonathan Fraser Light, "Ladies Day," *The Cultural Encyclopedia of Baseball*, (Jefferson, NC: McFarland, 1997).

8. Women in Baseball––Ladies Day file, National Baseball Hall of Fame Library.

9. Women in Baseball–Bloomer Girls file, National Baseball Hall of Fame Library.

10. Kathleen Birck, "Alta Weiss," in *Encyclopedia of Women and Baseball*, ed. Leslie A. Heaphy and Mel Anthony May (Jefferson, NC: McFarland, 2006).

HARRY GOES ELECTRIC

1. Tim Wiles, "Music of the Sphere," in *Baseball as America,* (Washington, D.C.; National Geographic, 2002), 133.

TIME LINE

1. Jonathan Fraser Light, "Seventh-Inning Stretch," *The Cultural Encyclopedia of Baseball* (Jefferson, NC: McFarland, 1997), 662.

2. *Los Angeles Times*, September 2, 1932.

3. *Detroit News*, October 6, 1935.

4. *Los Angeles Times*, March 27, 1934.

5. *The New York Times*, April 15, 1934.

6. *Los Angeles Times*, May 12, 1934.

7. *Los Angeles Times*, Oct 7, 1934.

8. *Chicago Tribune*, February 21, 1935.

9. *Los Angeles Times*, March 30, 1935.

10. *Los Angeles Times*, November 6, 1935.

11. *The Washington Post*, March 1, 1936.

12. *Chicago Tribune*, June 10, 1936.

13. *Chicago Tribune*, March 4, 1936.

14. *Los Angeles Times*, Aug 29, 1936.

15. *Los Angeles Times*, November 3, 1936.

16. Bob White, "Singers are No Prima Donnas," *Los Angeles Times*, March 14, 1937.

17. Charles B. Driscoll, "Pages from a Journalist's Diary," *The Washington Post*, January 1, 1939.

18. Orrin E. Dunlap Jr., "Batter Up! Baseball Telecast Seen in a Dark Room on a Sunny Afternoon in May," *The New York Times*, May 21, 1939.

19. *The New York Times*, June 13, 1939.

20. *The New York Times*, October 7, 1939.

21. *The New York Times*, July 16, 1940.

22. "Norworth to Be Honored," *The Sporting News*, June 20, 1940.

23. "Author of Game's Song Not Present Until 1940," *The Sporting News*, April 27, 1944.

24. *Chicago Tribune*, November 22, 1941.

25. "Jam Session Thrills 6,000," *Los Angeles Times*, January 31, 1944.

26. "Author of Game's Song Not Present Until 1940."

27. "Stars and Suds Open Baseball Race Today," *Los Angeles Times*, April 8, 1944, A6.

28. In the Wake of the News, *Chicago Tribune*, June 1, 1945.

29. Waldemar Kaempffert, "Science in Review," *The New York Times*, June 18, 1950.

30. Milton Bracker, "Music Is Loser as 2,426 Flail Muse in Weird Ebbets Field Cacophony," New York Times, August 14, 1951.

31. Clyde Snyder, "Lagunan Still Thrills to Baseball's Anthem," *Los Angeles Times*, April 13, 1958.

32. John Crosby, "Who Is This Abe Burrows?," *The Washington Post*, October 3, 1952, 49.

33. *The Sporting News*, February 18, 1953, and February 26, 1958.

34. Jeane Hoffman, "'Batter Up,' Stars' New Baseball Anthem, Won Over 1,000 Entries," *Los Angeles Times*, July 27, 1954.

35. "Albert Von Tilzer Is Dead at 78, Wrote 'Take Me Out

to the Ball Game," *The New York Times*, October 2, 1956, 35; "Von Tilzer Dies at 78; Wrote Ball Game Song," *Los Angeles Times*, October 2, 1956, B3; "Von Tilzer Rites Today," *Los Angeles Times*, October 3, 1956, B9.

36. *The Sporting News*, March 16, 1958.

37. "Previews of Today's TV," *Chicago Tribune*, April 13, 1958, 16.

38. *Los Angeles Times*, April 13, 1959.

39. "Jack Norworth, Famed Song Composer, Dies," *Los Angeles Times*, September 2, 1959, and "Jack Norworth, Song Writer, Dies," New York Times, September 2, 1959.

40. Mae Newman, "Credit Shared," *Los Angeles Times*, October 3, 1959.

41. Vogel press release, July 6, 1968, "Take Me Out to the Ball Game" file, National Baseball Hall of Fame Library, Cooperstown, NY.

42. "Curvy Hawaiian Hula Dancers Prove Big Hit at Dodger Stadium," *Major League Baseball News*, August 15, 1968.

43. Sharon Fay Koch, "Composers' Musical Legacies," *Los Angeles Times*, June 8, 1971.

44. "Rangers Change Tunes," *The Sporting News*, August 16, 1975.

45. John Schulian, *The Washington Post*, July 25, 1976.

46. "A Record Not to Be Missed," *Chicago Tribune*, September. 27, 1976, A1.

47. Bill Jauss, "Veeck Springs to Sox Neighborhood's Defense," *Chicago Tribune*, July 1, 1977.

48. C. C. Johnson Spink (editor and publisher of *The Sporting News*), editorial, *The Sporting News*, August 19, 1978.

49. Alfred E. Clark, "Larry Vogel, Longtime Publisher of Popular Music, Is Dead at 84," *The New York Times*, June 9, 1980.

50. George Vecsey, "The New Sounds of Music at Shea Stadium," *The New York Times*, June 30, 1980.

51. Bob Verdi, "Unsigned Caray Bit Itchy in Eden," *Chicago Tribune*, Jan 20, 1981.

52. David Margolick, "Arrested Yankee Fans Persist in Suit,' *The New York Times*, April 9, 1984.

53. "Caray, Hamilton Still Voicing Their Differences," *Los Angeles Times*, Sep 8, 1985.

54. Unsourced clipping, June 27, 1988, "Take Me Out to the Ball Game" file, National Baseball Hall of Fame Library.

55. George Vecsey, "The Giant Who Hired a Midget," Sports of the Times, *The New York Times*, February 28, 1991, D23.

56. Eleanor Blau, "P.D. Q. Bach Says Goodbye, But It's a Come-On," *The New York Times*, December 24, 1991, C9.

57. Michael Martinez, "The Fans Fill Candlestick, Not Sure If This Is Goodbye," *The New York Times*, September 28, 1992, C8.

58. Kirk Johnson, "Debating the Merits of Debate," *The New York Times*, October 4, 1992.

59. Joseph Skrec, "Baseball Gives Song Its Place in Documentary," 1994 (exact date and source unknown).

60. Jennifer Frey, "Gooden Goal: More Changeups, Less Pain," *The New York Times*, April 4, 1994, C9.

61. "Take Me Out to the Ball Game," *The News Tribune*, September 11, 1994.

62. Richard Sandomir, "Hits, Runs, and Memories," *The New York Times*, September 18, 1994.

63. Tom Pedulla, "Classic Baseball Tune Takes a Rap," *USA Today*, May 12, 1996; Richard Sandomir, "Baseball's Marketing Plan: Take an Old Familiar Score and Energize It With Some Cool and Soul," *The New York Times*, May 2, 1996, D8; and Claire Smith, "An Old Game Finally Gets New Beat," *The New York Times*, May 2, 1996. B13.

64. "Frito Lay to Buy Cracker Jack From Borden," *The New York Times*, October 9, 1997, D4.

65. Chuck Slater, "For Baseball Fans, Time on Their Side," *The New York Times*, August 6, 2000, WE3.

66. Jamie Allen, "Songs of the Century List: The Debate Goes On," CNN.com, March 8, 2001, and Andy Knobel, "If This Song Didn't Win, It's a Shame," *Baltimore Sun*, August 12, 2001.

67. Ira Berkow, "Eager to See the Return of Peanuts," *The New York Times*, October 11, 2001, S4.

68. William C. Rhoden, "Yankees' Seventh-Inning Stretch Shouldn't Be So Stretched Out," *The New York Times*, October 4, 2003, D3.

69. *Palatka (FL) Daily News*, May 18, 2007.

CAN PIGEONS CARRY A TUNE?

1. "Pigeons and People," *Time*, June 19, 1950.
2. Waldemar Kaempffert, "Science in Review: Harvard Pigeons Play Tunes and Ping-Pong, Match Colors and Count Off Seconds," *The New York Times*, June 18, 1950, E9.

WEDDINGS, FUNERALS, AND LL COOL J

1. Jay Posner, *The San Diego Union Tribune*, July 16, 2007.
2. Gay Talese, *The New York Times*, October 7, 1956.
3. "Baseball: The Music of Baseball," www.pbs.org/kenburns/baseball/about/music.html.
4. Clive Hirschhorn, *Gene Kelly* (Chicago: Regnery, 1974), 25.
5. Warren G. Harris, *Lucy and Desi* (New York: Simon and Schuster, 1991), 190.
6. John P. Carmichael, *The Sporting News*, September 9, 1959, 35.

SHOW ME THE MONEY

1. Statistics graciously provided by Jim Steinblatt, director of public relations, at ASCAP.

THE TIMES THEY ARE A-CHANGIN'

1. Murray Chass, "Old Ball Game Rocks to New Tune 'For Now Time,'" *The New York Times*, August 24, 1969.
2. Jeane Hoffman, "Pasadenian Takes Prize," *Los Angeles Times*, July 27, 1954, C2.

GOING, GOING, GONE...

1. Jonathan Fraser Light, "Organs/Organists," *The Cultural Encyclopedia of Baseball*, (Jefferson, NC: McFarland, 1997), 527.
2. Interview with Jane Jarvis, conducted by Tim Wiles, September 14, 2007.
3. www.ballparktour.com/organists.html.
4. Ibid.
5. Melissa Isaacson, "She Can Play: Ballpark Organists Are a Dying Breed, but After 35 Summers, Nancy Faust Is Still in Tune with White Sox Fans," *Chicago Tribune*, September 7, 2004.
6. Ibid.
7. Peter Sanders, "At Dodger Stadium, a Noteworthy Figure Loses Playing Time," *The Wall Street Journal*, August 11, 2004, 1.
8. Roy Rivenburg, "Ballpark Organists: They're Out," *Los Angeles Times*, June 11, 2005.
9. Dan Ankeles, "When Live Music Was King at Old Comiskey," *Chicago Maroon*, September 11, 2003; www.ballparktour.com.nancy_faust.html.
10. "Best 'Player' for Chisox: Harry," undated, unsourced clipping in Harry Caray biographical file, National Baseball Hall of Fame Library, Cooperstown, NY.
11. Roy Rivenburg, "Ballpark Organists: They're Out."
12. Interview with Jane Jarvis.

THE SOUND TRACK OF SUMMER

1. James Mote, *Everything Baseball*, (New York: Prentice Hall, 1989), 289.
2. About the Film: The Music of Baseball, www.pbs.org/kenburns/baseball/about/music.html.

AFTER PEANUTS—BEFORE CRACKER JACK

1. David Hinckley, "Toy, Joy, Oi: In Memory of the Worst Baseball Song Ever Written," *Daily News*, 32.
2. Over 1,000 songs were submitted in 1954 alone as part of a songwriting contest.

THE CRACKER JACK CONNECTION

1. Alex Jaramillo, *Cracker Jack Prizes* (New York: Abbeville, 1989), 7.
2. Ibid., 8.
3. First Annual Cracker Jack Old Timers Program (1982), 30.
4. Ibid.

Is Still in Tune with White Sox Fans." *Chicago Tribune*, September 7, 2004.

"Jack Norworth, Famed Song Composer, Dies." *Los Angeles Times*, September 2, 1959, 5.

Kriplen, Nancy. "Baseball's Anthem for All Ages." *Smithsonian* 35, no. 1 (April 2004): 47–48.

Mote, James. "The Anthem of Baseball." In *Everything Baseball*, edited by James Mote. New York: Prentice-Hall Press, 1989.

Ripley, John W. "Baseball's Forgotten Casey." *Ford Times*, June 1974, 20–23.

Ripley, John W. "Baseball's Greatest Song–Illuminated by the Hand-Tinted Slides That Helped Make It a Hit." *American Heritage* (June/July 1983): 76–78.

Rivenburg, Roy. "Ballpark Organists: They're Out." *Los Angeles Times*, June 11, 2005.

Rosenthal, Harold. "Take Me Out to Ball Game Written on Subway in '08." *The Sporting News*, March 16, 1958.

"Sailor Boy, Comedian, Songsmith." *The Washington Post*, April 11, 1909, M7.

Snyder, Clyde. "Lagunan Still Thrills to Baseball's Anthem." *Los Angeles Times*, April 13, 1958, OC1.

Spink, C. C. Johnson. "Baseball's Song of Songs." *The Sporting News*, August 19, 1978.

Weld, John. "Our Town" (column). *South Coast News*, September 4, 1959, 1.

Wiles, Tim. "Music of the Sphere." In *Baseball as America: Seeing Ourselves Through Our National Game*. Washington, D.C.: National Geographic, 2002.

COMPACT DISCS

1908: The Phonographic Yearbook, "Take Me Out With the Crowd." Archeophone 9009.

Debus, Allen G. "Bayes and Norworth: America's Happiest Couple." Liner Notes to *Nora Bayes and Jack Norworth: Together...and Alone*. St. Joseph, IL: Archeophone Records, 2004.

LIBRARY FILES

National Baseball Hall of Fame Library
Music–General
Music: "Take Me Out to the Ball Game"
Norworth, Jack
Women in Baseball–Bloomer Girls
Women in Baseball–Female Fans
Women in Baseball–Ladies Day
Women in Baseball–Women's Suffrage
Von Tilzer, Albert
New York Public Library of Performing Arts
Baseball Music
Berkeley, Busby
Norworth, Jack
Von Tilzer, Albert

ARCHIVAL MATERIALS

Letter, Alexander G. Law to Sid Keener, October 29, 1953. National Baseball Hall of Fame Library, Special Collections and Archives Dept.

Letter, Jack Norworth to A. G. Law, October 10, 1953. National Baseball Hall of Fame Library, Special Collections and Archives Dept.

WEB SITES

www.ballparktour.com/organists.html
Cracker Jack.com
IBDB.com
IMDB.com

Lagunahistory.org "Jack Norworth and 'Take Me Out to the Ball Game'"

Parlorsongs.com

www.SongwritersHallofFame.org

www.Wikipedia.org. See: Albert Von Tilzer, Jack Norworth, "Take Me Out to the Ball Game," Seventh-Inning Stretch.

INTERVIEWS

Lavonne "Pepper" Paire Davis, September 2007

Dr. Allen Debus, September 14, 2007

Roland Hemond, July 2007

Jane Jarvis, September 13, 2007

TEXT AND IMAGE
PERMISSIONS

Grateful acknowledgment is made to the following for permission to use previously published and unpublished material:

Ira Berkow: "The Return of Peanuts" and excerpts from his column "Sports of the Times," originally published in the *New York Times*, October 11, 2001.

LaVonne "Pepper" Paire Davis: Untitled parody of "Take Me Out to the Ball Game."

Ed Grainger and Jerry Vogel Music Company, Inc.: Lyrics from the 1927 version of "Take Me Out to the Ball Game."

David Headlam: "Professor Headlam's Formal Musical Theoretical Analysis of 'Take Me Out to the Ball Game'" and his contributions to the section "What's in a Song?"

Jeffrey Lyons: "Sinatra to Kelly to Williams" (a film review of *Take Me Out to the Ball Game*).

MLBP and LL Cool J (James Todd Smith): Additional lyrics to "Take Me Out Me Out to the Ball Game." Major League Baseball trademarks are used with permission of Major League Baseball Properties, Inc.

The National Baseball Hall of Fame: Letters by Alexander Law and Jack Norworth.

Lenore Skenazy and Creators Syndicate, Inc.: Parody "Take Me Out to the New Non-Competitive Ball Game" © 2007 Creators Syndicate, Inc. Used by permission of Lenore Skenazy and Creators Syndicate, Inc.

The images reproduced in this book are from the following sources:

ASCAP Foundation: Logo, p. 95. *Getty Images*: Harry Caray, pp. 5, 64, and 65. *Lester S. Levy Collection of Sheet Music, Special Collections at the Sheridan Libraries of the Johns Hopkins University*: "The Baseball March and Two-Step," p. 111; "Three Strikes Two-Step," p. 111; "The Umpire," p. 111; "At the Baseball Game," p. 112; "Back to the Bleacher for Me," p. 112; "That Baseball Rag," p. 112; "The National Game," p. 112; "Remember Me to My Old Gal," p. 112; "The Feds Are Here to Stay," p. 113; "Oh! You, Babe Ruth," p. 114; "Along Came Ruth," pp. 104 and 114; "Slide Kelly Slide," pp. 68, 110, and 116; "Tally One for Me," p. 110; "Silver Ball March," p. 110. *Laguna Historical Society*: Jack Norwoth, p. 134. *Library of Congress*: Christy Mathewson, pp. 2 and 33; Ty Cobb, p. 30; Fred Merkle, pp. 31 and 37; Honus Wagner, p. 31; Al Bridwell, p. 34; Joe McGinnity, p. 35; Joe Tinker, pp. 35 and 37. *Major League Baseball*: Team logos, pp. 40, 41, 42, 43, and 45; "Baseball Is More Than a Game," p. 97. The New York Times: obituary, p. 7. *The National Baseball Library/The National Baseball Hall of Fame*: Jack Norworth's handwritten lyrics, pp. 1 and 17; "Take Me Out to the Ball Game," p. 9; the National Baseball Hall of Fame, p. 16; lantern slides, pp. 26 and 27; "Take Me Out to the Ball Game" (sheet music covers), p. 28; three players in 1908,

p. 31; "Come On Play Ball with Me, Dearie," pp. 36 and 111; Tinker and Evers, p. 37; Children at the game, p. 38; Amanda Clement, p. 56; Alta Weiss, pp. 56 and 57; the Bobbies, p. 56; the Vassar College Resolutes, p. 57; female baseball team from the early 1900s, background, pp. 58 and 59; female pitcher, p. 60; band of ball players, p. 62; Bill Veeck plaque, p. 63; Ebbets Field, p. 71; Buck O'Neil (photo by Don Sparks), p. 79; Stan Musial, p. 80; Bob Wolff, p. 80; collage, pp. 82 and 83; Helen Dell, p. 98; Nancy Faust (black and white), p. 98; Eddie Layton, p. 99; Johnny Bench, p. 104; the Kennedy family, p. 127; fans, p. 129; collage (photo by Milo Stewart, Jr.), pp. 148 and 149; Jack Norworth, p. 150. *Publisher's collection:* Irving Berlin letter, p. 4; Kate Smith, p. 5; Norworth images, p. 10; Norworth Theatre, p. 13; the Amphion, p. 25; Babe Ruth, p. 32; John McGraw, p. 33; subway riders illustration, p. 46; 1908 postcard, p. 58; small inset of female batter, p. 58; Polo Ground game announcement, p. 59; Harry Caray album cover, p. 63; inset, p. 67; Bang the Drum Slowly, p. 70; Ed Sullivan, p. 73; LL Cool J, p. 80; the Goo Goo Dolls, p. 80; Cracker Jack, p. 80; B.F. Skinner, p. 84; *Meet John Doe*, p. 89; Roger Clemens, p. 101; Al Leiter, p. 10; Damn Yankees, p. 102; Peter Gammons, p. 103; Terry Cashman, p. 103; Simon and Garfunkel, p. 104; New York Clipper, pp. 107 and 113; Roger Maris stamp, p. 120; "Home Run Quick Step," p. 110. *Topps Baseball Cards:* Joe Jackson, p. 126; Cracker Jack card, p. 126. *United Press International:* Dodgers, p. 15. *United States Postal Service:* One-hundredth anniversary commemorative stamp image, end sheets, frontispiece, pp. 120 and 121. Take Me Out to the Ball Game Stamp Design © 2008 United States Postal Service. All rights reserved. Used with permission.

All other images are from the authors' personal collections. *Photos by Judith Armistead:* Armistead's miniature objects, pp. 135 and 136. *Photo by Mastro Auctions:* Music box, p. 2. *Photos (of Andy Strasberg's collection) by Duane Dimock:* "Let's Get the Umpire Goat," p. 13; "The Story the Picture Blocks Told," p. 14; "Take Me Out to the Ball Game," pp. 14 and 28; "Smarty," p. 16; "Baseball is More Than a Game," p. 97; "Baseball," p. 118; Ivan "Pudge" Rodriguez, p. 52; Little Nellie Kelly poster, p. Records, pp. 3, 14, 29, 61, 86, 87, 92, and 140–147; Cylinders, pp. 66, 68, and 141; Sinatra and Kelly base-54; Wheaties record, p. 90; Cracker Jack ad, p. 126. *Photos (of Andy Strasberg's collection) by Michael Oletta* ball cards, p. 35; Music box, p. 35; seventh-inning stretch, p. 45; "Take Me Out to the Ball Game," p. 86; "Army Hit Kit," p. 119; Take Me Out to the Ball Game film posters and card, pp. 88, 89, and 124; sou, p. 92; collage, p. 123; Cracker Jack baseball cards, p.125; Cracker Jack baseball, p. 126.

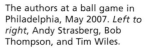
The authors at a ball game in Philadelphia, May 2007. *Left to right*, Andy Strasberg, Bob Thompson, and Tim Wiles.

THE AUTHORS

ANDY STRASBERG

IN HIS TWENTY-TWO years with the San Diego Padres, Andy Strasberg established himself as one of the sports world's most innovative marketers.

Upon leaving the Padres in 1996, Strasberg began to expand his horizons and created ACME (All-Star Corporate Marketing Enterprises) Marketing, which since that time has provided valuable service to a diverse roster of clients. They include: the National Baseball Hall of Fame, the HBO movie *61**, San Diego National Bank, baseball broadcaster Jerry Coleman, and baseball Hall of Famer Ozzie Smith and other retired major leaguers, for whom he coordinates media relations and marketing efforts.

Strasberg is a frequent guest lecturer at sports marketing symposia and a motivational speaker.

Because of his fascination with baseball music Strasberg owns an enormous collection of "Take Me Out to the Ball Game" recordings.

Strasberg is a native New Yorker and a cum laude graduate of Long Island University. His story regarding his relationship with Roger Maris has been published in *Reader's Digest, Chicken Soup for the Baseball Fan's Soul,* and *Sports Illustrated.*

BOB THOMPSON

PRODUCER, CONDUCTOR, publisher, professor, writer, and musician, Thompson grew up in Hawthorne, New York, the resting place of Babe Ruth and Lou Gehrig. He is the founder and co-producer of the Baseball Music Project (www.baseballmusicproject.com), a series of theatrical concerts presented in association with the National Baseball Hall of Fame, with Hall of Famer Dave Winfield as host and narrator. Working with Winfield, Thompson has conducted performances with the Seattle, Houston, Detroit, and Phoenix symphonies, among others. An acclaimed trumpet player, Thompson has performed with the Four Tops, the Temptations, and the Moody Blues. He holds a doctorate in music from the Eastman School of Music, University of Rochester, and was awarded the Distinguished Alumni Award from the University of South Florida in Tampa. He currently serves as associate dean of the Conservatory of Music at Purchase College, State University of New York, and director of its arts management program.

TIM WILES

TIM WILES IS director of research at the National Baseball Hall of Fame and Museum in Cooperstown, New York, a position he has held since 1995. In this position, Wiles oversees all public and professional research conducted in the library, which holds 2.5 million items in all formats, including audiovisual items. The clientele ranges from schoolchildren and genealogists to filmmakers, producers, screenwriters, the authors of most new baseball books, musicians and record companies, diverse media clients, including television, film, print, and Web-based media, sports teams, leagues, and licensees.

Wiles has written for, edited, proofread, and fact-checked hundreds of Hall of Fame publications in book, magazine, yearbook, and online forms. He is the co-editor, with Dr. Brooke Horvath, of the book *Line Drives: 100 Contemporary Baseball Poems* (Southern Illinois University Press, 2002). His freelance writing has appeared in many publications, including *The New York Times*, and in Major League Baseball's World Series, All-Star Game, and League Championship Series programs. From 1997 to 2000, he wrote a weekly column, "Letters in the Dirt," for the *Freeman's Journal*, Cooperstown's weekly newspaper. He was awarded the Illinois Central College Distinguished Alumnus Award in 2006.

His essay on "Take Me Out to the Ball Game" appeared in *Baseball as America*, the companion publication to the major traveling exhibition of the same name organized by the National Baseball Hall of Fame. He is on the editorial board of *Memories and Dreams*, the National Baseball Hall of Fame's magazine, and the editorial board of Writing Sports, a series from Kent State University Press. He has performed his costumed recitation of "Casey at the Bat" and "Take Me Out to the Ball Game" thousands of times since 1996, appearing in twenty-two states and at schools, conferences, conventions, ball games, and elsewhere.

INDEX

CD CONTENTS

Editor's note: Each track is a different recording of the song "Take Me Out to the Ball Game." We included as many versions as we could to give you a taste of the variety of interpretations that have been recorded. You can find a complete discography documenting all the recordings of "Take Me Out to the Ball Game" starting on page 158.

1. **"Take Me Out to the Ball Game"**

   by Norworth and Von Tilzer (2:33)

   Performed by Fred Lambert, from Oxford Disc Records 1185

2. **"Take Me Out to the Ball Game"**

   by Norworth and Von Tilzer (2:48)

   Performed by Leroy Holmes, from MGM 11016

3. **"Take Me Out to the Ball Game"**

   by Norworth and Von Tilzer (3:37)

   Performed by National Pastime Orchestra, from Cape Song Records

   Musical recording licensed under permission of Cape Song Records. All rights reserved. To buy *A Century of Baseball in Song*, go to CD Baby, or call 212-431-5485, or contact Worlds Records.

4. **"Take Me Out to the Ball Game"**

   by Norworth and Von Tilzer (2:57)

   Performed by Dr. John, from Nonesuch B000005J2P

   Musical recording licensed under permission of Colby Music. All rights reserved.

5. **"Take Me Out to the Ball Game"**

   by Norworth and Von Tilzer (4:48)

   Performed by the Ray Brown Trio, from Concord Records CCD-4520

   Musical recording licensed under permission of Concord Records. All rights reserved.

6. **"Take Me Out to the Ball Game"**

   by Norworth and Von Tilzer (2:48)

   Performed by Frank Rosolino, from Savoy Records MG-12062

   Musical recording licensed under permission of Savoy Records. All rights reserved.

7. **"Take Me Out to the Ball Game"**

   by Norworth and Von Tilzer (1:36)

   Performed by Arturo Sandoval, from HBO JBR-50472

   Musical recording licensed under permission of Home Box Office, a division of Time Warner Entertainment Company, L.P. All rights reserved.

8. **"Take Me Out to the Ball Game"**

   by Norworth and Von Tilzer (3:04)

   Performed by Johnny Guarnieri, from *Hungry for Music's Diamond Cuts: Grand Slam (Vol. IV)*

   Musical recording licensed under permission of Hungry for Music and the Guarnieri Family. All rights reserved.

9. **"Take Me Out to the Ball Game"**

   by Norworth and Von Tilzer (5:23)

   Performed by George Winston, from *Hungry for Music's Diamond Cuts: Turning Two (Vol. II)*

   Musical recording licensed under permission of Dancing Cat Records and Hungry for Music. All rights reserved.

 Hungry for Music is a grassroots volunteer-driven 501 (c)(3) charity organization with a nationwide and international outreach. Hungry for Music's mission is to inspire underprivileged children (and others) by bringing positive musical and creative experiences into their lives. Since becoming a non-profit in 1994, Hungry for Music has brought the healing quality of music to thousands of people through its musical instrument donations, concerts, and workshops. Hungry for Music supports its programs through memberships, benefit concerts and events, raffles, and the sale of Hungry for Music-produced compact discs. www.hungryformusic.org

"Hungry for Music's purpose is to embrace the positive qualities of music: its ability to create community, to express a talent, to unify all people, and most importantly to heal."

–Jeff Campbell, Executive Director

10. "Take Me Out to the Ball Game"

by Norworth and Von Tilzer (2:43)

Performed by Bruce Springstone, from Clean Cuts CC 1202

Musical recording licensed under permission of Clean Cuts Inc. All rights reserved.

11. "Take Me Out to the Ball Game"

by Norworth and Von Tilzer (1:39)

Performed by Albatross, from Pennsylvania Six 5000 PA 65000

Musical recording licensed under permission of Pennsylvania Six 5000. All rights reserved.

12. "Take Me Out to the Ball Game"

by Norworth and Von Tilzer (2:07)

Performed by Bob Stevens, from Erro J90W3159

13. "Take Me Out to the Ball Game"

by Norworth and Von Tilzer (3:53)

Performed by Eddie Burleton's Band, from Audiophile Records AP-43

Musical recording licensed under permission of Jazzology Records. All rights reserved.

14. "Take Me Out to the Ball Game"

by Norworth and Von Tilzer (1:28)

Performed by David Weiss, from a private recording David Weiss, musical saw; Alpha Hockett Walker, piano

Musical Recording licensed under permission of David Weiss. All rights reserved.

15. "Take Me Out to the Ball Game"

by Norworth and Von Tilzer (1:59)

Performed by Don Ippolito, from Deluxe Records 2035

Musical recording licensed under permission of Gusto. All rights reserved.

16. "Take Me Out to the Ball Game"

by Norworth and Von Tilzer (0:51)

Performed by Harry Caray, from Churchill Records

Musical recording licensed under permission of SONY/BMG. All rights reserved.

NORTH COUNTRY LIBRARY SYSTEM

0　　　　　　　　　　　　1

NORTH COUNTRY LIBRARY SYSTEM
Watertown, New York

CENTRAL LIBRARY
WATERTOWN

NOV   2008

BAKER & TAYLOR